THE AUTHORITATIVE REFERENCE ON BUFFALO NICKELS

Second Edition

By: John Wexler, Ron Pope
and Kevin Flynn

THE AUTHORITATIVE REFERENCE ON BUFFALO NICKELS

Second Edition

By: John Wexler, Ron Pope
and Kevin Flynn

Copyright © 2007
Kevin J. Flynn

Published by:
Zyrus Press Inc.
PO Box 17810, Irvine, CA 92623
Tel: (888) 622-7823 / Fax: (800) 215-9694
www.zyruspress.com
ISBN-10: 1-933990-03-1
ISBN-13: 978-1-933990-03-3

Dedication

This book is dedicated to Lloyd Hanson. Lloyd passed away in 2005 at the age of 67. Lloyd's primary passion in coins was his Buffalo nickel RPMs and OMMs, of which he had one of the most extensive collections of these varieties known. He enjoyed trading coins, debating and verifying mint anomalies. Lloyd shared his coins with others for the betterment of the hobby.

Lloyd lived in Henderson, NV. He was married 47 years to his wife Darlene. He had two children, his son Jeffery and daughter Kelly, three grandchildren and also several great grandchildren.

Lloyd will be missed by all.

Acknowledgements

We would like to thank Lloyd Hanson for his help in the Repunched Mintmark section of the book. Lloyd has been collecting Buffalo RPMs for many years and probably has the most extensive collection of RPMs in the Buffalo series. Most of the RPMs used in this book came from his collection. We would like to thank the Lafferty boys, Jim Jr. and Mark, and their father, Jim Lafferty Sr. The Lafferty boys are the essence of what young numismatists should strive to be. They believe in hard work, dedication, and have a passion like their father. Jim Sr. is a true numismatist, who believes in pure research.

We would like to thank Leroy VanAllen, who in 1992 found many of the Buffalo doubled die varieties with his wife by searching through a hoard of thousands of varieties. Mr. VanAllen is mostly known for his expertise on the Morgan and Peace Dollar series, but his expertise expands in other series as well. We would like to thank Sam Lukes, Bill VanNote, Bill Affanato, Bill Fivaz, Karen Peterson, Dennis Paulsen, and Brian Raines, who we can always count on to help with finding great, exciting varieties. They share their coins unselfishly for the good of others. We would like to thank JT Stanton for lending us some of the photos for this book. We would like to thank Larry Briggs for providing many of the varieties for this book and Tom McCarrow for letting us photograph his 1914/3.

We'd like to thank Tom Arch for lending us his coins and knowledge. Also thanks to Brian Allen for helping with the pricing in the RPM section. Most of the doubled die and over mintmark pricing, along with the comments on the strike, are the work of Ron Pope. Many doubled dies also came from Ron. He is one of the leading experts on this series. His overwhelming knowledge and expertise is obvious.

This information was so important and helpful that Mr. Pope was made a coauthor in this book.

We would like to thank Roger Burdette for helping with the Buffalo nickel proof section. We would like to thank Ken Bressett, Dave Bowers, Tom DeLorey, David Lange, Bill Fivaz, and John Dannreuther for sharing their knowledge on proofs.

Thanks to Heritage Galleries for permission to use the obverse and reverse photos in the Date-by-Date Analysis sections of the Business and Proof sections of this book.

Thanks to PCGS for permission to use their population totals. These totals are Copyright © 2005 Collectors Universe, Inc, and used with permission. PCGS, the world's largest third-party coin grading and authentication service was founded in February 1986 by David Hall and five other prominent professional numismatists: Bruce Amspacher, Steve Cyrkin, John W. Dannreuther, Silvano DiGenova, Van Simmons and Gordon Wrubel. Since then, PCGS has certified several of the world's most valuable rare coins, including: the finest known 1913 Liberty Head nickel (PCGS PF-66) which sold for $4.15 million; the $4.14 million Child's specimen 1804 Bust dollar (PCGS PF-67); the unique 1794 Flowing Hair dollar with a silver plug (PCGS Specimen-66); and the famous King of Siam proof set. In addition, PCGS experts authenticated the previously missing Walton specimen 1913 Liberty Head nickel in 2003. For additional information about PCGS or the PCGS Collectors Club, contact Professional Coin Grading Service, P.O. Box 9458, Newport Beach, CA 92658. Phone: (800) 447-8848. E-mail: info@pcgs.com. Web: www.pcgs.com.

Thank you to NGC for permission to use their certified coin census figures. The NGC Census is Copyright © 2005, Numismatic Guaranty Corporation, and reprinted with permission. NGC has become a leader in third-party impartial rare coin grading by offering consistent and accurate grading and unsurpassed customer service. In combination with certification and grading, NGC also offers VarietyPlus, a comprehensive variety attribution service for the specialist. NGC is the official grading service of the American Numismatic Association (ANA) and the Professional Numismatists Guild (PNG), the two most respected and recognized bodies in the rare coin hobby, representing the collector and dealer communities. For additional information about NGC contact NGC, PO Box 4776, Sarasota, FL 34230. Phone: (800) NGC-COIN. E-mail: service@ngccoin.com. Web: www.ngccoin.com.

Red Book values in the Date-by-Date section of the book are reprinted with permission from *The Official Red Book®: A Guide Book of United States Coins*, © Whitman Publishing, LLC. All Rights Reserved. The *Official Red Book and A Guide Book of United States Coins* are registered trademarks of Whitman Publishing, LLC, Atlanta, GA.

Table of Contents

Introduction

The Buffalo nickel series is considered by many to be one of the most popular and collectable of United States Mint issues. They replaced the Liberty Head nickel in 1913, and were struck until 1938. Created by James Earl Fraser, the Buffalo nickel is the very essence of an aesthetic design combined with historical significance. The American Indian on the obverse and the Buffalo on the reverse pay tribute to symbols of Native American heritage that played such an integral role in 19th century American history. The very definition of "coin lore" is epitomized in the Buffalo nickel.

New to this second edition is a date-by-date analysis of the Buffalo nickel series. With this, you will gain a general knowledge of rarity and striking characteristics for each date and mintmark. The mint state population reports are presented to help determine rarity. Of course, it cannot be emphasized enough that you must learn how to grade coins yourself. The more coins you study, the easier it becomes to determine grades yourself. Do not just rely on the certified grades; some of them are obviously over-graded. Go to coin shows and auctions, study the characteristics of a specific date and mintmark, and learn what to expect. With this knowledge, your collection an investment will gain.

The primary focus of the first edition of this book was Buffalo nickel die varieties. There are many series which contain an abundance of die varieties. The Buffalo nickel series is no exception. There are some monster doubled dies, overdates, over mintmarks, and repunched mintmarks. Varieties such as the 1916 doubled die obverse and 1918/7-D overdate are some of the most highly sought after varieties of any series and command near the highest premiums for a die variety. Just think of it, a 1916

DDO in grade G4 can sell for over $1,000. Not bad for a coin you can buy for under a dollar.

Varieties in general in this series, especially doubled dies and overdates, are prized by the collector. These coins are not normally bought and used as investments. They are purchased by collectors who enjoy the Buffalo series and treasure their collections. Dealers who regularly sell die varieties are usually quickly cleaned out of Buffalo doubled dies or overdates. Del Romines once put a 1916 doubled die for sale in a small ad in *Numismatic News*. Within a week, the coin was sold as well as the remaining 40 to 50 Buffalo nickel doubled dies that Mr. Romines had in his collection.

There are a large number of new Buffalo nickel varieties in this book. More will likely be found as more collectors become interested and start to search this series. This book lists double the number of RPMs compared to the number of Buffalo RPMs listed in the RPM book by John Wexler and Tom Miller. Some of these, such as the 1929-S RPM-004, are extremely dramatic; the repunched S is actually touching the rim on this variety. There are many new RPMs that are easily visible and highly collectable.

On overdates, the 1914/3 overdate was discovered in 1996 and verified in 1997. It's amazing how this variety could have been overlooked for over 80 years. It turns out that an estimated five to six different 1914 working dies from Philadelphia might show remnants of a 3, along with at least two dies from San Francisco. One from Denver also shows remnants of a 3. The logical conclusion is that these overdates originated from a 1913 working hub, in which the date was polished down, accidentally leaving part of the 3. The working hub was then used to make a new master die into which the 1914 date was punched. It was often normal procedure to use a working hub to make a new master die for the following year. This would save the wear and tear of the master hub. This book shows five absolutely different 1914/3 coins from different working dies. Two 1914/3 varieties from the first edition are delisted in this edition as further evidence and higher grade specimens proved they were not overdates. In future books, we will attempt to identify all 1914/3 Buffalo nickel varieties.

There are over 60 Buffalo nickel doubled dies listed in this book, including several new doubled dies that were not published in the first edition. Each doubled die contains pictures of all doubling, which makes distinguishing between varieties much easier. Photos are especially important for years such as 1930, which could have as many as 15 doubled die obverses and 8 doubled die reverses. There are 12 1930 doubled die obverses listed in the CONECA Master Listing, but without photographs it is extremely difficult to positively identify many of these varieties.

The goal of this book was to only publish varieties that have been examined and photographed. Even though this book contains more photographed Buffalo nickel doubled dies than any book ever published, it was expected that there would be a few known varieties that were not available to be photographed, and therefore could not be included. There will probably be a few new Buffalo doubled dies found before a third edition is published.

For now, collectors have a visual reference to identify many varieties, and will quickly know if they find a variety that is not published in this book.

This book was written to aid the collector in all aspects of collecting Buffalo nickels, and provides an invaluable tool allowing collectors to identify all Buffalo nickel die varieties that they have. The avid variety collectors will find much needed information, and the traditional collector will develop a greater awareness and appreciation for the rarity and desirability of these varieties.

We hope that you enjoy the book as you embark on your hunt for new treasures!

Chapter 1
Buffalo Nickel
Business Strikes

Business Strike Overview

This section provides you with the information needed to determine whether the Buffalo nickel you seek to purchase is rare, important, or valuable. With the proliferation of third party grading, it is important to note that the key to that answer is locked within the coin itself. You will not find it on the plastic around the coin, or the finite information a certified slab provides. Whether the Buffalo nickel you seek to purchase is raw or certified, you must know how to properly grade. And to properly grade, you will need to know how the elements of the coin and the striking characteristics of that particular date and mintmark factor into the equation.

Some certified coins are simply graded incorrectly; it is not uncommon to find a coin with an obvious over or under-grade. For some of the more expensive coins, a single increment of one grade can mean the difference in tens of thousands of dollars. Take a 1916 doubled die obverse. The value in MS63 is $175,000, but in MS64—just one grade increment higher—the price tag is $300,000. Such a dramatic difference in value provides a huge incentive for the owner to crack the slab open, remove the coin, and resubmit it to a grading service. An expensive coin is likely to be slabbed many times over in search of a higher certified grade.

The grading services deserve much credit; they provide a very valuable service to the hobby and draw on an unparallel level of expertise. But with your coins, the opinion you need to be able to trust the most is your own. The fact is, coins have been certified as Mint State that were actually Proof. Imagine purchasing a 1915 Buffalo nickel in MS65 for $150, only to discover later the coin is PR65 and worth $2,000. Or worse, imagine the opposite. You should examine as many Buffalo nickel proofs as you can set your eyes on until you can tell the difference. If you are considering investing in rare and/or expensive Buffalo nickels, you *must* learn how to grade them.

The best way to learn to grade is to go to coin shows, auctions, and coin stores. Examine as many Buffalo nickels as you can. Determine the acceptable number of nicks and scratches for a given grade. Learn to judge the luster, color, and overall eye appeal. An online auction archive, such as the one at Heritage Coins (www.ha.com), is a great place to see photos of thousands of coins right from the comfort of your own home. You can also gain much from reviewing auction catalogs.

Another aspect vital to collecting Buffalo nickels is striking characteristics. For example, 1924-S Buffalo nickels almost always come with weak strikes. A weak strike from a worn die can easily be confused as wear. Gaining knowledge through experience will help protect your investment. This chapter will help you learn what to generally expect for each date and mintmark.

Another useful tool in determining the rarity of a date and mintmark is the certified coin population reports published by third party grading services. Population reports have sparked a whole new angle on collecting. Registry set collecting, which is based entirely on the highest grade coins in a particular series, (as listed in a grading service's population report), is a fairly recent phenomenon. Registry sets have dramatically driven up the price of high grade coins as collectors compete to own the top coins for their set. However, the numbers found in these population reports often include coins that were slabbed several times. While population reports play an important role in knowing the rarity of a coin, they are just one of the many tools at your disposal.

It's important to remember that at the heart of coin collecting is a fun and exciting hobby. Choose coins that you will enjoy. At the same time, it is important to protect your financial investment. The more you learn about the coins, and the more you know about grading, strike characteristics, color, and rarity, the more you will feel a sense of accomplishment in assembling your collection.

This date-by-date section contains a great deal of information. Some of the information is useful in assembling a set of Buffalo nickels, such as the scarcity of a given date and mintmark. What follows is an overview of the major topics addressed for each date and mintmark.

Mintages: This section includes the number of business strikes or proofs that were produced at each of the mints for a given year for each of the series.

Die Varieties: This book covers Buffalo nickel doubled dies, overdates, over mintmarks and repunched mintmarks in great detail. The Die Varieties section lists some of the more desirable die varieties to search for.

Scarcity: This section discusses the scarcity and rarity of Buffalo nickels for each of the mints at which they were produced for that year.

Comments: This section includes some of the author's observations and comments. These are included simply to provide additional information that may be of interest.

Values: The values are the retail values listed in the *Red Book (A Guide Book of United States Coins)* for a given year and mintmark. The values are given in five year increments to show the changes in value over time. The values are given for coins struck at each mint.

Certified Populations: This section shows the number of certified Uncirculated Buffalo nickels for a given year from a given mint. Only coins certified between the grades of MS61 and above for business strikes are given. Population counts are shown from two grading services: NGC and PCGS, and are based upon the totals recorded in April of 2006. This section is useful in helping to determine rarity.

History Tidbits: This section lists major historical events that occurred during a given year. An old coin is a part of history, and it reminds us of the era during which it was struck. When we see a 1929 Buffalo nickel, we might think of the year of the Great Depression in the United States. Coins are an important part of our history, which is another reason to enjoy collecting.

1913
Variety I

BUSINESS STRIKE MINTAGES
Philadelphia: 30,993,520
Denver: 5,337,000
San Francisco: 2,105,000

PROOF MINTAGES
Philadelphia: 1,520

Images Courtesy of Heritage

DIE VARIETIES

Type I 1913 Buffalo nickels have several die varieties including one obverse and two reverse doubled dies, all on the 1913-P. There are no known doubled dies on the 1913-D or S. One RPM is known from Denver and San Francisco. A 3 ½ legged Buffalo from over polished dies has also been found on a 1913-P mintmark.

SCARCITY

Philadelphia: Very common in and near Mint State, but becomes rare at MS67 and better. The dates wore off very quickly on all the 1913 issues, making low grade coins with readable dates elusive.

Denver: Widely saved like the Philly coin, high grade specimens are easily available up to and including MS65.

San Francisco: Scarcer in all grades than the P and D mint coins and surprisingly difficult in the lower circulated grades.

COMMENTS

Philadelphia: Most are well struck. Full strikes are not uncommon. When found weak or incomplete in striking detail, the weakness is usually restricted to the tip of the small (uppermost) feather and adjacent area of the front of the Buffalo's head on the reverse and other peripheral details. This localized lack of detail is what prevents a true full strike on many coins.

Denver: Shares all of the striking characteristics with its Philadelphia Mint counterpart but is more frequently seen with striking weakness at the tip of the upper feather and front of the bison's head. A few incredibly struck coins—as nice as any Matte Proof—are very occasionally seen.

San Francisco: Like many of the later branch mint dates, it often exhibits an overall "mushy" appearance. The typical coin is fairly well struck, but not to the degree of the previous two. Full strikes are generally available, though none show the sharpness of detail found on the other two issues. Date lettering near the rim on both sides is often weak.

BUFFALO NICKEL RED BOOK VALUES

DATE	1913 Var I			1913-D Var I			1913-S Var I		
	FN	EF	MS60	FN	EF	MS60	FN	EF	MS60
1951	0.35	-----	0.75	0.75	-----	4.50	1.75	------	10.00
1955	0.40	-----	3.00	0.85	-----	5.00	2.00	-----	11.00
1960	0.75	1.25	3.00	2.00	4.00	9.00	5.50	9.00	17.50
1965	2.00	3.50	7.00	4.50	10.00	22.00	8.00	18.00	35.00
1970	2.00	4.50	11.00	6.00	10.00	24.00	8.50	15.00	37.50
1975	2.00	6.00	22.50	6.00	10.00	31.00	8.50	15.00	38.50
1980	4.00	10.00	35.00	7.00	14.00	42.50	10.00	20.00	60.00
1985	4.25	12.00	75.00	8.50	22.50	125.00	16.00	40.00	200.00
1990	4.50	12.00	80.00	8.75	22.50	125.00	16.00	40.00	175.00
1995	5.00	12.00	45.00	9.00	22.50	66.00	18.00	40.00	100.00
2000	6.00	12.00	45.00	10.00	23.00	67.00	19.00	42.00	110.00
2005	12.00	20.00	40.00	18.00	35.00	60.00	45.00	70.00	100.00

1913 CERTIFIED POPULATIONS

NGC	Total	MS61	MS62	MS63	MS64	MS65	MS66	MS67	MS68	MS69
1913	4942	21	111	323	1329	1821	1033	218	9	-----
1913-D	1348	14	97	162	472	397	133	9	-----	-----
1913-S	894	7	101	146	346	185	39	11	-----	-----
PCGS	**Total**	**MS61**	**MS62**	**MS63**	**MS64**	**MS65**	**MS66**	**MS67**	**MS68**	**MS69**
1913	8017	24	143	877	2748	2449	1268	311	8	-----
1913-D	2177	10	63	389	757	549	231	36	1	-----
1913-S	1427	13	58	323	553	248	79	11	1	-----

- WORLD HISTORY -

Jim Thorpe is stripped of his Olympic medals in the decathlon and pentathlon for earning $25 per week to play minor league baseball and branded a "professional." • United States Marines seize the port of Vera Cruz, Mexico. • King George of Greece is assassinated a few days before being king for 50 years. • Riots in India followed the jailing of Mohandas Gandhi after Gandhi refused to pay a fine for a law which prohibited Indians from entering the Tranvaal. • Grand Central station in New York opens; federal income tax is started in the United States. • Bulgaria attack Serbia and Greece. • Mongolia is granted independence from China. • The Panama Canal opens.

1913
Variety II

BUSINESS STRIKE MINTAGES
Philadelphia: 29,858,700
Denver: 4,156,000
San Francisco: 1,209,000

PROOF MINTAGES
Philadelphia: 1,114

Images Courtesy of Heritage

DIE VARIETIES

The Type II 1913 has a single obverse doubled die known on a 1913-P which shows nicely on the nose and eyelid. No doubled dies are known on the 1913-D or S. No RPMs are known.

SCARCITY

Philadelphia: Somewhat scarcer than the Variety I, especially in MS65 and better.

Denver: One of the semi-keys in the series, probably scarce due to the rapid wearing away of the date since the mintage is not exceptionally low.

San Francisco: The key date regular issue in the circulated grades. It is not nearly as tough in Mint State as many of the later dates in the series.

COMMENTS

Philadelphia: Not as well struck as the Variety I, especially in the center of the coin directly above the braid ribbon on the obverse and on the Buffalo's shoulder on the reverse. These two areas will be mentioned frequently throughout the text. They are the key places to determine full strikes for most dates. Full strikes are still relatively available.

Denver: Usually comes with an adequate strike. True full strikes are not especially rare.

San Francisco: Much more poorly produced than either the P or D Mint coins; those with weak central details periphery are not unusual. Full strikes are elusive.

BUFFALO NICKEL RED BOOK VALUES

DATE	1913 Var II			1913-D Var II			1913-S Var II		
	FN	EF	MS60	FN	EF	MS60	FN	EF	MS60
1951	0.45	------	1.50	3.50	------	11.00	8.50	------	25.00
1955	0.50	------	2.00	7.50	------	15.00	13.50	------	35.00
1960	0.85	1.50	3.50	15.00	22.50	37.50	27.50	45.00	70.00
1965	3.00	5.00	9.00	25.00	40.00	72.00	50.00	75.00	115.00
1970	3.25	5.25	12.50	27.50	42.00	76.50	46.00	70.00	120.00
1975	3.25	5.25	18.00	27.50	42.00	77.50	46.00	70.00	120.00
1980	4.75	9.00	30.00	35.00	55.00	100.00	62.50	90.00	175.00
1985	4.25	13.00	80.00	55.00	100.00	325.00	125.00	200.00	550.00
1990	4.25	13.00	80.00	55.00	100.00	325.00	115.00	200.00	550.00
1995	6.00	12.00	45.00	50.00	80.00	225.00	130.00	200.00	425.00
2000	7.50	12.00	50.00	60.00	80.00	250.00	155.00	240.00	500.00
2005	10.00	18.00	30.00	130.00	175.00	230.00	350.00	425.00	525.00

1913 VARIETY II CERTIFIED POPULATIONS

NGC	Total	MS61	MS62	MS63	MS64	MS65	MS66	MS67	MS68	MS69
1913	1099	9	93	187	448	252	61	6	------	------
1913-D	574	22	67	103	189	71	9	------	------	------
1913-S	768	35	113	129	188	52	16	2	-----	-----
PCGS	Total	MS61	MS62	MS63	MS64	MS65	MS66	MS67	MS68	MS69
1913	1844	10	70	342	766	349	126	10	------	------
1913-D	832	9	49	204	256	109	37	7	------	------
1913-S	1166	10	95	256	281	86	25	1	------	------

1914

BUSINESS STRIKE MINTAGES
Philadelphia: 20,665,738
Denver: 3,912,000
San Francisco: 3,470,000

PROOF MINTAGES
Philadelphia: 1275

Images Courtesy of Heritage

DIE VARIETIES

1914 is best known for the 1914/3 overdates, of which at least five have been confirmed on the 1914-P mintmarks. Several are believed to exist on 1914-D and S coins. These were created from a 1913 working die. The 3 was polished down and a 4 was struck into it to make a new working hub. 1914 DDO-001 and DDO-002 show the overdate the strongest and should command the highest premium. A nice RPM exists on a 1914-S, with none known on the 1914-D.

SCARCITY

Philadelphia: A little scarcer than the 1913 Variety II in all grades. The date was strengthened a little on the master die. Low grade coins can still be expected to have weak dates.

Denver: Another semi-key issue within the series. Though the mintage is comparable to the S mint coin, it is much more elusive.

San Francisco: It would be expected to be about as scarce as the 1914-D since the mintages are very close, but this is not the case except in MS65 or better. In all other grades it is much more frequently seen than the D mint coin.

COMMENTS

Philadelphia: Surprisingly, the P mint coin is the toughest for the year to find a fully struck coin, though these are of no great rarity. This is a very unusual situation with this series, as it is almost always the branch mint coins that suffer from striking deficiencies.

Denver: Usually very well struck. Finding a full strike should not present a serious problem.

San Francisco: Most often comes with a decent strike. Full strikes from this mint are a little more common than the Denver coins. Unlike the 1913 coins from all mints, the 1914 issue from all mints seldom show extreme weakness at the periphery.

BUFFALO NICKEL RED BOOK VALUES

DATE	1914			1914-D			1914-S		
	FN	EF	MS60	FN	EF	MS60	FN	EF	MS60
1951	0.60	------	3.00	3.00	------	15.00	1.25	------	13.50
1955	0.75	------	4.00	6.00	------	20.00	1.75	------	17.50
1960	1.75	3.00	6.00	14.00	22.50	40.00	5.00	16.00	35.00
1965	3.00	8.00	17.50	24.00	45.00	92.50	9.50	27.50	57.50
1970	3.25	8.75	23.00	27.50	50.00	115.00	9.00	22.50	67.50
1975	3.25	8.75	25.00	27.50	50.00	115.00	7.00	18.00	67.50
1980	5.75	13.50	35.00	33.50	57.50	150.00	8.00	19.00	90.00
1985	5.75	15.00	130.00	42.50	110.00	475.00	9.00	37.50	250.00
1990	5.75	16.00	130.00	45.00	100.00	425.00	9.00	37.50	250.00
1995	7.00	16.00	65.00	50.00	120.00	300.00	11.00	37.50	250.00
2000	9.00	18.00	70.00	60.00	120.00	325.00	13.00	37.50	350.00
2005	20.00	30.00	50.00	115.00	240.00	350.00	40.00	75.00	170.00

1914 CERTIFIED POPULATIONS

NGC	Total	MS61	MS62	MS63	MS64	MS65	MS66	MS67	MS68	MS69
1914	896	14	77	170	334	154	43	7	------	------
1914-D	599	18	84	118	183	60	9	1	------	------
1914-S	916	33	147	212	307	41	13	2	1	------
PCGS	**Total**	**MS61**	**MS62**	**MS63**	**MS64**	**MS65**	**MS66**	**MS67**	**MS68**	**MS69**
1914	1254	4	56	276	421	253	107	14	------	------
1914-D	837	6	58	195	253	118	33	4	------	------
1914-S	1104	4	106	338	328	81	21	------	------	------

1914/3 CERTIFIED POPULATIONS

NGC	Total	G	VG	F	VF	XF40	XF45	AU50	AU55	AU58
1914/3	123	2	7	11	12	10	3	5	12	16
		MS61	MS62	MS63	MS64	MS65	------	------	------	------
		6	14	12	8	3	------	------	------	------
PCGS	**Total**	**VG-VF**	**XF40/5**	**AU50/3**	**AU55**	**AU58**	**MS60/3**	**MS64**	**MS65**	**MS66**
1914/3	51	5	2	2	4	13	8	10	2	2

- WORLD HISTORY -

German Kaiser William II declares war on his cousin Czar Nicholas II. • Germany invades Luxemburg and Belgium, declares war on France. • Britain, Serbia, and Belgium declare war on Germany. • Austria declares war on Russia. • Britain and France declare war on Austria. • Europe is entrenched in war.

1915

BUSINESS STRIKE MINTAGES
Philadelphia: 20,987,270
Denver: 7,569,000
San Francisco: 1,505,000

PROOF MINTAGES
Philadelphia: 1,050

Images Courtesy of Heritage

DIE VARIETIES

The hottest variety in 1915 is the doubled die obverse (DDO-001), which shows nicely on the eye and nose. This variety has proved to be elusive, rare, and worth a nice premium for the lucky treasure hunter. No doubled dies are known on the 1915-D or S. One nice 1915-D RPM is known as well as two 1915-S RPMs.

SCARCITY

Philadelphia: A little more common in all grades than the 1914. This issue does not achieve any real rarity until the grade of MS67 is reached. The date was once again strengthened slightly on the master die to improve wearing abilities.

Denver: Not particularly scarce, even in high grade. Seems to be overpriced in the lower grades.

San Francisco: By far the scarcest coin for the year. This issue is difficult to find in VF to AU grades.

COMMENTS

Philadelphia: Almost without exception, this issue comes with an excellent strike and true full strikes are relatively common. Some of these are very easily confused with the Matte Proof issue for the year.

Denver: Usually comes with an adequate strike. True full strikes are occasionally seen.

San Francisco: Usually comes with a decent strike. True full strikes are available, and on a percentage basis, more available than the D mint issue.

BUFFALO NICKEL RED BOOK VALUES

DATE	1915			1915-D			1915-S		
	FN	EF	MS60	FN	EF	MS60	FN	EF	MS60
1951	0.60	------	3.50	2.00	------	15.00	1.75	------	13.50
1955	0.65	------	4.00	3.00	------	17.50	3.50	------	18.50
1960	1.50	3.50	7.50	5.00	12.50	27.50	3.50	17.50	35.00
1965	2.75	7.00	15.00	8.25	20.00	55.00	16.00	35.00	100.00
1970	3.00	10.00	22.50	10.50	24.00	65.00	16.00	44.00	130.00
1975	3.00	10.00	24.00	10.50	24.00	65.00	16.50	47.00	130.00
1980	3.25	11.50	35.00	11.25	25.00	90.00	22.50	52.50	165.00
1985	3.75	12.50	125.00	13.00	55.00	275.00	20.00	100.00	600.00
1990	3.75	12.50	125.00	15.00	55.00	275.00	20.00	100.00	600.00
1995	6.00	12.50	60.00	18.00	55.00	250.00	30.00	130.00	600.00
2000	6.25	14.00	65.00	22.00	55.00	300.00	45.00	150.00	750.00
2005	7.00	20.00	50.00	30.00	100.00	250.00	75.00	250.00	510.00

1915 CERTIFIED POPULATIONS

NGC	Total	MS61	MS62	MS63	MS64	MS65	MS66	MS67	MS68	MS69
1915	979	8	72	135	371	259	86	6	------	------
1915-D	587	29	109	103	158	41	9	------	------	------
1915-S	415	9	33	61	161	48	19	------	------	------
PCGS	Total	MS61	MS62	MS63	MS64	MS65	MS66	MS67	MS68	MS69
1915	1489	5	42	238	517	365	210	31	------	------
1915-D	754	10	63	196	173	97	19	2	------	------
1915-S	629	5	38	114	216	90	26	3	------	------

- WORLD HISTORY -

The Russian army was defeated by German forces in the battle at Tannenberg. • Four German cruisers are sunk by the British off the Falkland Islands. • German submarines cause havoc in the Atlantic. • Planes are used in battle to attack enemy troops. • Germany overruns Belgium. • The United States remains neutral.

1916

BUSINESS STRIKE MINTAGES
Philadelphia: 63,498,066
Denver: 13,333,000
San Francisco: 11,860,000

PROOF MINTAGES
Philadelphia: 600

Images Courtesy of Heritage

DIE VARIETIES

The 1916 doubled die obverse (DDO-001) is the king of Buffalo nickel die varieties. This coin also is the most expensive 20th century non-gold U.S. coin in higher grade levels. It has a wider spread than the 1955 Lincoln cent doubled die. It has also proved to be extremely rare in Mint State grades. No MS65 specimens have been certified to date. The 1916 doubled die is by far the rarest of the regularly collected varieties in the series, though it is exceeded in rarity by several of the lesser known but still significant doubled dies, such as the 1917 DDR-001. Mint State examples are exceedingly rare. For some reason, this variety is not as well struck as the regular issue. Most show no better than a typical strike. No true full strike is known.

SCARCITY

Philadelphia: Not difficult in any grade short of MS67. For some reason, thinner date numerals were once again used on the master die this year, which worsened its wearing quality. Low grade coins should be expected to show a weak date, much like the 1914 issue.

Denver: Not uncommon in the higher circulated grades. It becomes elusive in MS65 and better.

San Francisco: Similar in scarcity to the Denver coin, though very high grade Mint State pieces seem to be a little more available.

COMMENTS

Philadelphia: Well struck coins are commonplace. Full strikes are also easily obtainable.

Denver: Very weak strikes with a total lack of central detail start to show up with some frequency beginning this year, but full strikes are sometimes obtainable.

San Francisco: This issue is nearly identical to the D mint in striking quality. A few exceptionally struck coins with matte-like surfaces are seen from time to time.

BUFFALO NICKEL RED BOOK VALUES

DATE	1916			1916-D			1916-S		
	FN	EF	MS60	FN	EF	MS60	FN	EF	MS60
1951	0.40	------	2.25	1.00	------	13.50	1.00	------	13.50
1955	0.50	------	3.00	1.75	------	18.50	1.75	------	18.50
1960	1.00	2.50	6.00	3.50	9.00	25.00	4.00	11.00	32.50
1965	1.50	4.50	11.00	5.25	20.00	52.50	6.00	20.00	55.00
1970	1.50	4.50	16.50	6.50	18.50	60.00	6.00	20.00	65.00
1975	1.50	4.50	18.00	6.50	18.50	60.00	6.00	20.00	65.00
1980	1.75	6.50	27.50	7.50	19.00	82.00	6.00	19.00	100.00
1985	1.75	5.00	90.00	8.00	45.00	275.00	6.00	42.50	260.00
1990	1.75	5.00	90.00	8.00	45.00	275.00	6.00	42.50	260.00
1995	1.75	7.00	55.00	10.00	45.00	225.00	8.00	40.00	300.00
2000	2.00	7.00	60.00	13.00	50.00	230.00	9.00	40.00	300.00
2005	6.00	9.00	40.00	20.00	80.00	150.00	15.00	70.00	175.00

1916 CERTIFIED POPULATIONS

NGC	Total	MS61	MS62	MS63	MS64	MS65	MS66	MS67	MS68	MS69
1916	1288	17	123	209	543	262	60	5	1	------
1916-D	736	35	132	185	244	31	4	------	------	------
1916-S	550	26	97	120	177	26	9	1	------	------
PCGS	Total	MS61	MS62	MS63	MS64	MS65	MS66	MS67	MS68	MS69
1916	1873	6	69	408	750	354	109	9	------	------
1916-D	1122	9	132	313	315	83	8	------	------	------
1916-S	798	8	75	210	237	65	23	4	------	------

1916 DOUBLED DIE

NGC	Total	G	VG	F	VF	XF40	XF45	AU50	AU53	AU55
1916	73	2	3	7	9	7	8	4	2	17
		AU58	MS63	MS64	------	------	------	------	------	------
		6	3	5	------	------	------	------	------	------
PCGS	Total	VG-VF	XF40/5	AU50/3	AU55	AU58	MS62	MS64	------	------
1916	115	58	6,11	7,5	19	4	3	2	------	------

- WORLD HISTORY -

A German submarine torpedoes and sinks the liner Lusitania, killing more than 1,400 people. • Italy signs a treaty with Britain, France, and Russia, agreeing to enter the war in return for territory. • Albert Einstein proposes a new theory on gravity. • Germany uses chemical weapons during the war. • The United States entered World War I in 1917. • The war continued until 1918. Over 10 million people were killed during World War I.

1917

BUSINESS STRIKE MINTAGES
Philadelphia: 51,424,019
Denver: 9,910,000
San Francisco: 4,193,000

PROOF MINTAGES
None

Images Courtesy of Heritage

DIE VARIETIES

Two nice doubled die reverses are known on 1917-P. The first is very dramatic, especially on EPU. This variety is probably fourth in line in terms of Buffalo doubled dies, behind only the 1916 DDO-001, 1918/7 OVD-001, and 1935 DDR-001. No doubled dies are known on 1917-D or S. No RPMs are known. A 1917-D 3 ½ legged is known which only shows remnants of the center of the right front leg.

SCARCITY

Philadelphia: This issue is decidedly scarcer than the very common 1916 in all grades. Like the 1916, the numerals are thin and have a tendency to wear away quickly.

Denver: The 1917-D and S mark the beginning of the branch mint issues which are consistently difficult to find with a complete, full horn. They are scarce in Mint State condition.

San Francisco: Tougher to find in all grades than the D mint coin. Full horn coins are scarce.

COMMENTS

Philadelphia: Well struck and fully struck coins are available for this date but are not as common as the 1916. A controversial "Matte Proof" exists for the year.

Denver: Many show weak central detail as well as a poor strike at the front of the Buffalo's head, including the horn, although true full strikes are not of great rarity.

San Francisco: Usually shows a typical to good strike, though the striking weaknesses present for the Denver issue are repeated with this coin to a lesser degree.

BUFFALO NICKEL RED BOOK VALUES

DATE	1917			1917-D			1917-S		
	FN	EF	MS60	FN	EF	MS60	FN	EF	MS60
1951	0.35	------	2.50	1.75	------	20.00	2.00	------	25.00
1955	0.35	------	2.50	3.50	------	30.00	3.75	------	42.50
1960	0.65	1.50	6.50	6.00	20.00	42.50	6.00	25.00	60.00
1965	1.35	4.50	10.00	9.00	30.00	75.00	9.50	32.50	90.00
1970	1.30	5.00	18.00	9.50	40.00	80.00	10.50	42.50	120.00
1975	1.30	5.00	20.00	8.00	40.00	90.00	9.00	40.00	120.00
1980	1.90	10.00	35.00	9.25	45.00	140.00	9.25	45.00	175.00
1985	1.90	8.00	90.00	11.00	85.00	365.00	10.00	70.00	390.00
1990	1.90	8.00	110.00	11.00	85.00	365.00	10.00	70.00	390.00
1995	2.00	10.00	65.00	14.00	80.00	425.00	15.00	100.00	600.00
2000	2.50	10.00	65.00	20.00	85.00	450.00	25.00	110.00	625.00
2005	6.00	13.00	50.00	35.00	125.00	300.00	65.00	175.00	375.00

1917 CERTIFIED POPULATIONS

NGC	Total	MS61	MS62	MS63	MS64	MS65	MS66	MS67	MS68	MS69
1917	626	7	56	103	281	116	28	3	1	------
1917-D	469	19	70	95	146	32	1	------	------	------
1917-S	306	15	27	38	116	24	8	------	------	------
PCGS	Total	MS61	MS62	MS63	MS64	MS65	MS66	MS67	MS68	MS69
1917	1038	5	31	197	397	223	101	10	2	------
1917-D	770	5	53	160	257	106	12	------	------	------
1917-S	481	4	31	80	143	64	21	------	------	------

- WORLD HISTORY -

Puerto Rico becomes U.S. territory after Congress passes the Jones Act. • President Wilson signs a declaration taking the U.S. into World War I. • The first U.S. troops land in France. • Visions of the Virgin Mary are seen in Fatima, Portugal. • French dancer Mata Hari is sentenced to death for spying. • The German army penetrates deep within Italy. • German U-boats menace the Atlantic Ocean. • Czar Nicholas II abdicates his throne in Russia.

1918

BUSINESS STRIKE MINTAGES
Philadelphia: 32,086,314
Denver: 8,362,000
San Francisco: 4,882,000

PROOF MINTAGES
None

Images Courtesy of Heritage

DIE VARIETIES

The second hottest doubled die in the series is the 1918/7-D overdate. The bold remains of the 7 are clearly seen under the 8. No attempt was made to remove the 7. MS65 specimens are worth over $300,000. They usually come with an adequate strike, but many are seen from a very late state of the dies. The most serious striking issue often seen with this date is a lack of a full horn and adjacent weakness in the hair detail surrounding it. No true full strike of this variety is known. A single doubled die reverse is known for a 1918-P, and no doubled dies are known for 1918-S. One new RPM has been found on a 1918-D.

SCARCITY

Philadelphia: Much tougher than any of the previous P mintmark coins in the better circulated grades and in Mint State in general.

Denver: Scarce with a full horn and at all Mint State levels. The grade is often limited due to a poor strike.

San Francisco: One of the most difficult issues in the series in Mint State, especially MS65 or better, where the grade is greatly affected by the typically lousy strike.

COMMENTS

Philadelphia: Well struck coins are somewhat scarce. True full strikes are rare.

Denver: Serious striking deficiencies are present on a significant number of D mint coins. Central weakness on both obverse and reverse is most commonly seen. A lack of hair and horn detail on the bison is not uncommon.

San Francisco: In the opinion of many, this is the most poorly produced date in the series when STRIKE (not re-used, worn out dies) is the consideration. A very high percentage show absolute flatness and a total lack of any detail at the center of both the obverse and reverse.

BUFFALO NICKEL RED BOOK VALUES

DATE	1918			1918-D			1918-S		
	FN	EF	MS60	FN	EF	MS60	FN	EF	MS60
1951	0.70	------	6.00	2.00	------	35.00	2.00	------	35.00
1955	0.70	------	8.50	3.50	------	45.00	3.50	------	45.00
1960	1.50	3.00	16.50	5.50	22.50	57.50	6.00	27.50	67.50
1965	2.50	8.50	32.50	8.00	40.00	140.00	8.50	45.00	150.00
1970	1.85	10.75	47.50	9.00	50.00	165.00	9.00	47.50	175.00
1975	1.85	10.75	47.50	9.00	47.50	165.00	7.50	47.50	155.00
1980	2.75	12.50	60.00	10.00	55.00	250.00	9.50	52.50	225.00
1985	2.50	15.00	180.00	12.00	85.00	550.00	9.50	75.00	475.00
1990	2.50	15.00	180.00	12.00	85.00	550.00	9.50	75.00	475.00
1995	2.50	16.00	90.00	17.00	145.00	450.00	13.00	135.00	1000.00
2000	2.50	16.00	125.00	22.00	160.00	650.00	19.00	150.00	2000.00
2005	6.00	30.00	95.00	40.00	20.00	375.00	42.00	175.00	500.00

1918 CERTIFIED POPULATIONS

NGC	Total	MS61	MS62	MS63	MS64	MS65	MS66	MS67	MS68	MS69
1918	390	5	44	74	175	57	10	1	------	------
1918-D	377	7	50	58	109	18	5	------	------	------
1918-S	323	23	47	54	119	9	------	------	------	------
PCGS	Total	MS61	MS62	MS63	MS64	MS65	MS66	MS67	MS68	MS69
1918	721	3	26	144	297	142	31	7	------	------
1918-D	564	7	43	131	187	55	18	1	------	------
1918-S	494	5	47	116	163	26	1	------	------	------

- WORLD HISTORY -

Vladimir Lenin, a former law student, creates a Red Army and a security police force. • The Royal Air Force is formed in Britain. • British Major T.E. Lawrence (Lawrence of Arabia) led the Arab army into Damascus. • In Russia, the former Czar Nicholas II and his family are slaughtered. • President Woodrow Wilson presents his 14-point Wilson Plan for a post-war peace plan. • The Allies smash through the German lines. • Bulgaria surrenders. • The Republic of Czechoslovakia is formed. • Hungary declares independence from Austria. • Germany signs the armistice at Compiègne ending World War I.

1919

BUSINESS STRIKE MINTAGES
Philadelphia: 60,868,000
Denver: 8,006,000
San Francisco: 7,521,000

PROOF MINTAGES
None

Images Courtesy of Heritage

DIE VARIETIES

One minor doubled die obverse and reverse are known for 1919-P. No doubled dies are known for 1919-D or S. No RPMs are known.

SCARCITY

Philadelphia: This issue is comparable to the 1917 in overall availability. It gets really rare only in MS67 and above.

Denver: Tougher than the following S mint in XF, AU, and the lower levels of Mint State, but not nearly as rare in MS65 or better.

San Francisco: Poorly produced, lower-end Mint State coins are typical. This is one of the toughest coins in the series to find in MS65 or better.

COMMENTS

Philadelphia: The typical coin comes well struck. True full strikes are found without too much trouble. A possible specimen striking exists, but it has yet to be authenticated as such by any of the certification companies. Once again, the date was strengthened in the master die in an attempt to improve its wearing qualities.

Denver: This date has a reputation for crummy strikes. However, specimens are found that come frequently well struck and even true full strikes are in no way great rarities. That's not to say that a number do not show a miserable strike—they do. But it is believed that well struck coins of this issue are highly overrated as a major strike rarity.

San Francisco: Much tougher to find well struck than the D mint issue. Often seen struck from a badly eroded reverse die. This seems to be the first date in the series where this presents a major problem—one that continues for the next decade. True full strikes are virtually unknown.

BUFFALO NICKEL RED BOOK VALUES

DATE	1919			1919-D			1919-S		
	FN	EF	MS60	FN	EF	MS60	FN	EF	MS60
1951	0.40	------	3.25	2.00	------	32.50	2.00	------	35.00
1955	0.50	------	4.50	3.50	------	50.00	3.50	------	60.00
1960	0.60	1.75	7.50	7.50	37.50	80.00	7.50	45.00	95.00
1965	1.50	5.00	17.50	11.00	65.00	150.00	13.00	75.00	160.00
1970	1.25	5.50	24.00	11.50	70.00	205.00	11.50	67.50	200.00
1975	1.25	5.50	24.00	10.00	70.00	205.00	8.00	67.50	200.00
1980	1.50	7.50	32.50	11.50	75.00	325.00	8.75	65.00	300.00
1985	1.50	7.50	80.00	11.50	100.00	650.00	9.00	80.00	525.00
1990	1.50	7.50	85.00	11.50	100.00	650.00	9.00	80.00	525.00
1995	1.50	7.50	60.00	17.00	160.00	650.00	10.00	160.00	700.00
2000	1.50	7.50	75.00	28.00	165.00	900.00	18.00	350.00	950.00
2005	2.50	12.00	45.00	50.00	250.00	550.00	40.00	250.00	500.00

1919 CERTIFIED POPULATIONS

NGC	Total	MS61	MS62	MS63	MS64	MS65	MS66	MS67	MS68	MS69
1919	751	9	54	132	336	142	36	5	1	------
1919-D	515	17	36	38	108	11	2	------	------	------
1919-S	409	12	55	79	84	11	------	------	------	------
PCGS	Total	MS61	MS62	MS63	MS64	MS65	MS66	MS67	MS68	MS69
1919	1217	3	39	192	503	289	103	7	------	------
1919-D	515	7	32	89	169	48	13	------	------	------
1919-S	600	4	42	166	149	26	1	------	------	------

- WORLD HISTORY -

In Italy, Benito Mussolini founds the Fasci di Combattimento party. • A U.S. NC4 seaplane completes the first flight across the Atlantic. • The Allies and Germany sign the treaty of Versailles. • Britain permits Egypt a constitution. • Lady Astor becomes the first female in the British House of Commons. • The League of Nations is formed. • Professor Rutherford, an English Scientist, develops a process for splitting atoms.

1920

BUSINESS STRIKE MINTAGES
Philadelphia: 63,093,000
Denver: 9,418,000
San Francisco: 9,689,000

PROOF MINTAGES
None

Images Courtesy of Heritage

DIE VARIETIES

No doubled dies are known for 1920. One RPM is known on a 1920-D.

SCARCITY

Philadelphia: P mint is a tougher issue to find in high Mint State grades, approaching the 1918 in this regard.

Denver: Scarce with a full horn. Some show the badly eroded dies so common to branch mint coins of this era, and this does limit their technical grade.

San Francisco: Tougher than the 1918-S in MS65. Low-end Mint State coins are the rule for this date when they are found in Uncirculated condition.

COMMENTS

Philadelphia: Most seen exhibit no better than a typical strike. Well struck coins can be somewhat difficult to locate. True full strikes are rare.

Denver: Coins struck from badly eroded dies exist in large numbers. This is another overrated strike rarity in the opinion of some specialists, but not as bad as the 1919-D in this regard. Well struck coins can be located with some effort; full strikes are of considerable rarity, but do exist.

San Francisco: No true full strike of this date has been examined. A very large percentage come from very badly eroded, worn out reverse (and sometimes, obverse) dies.

BUFFALO NICKEL RED BOOK VALUES

DATE	1920			1920-D			1920-S		
	FN	EF	MS60	FN	EF	MS60	FN	EF	MS60
1951	0.40	------	3.25	1.75	------	32.50	1.75	------	35.00
1955	0.50	------	4.50	2.25	------	50.00	2.25	------	50.00
1960	0.75	1.75	7.50	5.00	35.00	80.00	5.00	35.00	80.00
1965	1.25	6.00	15.00	8.50	50.00	160.00	8.50	50.00	150.00
1970	1.15	5.25	22.50	9.00	55.00	195.00	8.00	48.50	195.00
1975	1.15	5.75	24.00	8.50	50.00	175.00	6.00	47.50	175.00
1980	1.50	7.50	30.00	8.75	55.00	275.00	6.25	51.50	285.00
1985	1.50	7.50	85.00	8.75	100.00	700.00	6.25	75.00	500.00
1990	1.50	7.50	90.00	8.75	100.00	700.00	6.25	75.00	500.00
1995	1.50	9.00	60.00	13.00	200.00	725.00	8.00	130.00	750.00
2000	1.50	9.00	75.00	17.00	220.00	1100.00	13.00	150.00	1000.00
2005	2.50	12.00	50.00	25.00	275.00	500.00	20.00	175.00	500.00

1920 CERTIFIED POPULATIONS

NGC	Total	MS61	MS62	MS63	MS64	MS65	MS66	MS67	MS68	MS69
1920	546	7	51	94	266	89	18	3	------	------
1920-D	385	16	37	51	139	13	1	------	------	------
1920-S	422	17	50	58	157	6	------	------	------	------
PCGS	**Total**	**MS61**	**MS62**	**MS63**	**MS64**	**MS65**	**MS66**	**MS67**	**MS68**	**MS69**
1920	993	3	40	198	385	190	88	8	------	------
1920-D	464	5	22	71	191	46	1	------	------	------
1920-S	593	4	37	99	227	15	1	------	------	------

- WORLD HISTORY -

The 18th Amendment to the Constitution prohibiting the manufacture and sale of alcohol is enforced. • The Anti-Saloon League pushed the Volstead Act through Congress against the "demon drink." • Adolf Hitler publishes a program for a third reich as the leader of the National Socialist Worker's Party. • War is declared between Poland and Russia. • A Communist party in Britain is founded. • The first 100 women are admitted to Oxford University. • Warren Harding is elected President. • Mohandas Gandhi presents a program to the Indian National Congress for non-cooperation with the British Government.

1921

BUSINESS STRIKE MINTAGES
Philadelphia: 10,663,000
Denver: None
San Francisco: 1,557,000

PROOF MINTAGES
None

Images Courtesy of Heritage

DIE VARIETIES

One 1921 doubled die is found on a 1921-P obverse. No doubled dies are known for 1921-S. No RPMs are known.

SCARCITY

Philadelphia: Not quite as scarce as the relatively low mintage would indicate. Partially due to the re-working of the master die and the resulting improvement in strike, very high grade Mint State pieces are not all that uncommon.

San Francisco: Not as tough in the higher levels of Mint State as other S mint dates of the era. VF and XF coins are very scarce with a full horn; the vast majority offered in this grade are badly overgraded and in reality are no better than Fine.

COMMENTS

Philadelphia: The Master die was re-worked this year, as is evidenced by the unique date style and completely different configuration of the hair detail directly above the braid ribbon. For this reason, fully struck coins comprise the majority of this issue.

San Francisco: The reworked obverse die allows for a number of full obverse strikes for this coin. The reverse, however, suffers from the same general weakness found on other S mint coins from the '20s, though not to the same degree as most other dates.

BUFFALO NICKEL RED BOOK VALUES

DATE	1921			1921-S		
	FN	EF	MS60	FN	EF	MS60
1951	0.50	------	5.50	3.50	------	40.00
1955	0.65	------	6.50	6.00	------	50.00
1960	1.25	3.00	11.00	9.50	40.00	90.00
1965	2.50	7.50	30.00	22.50	75.00	225.00
1970	2.60	11.50	59.00	25.00	95.00	335.00
1975	2.60	11.50	65.00	25.00	95.00	335.00
1980	3.00	14.50	75.00	30.00	115.00	475.00
1985	3.00	17.00	175.00	38.00	275.00	800.00
1990	3.00	17.00	180.00	40.00	325.00	1000.00
1995	3.00	20.00	120.00	50.00	625.00	1700.00
2000	3.00	20.00	135.00	70.00	675.00	1900.00
2005	6.00	50.00	100.00	175.00	850.00	1500.00

1921 CERTIFIED POPULATIONS

NGC	Total	MS61	MS62	MS63	MS64	MS65	MS66	MS67	MS68	MS69
1921	473	3	31	74	170	113	50	8	------	------
1921-S	455	4	11	29	89	21	3	------	------	------
PCGS	Total	MS61	MS62	MS63	MS64	MS65	MS66	MS67	MS68	MS69
1921	808	2	24	119	269	213	111	16	------	------
1921-S	731	1	11	65	188	50	7	------	------	------

- WORLD HISTORY -

Sun Yat-sen is elected president in China. • The Chinese Communist Party holds its first congress in Shanghai. • Britain, France, Japan, and the United States sign a treaty to control Naval build up in the Pacific. • Agatha Christie publishes *The Mysterious Affair at Styles*, her first detective novel. • The first gyroplane, an early form of helicopter, is designed by Etienne Oehmichen of France. • Benito Mussolini declares himself the leader of Italy's Fascists. • A severe drought in Russia causes famine and millions die of starvation. • Mohandas Gandhi is sentenced to six years for sedition.

1923

BUSINESS STRIKE MINTAGES
Philadelphia: 35,715,000
Denver: None
San Francisco: 6,142,000

PROOF MINTAGES
None

Images Courtesy of Heritage

DIE VARIETIES

A minor doubled die obverse is found on both the 1923-P and 1923-S. No RPMs are known. A possible S over D, as listed in the Breen reference on U.S. coinage is reported, but has yet to be authenticated. A few which have been examined look pretty convincing. Regardless, further study is needed, such as photographic overlays on high grade early die state coins, to once and for all confirm or deny its existence.

SCARCITY

Philadelphia: Scarcer in the higher Mint State grades than the previous year, despite a much higher mintage.

San Francisco: Not as difficult in Mint State as once thought. Full horn and MS65 examples are of some rarity but seem to be somewhat overrated.

COMMENTS

Philadelphia: Good strikes are typical for the issue, with true full strikes sometimes available as well.

San Francisco: This issue has its share of coins struck from eroded reverse dies, but well struck coins are not the great rarities found in other dates. Full strikes, though rare, can be found with some persistence.

BUFFALO NICKEL RED BOOK VALUES

DATE	1923			1923-S		
	FN	EF	MS60	FN	EF	MS60
1951	0.40	------	3.25	1.50	------	35.00
1955	0.40	------	4.00	2.00	------	42.50
1960	0.60	1.50	6.50	4.50	29.00	65.00
1965	1.25	4.00	12.50	8.00	45.00	140.00
1970	1.10	4.85	21.00	6.00	42.50	165.00
1975	1.10	4.75	23.00	6.00	42.50	165.00
1980	1.25	7.00	32.50	5.50	50.00	225.00
1985	1.25	7.00	90.00	5.50	60.00	400.00
1990	1.25	7.00	90.00	5.50	60.00	250.00
1995	1.50	8.00	60.00	8.00	185.00	550.00
2000	1.50	8.00	75.00	9.00	225.00	650.00
2005	3.00	12.00	50.00	18.00	275.00	450.00

1923 CERTIFIED POPULATIONS

NGC	Total	MS61	MS62	MS63	MS64	MS65	MS66	MS67	MS68	MS69
1923	631	9	40	98	269	150	31	7	------	------
1923-S	747	23	98	159	257	22	3	------	------	------
PCGS	Total	MS61	MS62	MS63	MS64	MS65	MS66	MS67	MS68	MS69
1923	968	5	28	164	385	232	82	8	------	------
1923-S	908	12	79	209	335	27	2	------	------	------

- WORLD HISTORY -

An earthquake in Tokyo kills 132,807, destroying half a million homes. • Vladimir Lenin retires in Russia after a stroke. • In London, the Matrimonial Causes Bill permits women to divorce their husbands for adultery. • President Warren Harding dies suddenly and is succeeded by Vice President Calvin Coolidge. • The first transatlantic wireless broadcast is made from Britain to the U.S. • In the U.S., the Ku Klux Klan claims a million members. • King George II is deposed by the Greek National Parliament.

1924

BUSINESS STRIKE MINTAGES
Philadelphia: 21,620,000
Denver: 5,258,000
San Francisco: 1,437,000

PROOF MINTAGES
None

Images Courtesy of Heritage

DIE VARIETIES

No doubled dies are known. Three nice RPMs are known on the 1924-D and two on the 1924-S.

SCARCITY

Philadelphia: Second only to the 1918 in Mint State rarity. AUs are scarce, but it is not difficult to find in all other grades.

Denver: Mint State pieces are typically low-end. It is scarce in MS65, as are circulated coins showing a full horn.

San Francisco: Like the 1921-S, most offered in VF or better are only Fines. Very difficult to find in true VF and especially difficult in true XF grade. Upper levels of Mint State coins are limited due to the poor strike shown by many examples.

COMMENTS

Philadelphia: The large majority are found with a typical strike, but well struck coins are sometimes seen. True full strikes are rare.

Denver: Almost always weak at the very front of the bison's head and the corresponding tip of the small feather on the obverse. The few that do show full detailing in these places invariably show incompleteness on the hair above the braid ribbon and/or on the bison's shoulder. A true full strike of this date is not known.

San Francisco: No true full strike for this date has been examined, though a very few have come close. Many are seen with a badly eroded reverse that is typical for the branch mint coins of the era. Some are so bad that they show no better than Good or Very Good detail even though they are technically Mint State in grade.

BUFFALO NICKEL RED BOOK VALUES

DATE	1924			1924-D			1924-S		
	FN	EF	MS60	FN	EF	MS60	FN	EF	MS60
1951	0.40	------	4.00	1.50	------	30.00	3.00	------	45.00
1955	0.40	------	5.00	1.75	------	40.00	5.00	------	75.00
1960	0.50	1.75	8.50	4.00	22.50	62.50	9.50	45.00	110.00
1965	1.30	3.00	15.00	7.00	45.00	125.00	19.00	80.00	250.00
1970	1.20	4.80	22.50	8.00	48.00	175.00	10.50	115.00	675.00
1975	1.25	7.50	37.50	8.00	48.00	200.00	13.50	125.00	675.00
1980	1.25	8.00	55.00	7.75	45.00	285.00	14.50	140.00	800.00
1985	1.25	8.00	135.00	8.00	85.00	450.00	14.50	225.00	1000.00
1990	1.25	8.00	135.00	8.00	85.00	450.00	14.50	400.00	1450.00
1995	1.50	9.00	75.00	8.00	130.00	475.00	30.00	900.00	2000.00
2000	1.50	10.00	85.00	12.00	150.00	650.00	45.00	1000.00	2900.00
2005	5.00	18.00	65.00	25.00	225.00	350.00	100.00	1250.00	2400.00

1924 CERTIFIED POPULATIONS

NGC	Total	MS61	MS62	MS63	MS64	MS65	MS66	MS67	MS68	MS69
1924	439	3	35	75	191	81	29	------	------	------
1924-D	413	9	29	46	195	16	1	------	------	------
1924-S	478	7	13	24	80	12	1	------	------	------
PCGS	Total	MS61	MS62	MS63	MS64	MS65	MS66	MS67	MS68	MS69
1924	717	4	23	130	296	159	48	3	------	------
1924-D	612	3	38	92	269	71	1	------	------	------
1924-S	578	0	24	46	124	32	1	------	------	------

- WORLD HISTORY -

Vladimir Lenin, founder of Soviet Russia, died. • The first Olympic winter games are held in France. • Mohandas Gandhi goes on a hunger strike in India. While serving his 6 year prison term, he is released from prison. • Adolph Hitler is sentenced to five years in prison, only to be set free after serving 8 months. • In Italy, Mussolini's Fascist party wins elections. • Calvin Coolidge is reelected President of the U.S. and James MacDonald becomes the first Labour Party Prime Minister in Britain.

1925

BUSINESS STRIKE MINTAGES
Philadelphia: 35,565,100
Denver: 4,450,000
San Francisco: 6,256,000

PROOF MINTAGES
None

Images Courtesy of Heritage

DIE VARIETIES

A master doubled die obverse is known and is found on coins from all three mints. Five RPMs are found on 1925-S coins.

SCARCITY

Philadelphia: Nearly as rare as the 1924 in MS65. Otherwise, Mint State coins are readily available.

Denver: Scarce at any level of Mint State and tough to find with a full, rounded (in relief) horn.

San Francisco: One of the premier rarities in the series at the MS65 level. Lower-end Mint State coins are slightly more often seen than those from the Denver Mint.

COMMENTS

Philadelphia: By this time the master hub had lost much of its fine detailing with the result that all coins from all three mints present a generally "mushy" appearance to one degree or another—especially on the obverse. Full strikes—to the limit of the detail remaining in the master hub—can sometimes be found, though they are rare. This applies to the following branch mint issues as well.

Denver: The same comments apply to this coin as to the P mint coin above. Of course, full strikes are much rarer.

San Francisco: Same comments as to the previous two. Full strikes are virtually unknown, though a few do exist.

BUFFALO NICKEL RED BOOK VALUES

DATE	1925			1925-D			1925-S		
	FN	EF	MS60	FN	EF	MS60	FN	EF	MS60
1951	0.30	------	3.00	1.75	------	15.00	2.50	------	50.00
1955	0.30	------	4.00	2.50	------	16.50	3.00	------	60.00
1960	0.50	3.50	8.50	7.50	17.50	33.00	7.50	30.00	100.00
1965	1.35	3.50	16.00	13.50	37.50	135.00	10.00	42.50	200.00
1970	1.35	4.75	22.50	12.00	50.00	210.00	8.50	48.00	230.00
1975	1.15	4.75	25.00	9.00	55.00	215.00	6.25	45.00	230.00
1980	1.25	7.00	30.00	11.00	65.00	300.00	6.75	52.50	300.00
1985	1.25	7.00	90.00	11.00	90.00	550.00	6.75	55.00	450.00
1990	1.25	7.00	90.00	11.00	90.00	550.00	6.75	55.00	450.00
1995	2.00	8.00	55.00	18.00	60.00	425.00	8.00	140.00	1200.00
2000	2.50	8.00	70.00	25.00	160.00	575.00	12.00	140.00	1700.00
2005	4.00	15.00	40.00	35.00	175.00	400.00	18.00	175.00	450.00

1925 CERTIFIED POPULATIONS

NGC	Total	MS61	MS62	MS63	MS64	MS65	MS66	MS67	MS68	MS69
1925	597	0	35	64	285	158	43	1	------	------
1925-D	489	10	52	86	202	49	4	------	------	------
1925-S	543	24	66	100	144	14	------	------	------	------
PCGS	Total	MS61	MS62	MS63	MS64	MS65	MS66	MS67	MS68	MS69
1925	1079	1	10	125	454	353	106	1	------	------
1925-D	676	6	56	151	275	53	2	------	------	------
1925-S	669	6	43	158	211	15	1	------	------	------

- WORLD HISTORY -

Three million people die in China from famine. • John Scopes, a teacher in Tennessee is convicted of teaching evolution in a state school and fined 100 dollars. • Adolph Hitler writes his book *Mein Kampf*. • Paul von Hindenburg becomes Germany's first elected president. • Cyprus becomes a British colony. • Walter Chrysler founds the Chrysler Motor Company. • The Ku Klux Klan has its first national congress. • The first motel in the U.S. opens in California. • Henry Souttar performs the first surgical operation inside the heart.

1926

BUSINESS STRIKE MINTAGES
Philadelphia: 44,693,000
Denver: 5,638,000
San Francisco: 970,000

PROOF MINTAGES
None

Images Courtesy of Heritage

DIE VARIETIES

One moderate Class VI is found on a 1926-P. No doubled dies are known for 1926-D or S. No RPMs are known. A 1926-D 3 ½ legged is known which only shows remnants of the center of the right front leg.

SCARCITY

Philadelphia: Common up to and including MS65.

Denver: Mint State coins are plentiful but most are struck from very worn out, eroded dies, both obverse and reverse. This poor quality of strike affects the higher levels of circulated grades to a great degree as well.

San Francisco: This is the rarest regular issue in Mint State. MS65 examples are notable 20th century rarities and are worth close to $100,000. VF coins are somewhat scarce; in XF grade it becomes much tougher. As with the 1921-S and 1924-S, many advertised in VF and XF are, at best, Choice Fine.

COMMENTS

Philadelphia: Apparently, the master hub was completely re-worked in 1926. Note that the date is larger and the numerals are thicker than in previous years and that the last digit of the date now lies on top of, instead of to the left of, the ribbon tie closest to the date. All other details, especially on the obverse, have been sharpened. In spite of these changes, most 1926-P coins show only a typical strike without the general "mushiness" of the 1925 issues. A good number show well struck devices, and a few exhibit a true full strike.

Denver: The bad reputation this date has applies much more because of worn dies than an actual deficiency of the strike, unlike the 1918-S. Some actual Mint State coins show only Good-VG detail on the reverse, much like the 1924-S. No true full strike is known.

San Francisco: Counter to its reputation, this coin sometimes comes with a decent strike—a trend that occurs for the next four years with regard to the San Francisco issues. Some are found struck from worn dies, but not to the degree of previous years. Horn and hair detail on the bison is usually complete but not sharp. Any true full strikes for this issue have yet to be seen.

BUFFALO NICKEL RED BOOK VALUES

DATE	1926			1926-D			1926-S		
	FN	EF	MS60	FN	EF	MS60	FN	EF	MS60
1951	0.25	------	2.25	0.50	------	4.50	3.00	------	70.00
1955	0.25	------	3.00	0.60	------	5.50	5.00	------	90.00
1960	0.35	1.00	6.00	1.00	2.25	10.00	12.50	60.00	165.00
1965	1.10	3.00	12.00	8.50	30.00	250.00	20.00	100.00	325.00
1970	0.95	4.75	18.00	10.00	50.00	315.00	16.50	115.00	440.00
1975	0.95	4.75	20.00	7.75	55.00	290.00	13.00	125.00	410.00
1980	0.95	5.00	27.00	9.00	60.00	300.00	15.50	150.00	625.00
1985	0.95	5.00	75.00	9.00	90.00	425.00	14.00	225.00	900.00
1990	0.95	5.00	80.00	9.00	90.00	425.00	14.00	300.00	1300.00
1995	0.95	5.00	40.00	14.00	110.00	400.00	25.00	775.00	2900.00
2000	1.00	5.00	50.00	16.00	110.00	450.00	35.00	760.00	5000.00
2005	2.50	10.00	35.00	24.00	175.00	300.00	75.00	900.00	4200.00

1926 CERTIFIED POPULATIONS

NGC	Total	MS61	MS62	MS63	MS64	MS65	MS66	MS67	MS68	MS69
1926	1050	2	19	61	352	435	159	12	1	------
1926-D	478	18	110	131	93	21	7	------	------	------
1926-S	739	7	18	38	76	5	1	------	------	------
PCGS	Total	MS61	MS62	MS63	MS64	MS65	MS66	MS67	MS68	MS69
1926	1984	2	9	112	790	779	254	20	------	------
1926-D	829	15	169	308	150	74	18	1	------	------
1926-S	953	3	13	85	111	10	------	------	------	------

- WORLD HISTORY -

For the first time, women are granted the right to run for public office in India. • Gertrude Ederle becomes the first female to swim the English Channel. • Film star Rudolf Valentino dies. • The book *Winnie-the-Pooh* is published by A. Milne. • Escape artist Harry Houdini dies. • In Persia, Ali Reza Kahn Pahavi is crowned the shah.

1927

BUSINESS STRIKE MINTAGES
Philadelphia: 37,981,000
Denver: 5,730,000
San Francisco: 3,430,000

PROOF MINTAGES
None

Images Courtesy of Heritage

DIE VARIETIES

A minor doubled die obverse is known on both the 1927-P and 1927-D. A nice 1927-S doubled die obverse shows mainly on the date. A 6-legged (doubling showing on both front legs) is found on a 1927-S reverse. There are two 1927-D RPMs, with one showing nice triple punching. No RPMs are known for 1927-S. A 1927-D 3 ½ legged is known which only shows remnants of the center of the right front leg.

SCARCITY

Philadelphia: Readily available in all grades up to and including MS65.

Denver: Common through the grade of VF. XF coins are slightly scarce, as are lower-end Mint State pieces. It becomes rare in MS65.

San Francisco: Years ago, this date and mint was considered to be rarer than the 1926-S in Mint State. While this is no longer the case, it is still one of the more difficult issues in the series at all Uncirculated levels and especially so in MS65.

COMMENTS

Philadelphia: True full strikes are *much rarer* than would be expected—only one has been seen. Typical strikes predominate; well struck coins can be found with some effort. The specimen strike coins show full, sharp detail comparable to the earlier Matte Proofs and the Satin Proofs of 1936.

Denver: Most Denver issues fall in the typical strike range; a true full strike of this date is unknown. Sometimes they are seen struck from the eroded dies used so frequently in past years.

San Francisco: This is a generally well produced issue—meaning they are well struck from dies that are in decent condition. Full strikes, though rare, are not unheard of. Coins struck from eroded dies are sometimes encountered.

BUFFALO NICKEL RED BOOK VALUES

DATE	1927			1927-D			1927-S		
	FN	EF	MS60	FN	EF	MS60	FN	EF	MS60
1951	0.25	------	2.50	0.50	------	5.50	3.00	------	70.00
1955	0.40	------	3.00	0.75	------	8.00	5.00	------	80.00
1960	0.45	1.00	5.00	1.50	3.50	14.00	8.50	40.00	130.00
1965	0.85	2.00	10.00	2.75	11.00	32.50	12.00	50.00	250.00
1970	0.85	4.00	15.50	3.75	15.00	45.00	6.50	45.00	250.00
1975	0.85	4.00	17.50	3.00	17.00	47.50	4.00	37.50	235.00
1980	0.95	5.00	26.00	3.00	20.00	65.00	3.00	41.00	300.00
1985	0.95	5.00	75.00	3.00	35.00	225.00	3.00	50.00	300.00
1990	0.95	5.00	75.00	3.00	35.00	260.00	3.00	60.00	325.00
1995	1.00	5.00	40.00	4.00	40.00	200.00	2.25	65.00	900.00
2000	1.00	5.00	45.00	4.00	40.00	235.00	2.25	65.00	1800.00
2005	2.50	10.00	30.00	7.00	75.00	15.00	5.00	85.00	500.00

1927 CERTIFIED POPULATIONS

NGC	Total	MS61	MS62	MS63	MS64	MS65	MS66	MS67	MS68	MS69
1927	684	3	32	58	271	237	66	7	------	------
1927-D	485	14	72	168	171	15	------	------	------	------
1927-S	371	19	57	64	110	10	1	------	------	------
PCGS	Total	MS61	MS62	MS63	MS64	MS65	MS66	MS67	MS68	MS69
1927	1446	2	13	120	501	562	206	4	------	------
1927-D	722	2	47	271	292	47	2	------	------	------
1927-S	570	7	30	136	216	20	------	------	------	------

- WORLD HISTORY -

Henry Segrave sets a land speed record of 203.841 mph. • In golf, the U.S. team wins the first Ryder Cup in Britain. • In Romania, 5-year-old Prince Mihail succeeds his father King Ferdinand. • Iraq's first oil strike is made in Kirkuk. • Charles Lindbergh becomes the first to make a solo crossing across the Atlantic in his Spirit of St. Louis. • Al Jolson becomes the first person to talk in a film. • In Russia, Joseph Stalin exiles his opponents to Siberia.

1928

BUSINESS STRIKE MINTAGES
Philadelphia: 23,411,000
Denver: 6,436,000
San Francisco: 6,936,000

PROOF MINTAGES
None

Images Courtesy of Heritage

DIE VARIETIES

No doubled dies or RPMs are known for 1928.

SCARCITY

Philadelphia: Compares favorably with the two previous Philadelphia coins, though it seems to be slightly tougher in MS65.

Denver: Common in low end Mint State, up to MS64. The poor strike quality of many coins limits MS65 and better grades.

San Francisco: Another generally well produced coin, often found with a good strike, even though many of these are from late state dies. Some are seen struck from eroded dies, especially on the reverse.

COMMENTS

Philadelphia: The same can be said for this date as the 1927, almost word for word. Only one full strike has been seen, and this from late state dies. Others doubtlessly exist but, like many of the coins from the late '20s into the early '30s, it is an unrecognized strike rarity.

Denver: Often seen with a very substandard strike. Well struck coins exist in small numbers. This is another date that has not been seen with a true full strike.

San Francisco: Another generally well produced coin, often found with a good strike, although many are from late state dies. A few full strikes are known.

BUFFALO NICKEL RED BOOK VALUES

DATE	1928			1928-D			1928-S		
	FN	EF	MS60	FN	EF	MS60	FN	EF	MS60
1951	0.20	------	2.00	0.25	------	1.50	0.40	------	7.50
1955	0.20	------	2.50	0.35	------	2.50	0.40	------	12.50
1960	0.25	0.75	4.50	0.45	1.25	4.50	0.85	3.00	24.00
1965	0.75	2.00	10.00	1.00	2.50	11.00	2.25	10.00	40.00
1970	0.80	3.75	16.00	1.40	4.75	17.50	2.00	8.75	52.50
1975	0.80	3.75	17.50	1.40	4.75	19.00	2.00	8.75	52.50
1980	0.95	4.50	26.00	2.25	8.00	30.00	1.50	9.50	75.00
1985	0.95	4.50	75.00	2.25	11.00	110.00	1.50	10.00	160.00
1990	0.95	4.60	75.00	2.25	11.00	110.00	1.50	10.00	175.00
1995	1.00	5.00	35.00	2.25	15.00	55.00	2.00	13.00	360.00
2000	1.00	6.00	50.00	2.25	16.00	75.00	2.00	13.00	550.00
2005	2.50	10.00	30.00	5.00	40.00	50.00	3.00	27.00	250.00

1928 CERTIFIED POPULATIONS

NGC	Total	MS61	MS62	MS63	MS64	MS65	MS66	MS67	MS68	MS69
1928	581	2	22	58	253	175	40	5	------	------
1928-D	1103	3	60	242	670	111	4	------	------	------
1928-S	494	17	77	113	177	36	3	------	------	------
PCGS	**Total**	**MS61**	**MS62**	**MS63**	**MS64**	**MS65**	**MS66**	**MS67**	**MS68**	**MS69**
1928	1247	1	15	162	495	396	130	11	------	------
1928-D	1748	6	50	449	944	251	28	------	------	------
1928-S	648	2	44	178	269	50	5	------	------	------

- WORLD HISTORY -

Walt Disney introduces Mickey Mouse in the first animated cartoon to have a sound track named Steamboat Willie. • After 70 years of work, the Oxford English Dictionary is complete. • In Turkey, Islam is abolished as the state religion. • Shares plunge on Wall Street on panic selling. • King Fuad of Egypt ends parliamentary government and makes himself dictator. • In Russia, Joseph Stalin creates a five year economic plan. • Herbert Hoover is elected President. • Hirohito is crowned Emperor in Japan at 27 years old. • In what was dubbed the "Valentine's Day Massacre," George "Bugsy" Moran and six other gang members were gunned down in Chicago.

1929

BUSINESS STRIKE MINTAGES
Philadelphia: 36,446,000
Denver: 8,370,000
San Francisco: 7,754,000

PROOF MINTAGES
None

Images Courtesy of Heritage

DIE VARIETIES

A moderate 1929-P doubled die obverse shows nice doubling on the date. A 1929-P doubled die reverse is one of the few Class I doubled dies in the Buffalo series. No doubled dies are known for 1929-D or S. Five different 1929-S RPMs are listed, with one in which the S is seen extending into the rim.

SCARCITY

Philadelphia: Common in all grades short of MS66.

Denver: The toughest of the three mints for 1929, though not rare, except in better than MS65.

San Francisco: Common in all grades up to and including MS65.

COMMENTS

Philadelphia: There is doubt that this date exists as a true full strike on the obverse—not one has ever been seen that even comes close. The main area of weakness is the hair detail directly above the braid ribbon. This issue is generally seen with a typical obverse strike at best, but sometimes shows a near full strike on the reverse. This coin is a true strike rarity.

Denver: One true full strike is seen for this issue. Otherwise, it often comes very poorly struck, especially on the reverse.

San Francisco: By far the best produced of the three mints for the year. About half will show a good strike. Full strikes exist.

BUFFALO NICKEL RED BOOK VALUES

DATE	1929			1929-D			1929-S		
	FN	EF	MS60	FN	EF	MS60	FN	EF	MS60
1951	0.15	------	0.75	0.25	------	1.50	0.25	------	1.25
1955	0.15	------	1.50	0.35	------	2.75	0.35	------	2.25
1960	0.15	0.75	3.25	0.40	1.50	5.00	0.40	1.25	4.50
1965	0.60	2.00	8.00	0.80	3.00	11.00	0.80	3.50	12.00
1970	0.75	2.50	11.75	0.90	3.50	36.50	0.90	3.50	16.50
1975	0.75	2.50	12.50	0.90	3.50	18.00	0.90	3.50	18.00
1980	0.85	4.00	24.00	1.40	5.00	40.00	1.00	4.00	30.00
1985	0.85	4.00	60.00	1.40	10.00	115.00	1.00	7.00	70.00
1990	0.85	4.00	65.00	1.40	10.00	125.00	1.00	7.00	90.00
1995	1.00	4.50	35.00	1.50	13.00	60.00	1.00	8.00	60.00
2000	1.00	4.50	45.00	1.50	13.00	75.00	1.00	8.00	70.00
2005	2.50	10.00	35.00	2.50	35.00	60.00	2.00	14.00	50.00

1929 CERTIFIED POPULATIONS

NGC	Total	MS61	MS62	MS63	MS64	MS65	MS66	MS67	MS68	MS69
1929	784	3	38	89	400	210	31	------	------	------
1929-D	542	12	54	119	285	49	11	------	------	------
1929-S	611	3	26	83	306	143	34	2	------	------
PCGS	**Total**	**MS61**	**MS62**	**MS63**	**MS64**	**MS65**	**MS66**	**MS67**	**MS68**	**MS69**
1929	1349	4	14	185	660	357	91	1	------	------
1929-D	861	4	36	232	404	115	40	1	------	------
1929-S	1209	1	18	174	504	345	119	4	------	------

- WORLD HISTORY -

The Great Depression starts in the United States after the stock market crashed. • The first Academy Awards are held, and the first one is awarded to Janet Gaynor. • The Vatican becomes a state. • Mahatma Gandhi is elected President of the Indian National Congress, but refuses to accept. • Margaret Bondfield is the first female to become a cabinet minister in Britain. • In Russia, Stalin declares all farms are to be part of a cooperative system.

1930

BUSINESS STRIKE MINTAGES
Philadelphia: 22,849,000
Denver: None
San Francisco: 5,435,000

PROOF MINTAGES
None

Images Courtesy of Heritage

DIE VARIETIES

1930 is the hottest year for Buffalo nickel doubled dies. Seven obverse and seven reverse doubled dies are listed in this book. Several of the obverse doubled dies show nicely on the eye, especially for DDO-004 and DDO-006. On the reverse doubled dies, the hottest is DDR-001, which is also called the "five-legged Buffalo." One doubled die reverse is known for a 1930-S. Eight RPMs are known for 1930-S.

SCARCITY

Philadelphia: Common up to and including MS65.

San Francisco: Only those coins grading MS66 or better can be considered rare. Most often they are seen in low-end Mint State.

COMMENTS

Philadelphia: Like the 1929, it would be a tremendous rarity with a full strike if one were to turn up. Unfortunately, no true full strike coin has ever been examined. Good strikes are more frequently seen for this issue than for the 1929 and they can be located without too much difficulty. Once again, the problem lies with the obverse; coins with a fully struck reverse are sometimes seen.

San Francisco: Generally a little better struck than the Philadelphia issue, but, as with that coin, no true full strike has been examined.

BUFFALO NICKEL RED BOOK VALUES

DATE	1930			1930-S		
	FN	EF	MS60	FN	EF	MS60
1951	0.10	------	1.50	0.30	------	2.50
1955	0.10	------	2.25	0.50	------	5.00
1960	0.15	0.75	4.00	1.00	2.00	10.00
1965	0.45	1.50	11.00	2.50	6.00	35.00
1970	0.65	2.00	14.00	1.60	5.50	40.00
1975	0.65	2.00	15.00	1.60	5.50	40.00
1980	0.85	4.00	25.00	1.00	5.75	50.00
1985	0.85	4.00	65.00	1.00	6.75	100.00
1990	0.85	4.00	65.00	1.00	6.75	125.00
1995	1.00	4.00	35.00	1.00	7.00	60.00
2000	1.00	4.00	40.00	1.00	7.00	75.00
2005	2.50	10.00	30.00	2.50	12.00	50.00

1930 CERTIFIED POPULATIONS

NGC	Total	MS61	MS62	MS63	MS64	MS65	MS66	MS67	MS68	MS69
1930	866	1	24	63	352	331	69	3	------	------
1930-S	481	2	33	55	207	144	20	1	------	------
PCGS	Total	MS61	MS62	MS63	MS64	MS65	MS66	MS67	MS68	MS69
1930	1836	0	18	113	622	825	205	18	------	------
1930-S	938	1	14	92	386	289	93	4	------	------

- WORLD HISTORY -

Mahatma Ganhdi makes his famous walk of 300 miles to defy the British salt tax. • Amy Johnson becomes the first woman to fly solo from Britain to Australia. • Pluto is discovered by Clyde Tombaugh. • White women are given the right to vote in South Africa. • Iraq's independence is recognized by Britain. • The Nazi party wins 107 seats in elections and becomes the second largest party in Germany behind the Socialists. • The radio-telescope is developed by Karl Jansky.

1931

BUSINESS STRIKE MINTAGES
Philadelphia: None
Denver: None
San Francisco: 1,200,000

PROOF MINTAGES
None

Images Courtesy of Heritage

DIE VARIETIES

Three doubled die reverses are known for 1931-S, with DDR-003 showing tripling on parts of EPU. One RPM is known for 1931-S.

SCARCITY

San Francisco: Common in all grades short of MS66.

COMMENTS

San Francisco: The vast majority of this date show a typical strike. Weak strikes are seen with some frequency and well struck coins are scarce. This is yet another date from the late '20s and early '30s that is unknown with a full strike, as the hair detail above the braid ribbon is always incomplete.

BUFFALO NICKEL RED BOOK VALUES

	1931-S		
DATE	FN	EF	MS60
1951	0.30	------	2.50
1955	0.45	------	4.00
1960	1.25	3.50	9.50
1965	5.50	12.50	50.00
1970	6.00	15.00	60.00
1975	5.00	10.00	55.00
1980	5.50	10.00	62.50
1985	5.50	10.00	100.00
1990	5.50	10.00	125.00
1995	5.50	10.00	65.00
2000	5.50	10.00	65.00
2005	18.00	22.00	50.00

1931 CERTIFIED POPULATIONS

NGC	Total	MS61	MS62	MS63	MS64	MS65	MS66	MS67	MS68	MS69
1931-S	1263	2	13	73	516	573	57	2	------	------
PCGS	**Total**	**MS61**	**MS62**	**MS63**	**MS64**	**MS65**	**MS66**	**MS67**	**MS68**	**MS69**
1931-S	2699	4	19	183	1073	1103	274	1	------	------

- WORLD HISTORY -

Inventor Thomas Edison dies. • The "Star Spangled Banner" becomes the national anthem of the U.S. • King Alfonso XIII abdicates his throne in Spain. • The Empire State Building opens in New York. • Britain, Denmark, Norway, Sweden, Japan, and Egypt abandon the gold standard. • Mao Zedong is appointed Chairman of the central executive committee of the Chinese Soviet Republic. • The Indian National Congress is outlawed and Gandhi is arrested.

1934

BUSINESS STRIKE MINTAGES
Philadelphia: 20,213,003
Denver: 7,480,000
San Francisco: None

PROOF MINTAGES
None

Images Courtesy of Heritage

DIE VARIETIES

One doubled die obverse and three doubled die reverses are known for 1934-P. One obverse and two reverse doubled dies are known for 1934-D. One RPM is known for 1934-D.

SCARCITY

Philadelphia: Common up to and including MS65.

Denver: Scarce in MS65 or better; otherwise common in Mint State.

COMMENTS

Philadelphia: The most common date with a full strike of this era. A number are known. Most often they are seen with a typical strike, but well struck coins are not by any means rare.

Denver: The last regular issue date in the series that has not been seen with a true full strike. A few have come close. Usually shows a typical strike, though very weak coins from badly eroded dies are not uncommon.

BUFFALO NICKEL RED BOOK VALUES

DATE	1934			1934-D		
	FN	EF	MS60	FN	EF	MS60
1951	------	------	1.25	------	------	1.50
1955	------	------	1.85	------	------	2.75
1960	0.25	0.75	3.75	0.45	1.25	4.75
1965	0.35	1.00	8.00	0.75	2.25	11.00
1970	0.65	2.00	11.00	0.70	2.50	13.50
1975	0.65	2.00	12.00	0.70	2.50	16.50
1980	0.60	3.50	26.00	0.85	5.00	32.00
1985	0.60	3.50	55.00	0.85	5.00	115.00
1990	0.60	3.50	60.00	0.85	5.00	115.00
1995	1.00	4.00	35.00	1.00	8.00	60.00
2000	1.00	4.00	35.00	1.00	8.00	70.00
2005	2.50	10.00	50.00	2.50	15.00	70.00

1934 CERTIFIED POPULATIONS

NGC	Total	MS61	MS62	MS63	MS64	MS65	MS66	MS67	MS68	MS69
1934	676	2	30	68	246	234	66	2	------	------
1934-D	783	7	51	165	452	89	8	------	------	------
PCGS	**Total**	**MS61**	**MS62**	**MS63**	**MS64**	**MS65**	**MS66**	**MS67**	**MS68**	**MS69**
1934	1262	4	15	117	480	427	142	17	------	------
1934-D	1513	4	71	435	675	249	32	------	------	------

- WORLD HISTORY -

Germany signs a 10-year non-aggression pact with Poland. • Bonnie and Clyde are killed in a police ambush. • Adolph Hitler takes the title of Fuhrer after the death of Hindenburg. • Women get the right to vote in Turkey. • Persia is renamed to Iran. • Radar is invented in Britain. • Japan installs Puyi, the last emperor of China, as the emperor of Manchuria.

1935

BUSINESS STRIKE MINTAGES
Philadelphia: 58,264,000
Denver: 12,092,000
San Francisco: 10,300,000

PROOF MINTAGES
None

Images Courtesy of Heritage

DIE VARIETIES

After 1930, this is the second best year for total number of doubled dies. One obverse and four reverse doubled dies are known for 1935-P. One doubled die obverse and three doubled die reverses are known for 1935-S. Of course, the nicest 1935 doubled die is the dramatic 1935 DDR-001. This variety is the third hottest doubled die in the Buffalo series, worth over $25,000 in MS65. Many of the other 1935 doubled dies show nice doubling. Some are rare, such as the 1935 DDO-001, which has proven difficult to locate. Eleven 1935-D RPMs are known as are eleven 1935-S RPMs, some of which are dramatic and highly sought after.

SCARCITY

Philadelphia: Common up to and including MS66. MS67s are very scarce.

Denver: Common up to and including MS64. Scarce in MS65 or better.

San Francisco: Common up to and including MS65.

COMMENTS

Philadelphia: Typical strikes predominate, but well struck coins exist in large numbers. Full strikes, on the other hand, are rarely seen. DOUBLED DIE REVERSE—As would be expected, it generally follows the pattern of the regular issue regarding the strike. It is rare enough in Mint State, however, that no full strike of this variety has yet turned up.

Denver: Weak strikes and coins struck from very late state dies are common. Despite a reputation to the contrary, a much higher percentage of weak strikes are seen on the S mint coin than on the Denver issue. True full strikes are virtually unknown for this date.

San Francisco: Very poor strikes are a serious problem with this issue—more so than with the Denver issue. As with the D mint coin, true full strikes are excessively rare. Fewer are seen from badly worn dies than the D mint.

BUFFALO NICKEL RED BOOK VALUES

DATE	1935			1935-D			1935-S		
	FN	EF	MS60	FN	EF	MS60	FN	EF	MS60
1951	------	------	0.50	------	------	0.75	------	------	0.75
1955	------	------	0.50	------	------	0.85	------	------	1.25
1960	0.15	0.35	1.25	0.20	0.75	2.50	0.25	0.90	3.00
1965	0.25	0.70	4.00	0.40	1.75	8.50	0.50	1.50	7.50
1970	0.35	1.10	5.50	0.50	2.00	10.50	0.50	1.90	9.75
1975	0.35	1.10	7.25	0.50	2.00	11.25	0.50	1.90	9.75
1980	0.45	2.00	20.00	0.60	3.50	22.50	0.50	2.50	22.00
1985	0.45	2.00	35.00	0.60	3.50	100.00	0.50	2.50	50.00
1990	0.45	2.25	35.00	0.60	3.50	110.00	0.50	2.50	50.00
1995	1.00	2.25	20.00	1.25	8.00	45.00	1.00	2.50	35.00
2000	1.00	2.25	20.00	1.25	8.00	50.00	1.00	2.50	35.00
2005	1.75	2.50	20.00	2.50	15.00	60.00	2.00	4.00	50.00

1935 CERTIFIED POPULATIONS

NGC	Total	MS61	MS62	MS63	MS64	MS65	MS66	MS67	MS68	MS69
1935	939	4	19	39	141	426	257	25	------	------
1935-D	856	3	30	101	442	233	28	2	------	------
1935-S	983	3	12	8	13	3	2	------	------	------
PCGS	Total	MS61	MS62	MS63	MS64	MS65	MS66	MS67	MS68	MS69
1935	1867	2	18	89	423	833	386	56	------	------
1935-D	1593	2	19	297	836	320	96	6	------	------
1935-S	1914	1	8	158	682	752	268	24	------	------

1935 DOUBLED DIE REVERSE

PCGS	Total	VG-VF	XF40/5	AU50/3	AU55	AU58	MS61-3	MS64	------	------
1935	74	49	4,4	3,3	3	3	3,3,3	3	------	------

- WORLD HISTORY -

The German air force Luftwaffe is created. • France and the USSR sign a mutual defense pact if either is attacked. • Pierre Laval becomes Prime Minister of France. • Stanley Baldwin becomes Prime Minister in Britain. • Franklin Roosevelt signs the Social Security Bill. • Sir Malcolm Campbell sets a land-speed record of 301.337 mph. • Mussolini's troops invade Ethiopia.

1936

BUSINESS STRIKE MINTAGES
Philadelphia: 119,001,420
Denver: 24,814,000
San Francisco: 14,930,000

PROOF MINTAGES
Philadelphia: 4,420

Images Courtesy of Heritage

DIE VARIETIES

Two doubled die obverses and one doubled reverse is known for a 1936-P. One doubled die reverse is known for 1936-D. 1936 DDO-001 and DDR-001 are two of the most dramatic Class VI doubled dies of the series. Both show extra thickness on the lettering around the rim. 1936 DDO-001 is worth over $1,200 in MS65, while 1936 DDR-001 is worth around $500 in MS65. Fourteen RPMs are known for 1936-D and eleven are known for 1936-S. Several of these are very dramatic RPMs, including a 1936-S (RPM-001), which shows the second S extending into the rim. A 1936-D 3 ½ legged is known which only shows remnants of the center of the right front leg.

SCARCITY

Philadelphia: Common in all grades short of MS67.

Denver: Common in all grades short of MS67. All dates and mints from 1936 to the end of the series were saved in roll quantity.

San Francisco: Common in all grades up to and including MS66.

COMMENTS

Philadelphia: Typical strikes slightly outnumber well struck coins, determined by the hair detail above the braid ribbon. They are usually well struck to fully struck elsewhere. Striking extremes—both weak strikes and true full strikes—are unusual.

Denver: Typical strikes predominate to a greater degree than on the P mint issue but full strikes are a little more common percentage wise.

San Francisco: Generally, better struck than either the Philly or Denver issue, but true full strikes on the obverse, with full hair detail above the braid ribbon and on the bison, especially at the top of the left front leg, are quite rare.

BUFFALO NICKEL RED BOOK VALUES

DATE	1936			1936-D			1936-S		
	FN	EF	MS60	FN	EF	MS60	FN	EF	MS60
1951	------	------	0.50	------	------	0.60	------	------	0.70
1955	------	------	0.50	------	------	0.75	------	------	0.85
1960	------	0.35	1.25	------	0.35	1.25	------	0.45	1.50
1965	0.25	0.60	3.25	0.35	0.70	3.75	0.35	1.00	4.00
1970	0.30	0.65	4.50	0.40	1.15	4.75	0.40	1.20	5.50
1975	0.30	0.65	6.25	0.40	1.15	6.25	0.40	1.20	7.00
1980	0.40	1.50	18.00	0.50	2.00	20.00	0.50	1.90	20.00
1985	0.40	1.50	25.00	0.60	2.00	35.00	0.50	1.90	37.50
1990	0.40	2.25	25.00	0.50	2.25	35.00	0.50	2.35	37.50
1995	1.00	2.25	20.00	1.00	2.50	22.00	1.00	2.25	20.00
2000	1.00	2.25	20.00	1.00	2.50	22.00	1.00	2.25	20.00
2005	1.75	4.00	15.00	1.75	4.00	35.00	1.75	3.50	35.00

1936 CERTIFIED POPULATIONS

NGC	Total	MS61	MS62	MS63	MS64	MS65	MS66	MS67	MS68	MS69
1936	1759	7	35	45	220	625	712	46	2	------
1936-D	1392	0	6	23	185	734	421	12	------	------
1936-S	1080	2	6	15	193	543	286	25	------	------
PCGS	**Total**	**MS61**	**MS62**	**MS63**	**MS64**	**MS65**	**MS66**	**MS67**	**MS68**	**MS69**
1936	3410	3	21	122	693	1538	833	67	------	------
1936-D	2474	0	5	91	603	1229	466	52	2	------
1936-S	2460	1	9	39	518	1300	501	52	------	------

- WORLD HISTORY -

Spain falls into civil war. • The Olympic Games are held in Berlin. • The great Jesse Owens sets several sprint records and upsets the Nazis after winning four gold medals. • In Britain, after the death of George V, Edward VIII is proclaimed king and later abdicates. • 16-year-old Prince Farouk succeeds King Fuad in Egypt. • Mussolini announces anti-communist axis with Germany. • President Roosevelt is elected President for a second term.

1937

BUSINESS STRIKE MINTAGES
Philadelphia: 79,485,769
Denver: 17,826,000
San Francisco: 5,635,000

PROOF MINTAGES
Philadelphia: 5,769

Images Courtesy of Heritage

DIE VARIETIES

One minor doubled die obverse is found on a 1937-P. No doubled dies are known for 1937-D or S. Fifteen RPMs are known for 1937-D and seven are known for 1937-S. The 1937-D "3 legged" Buffalo is the true and original three legged Buffalo nickel. The entire right front leg was completely polished off. This variety can be worth $30,000 in MS65.

SCARCITY

Philadelphia: Very common in all grades below MS67.

Denver: Very common in all grades through MS66.

San Francisco: Very common in all grades below MS67.

COMMENTS

Philadelphia: As with the 1936 issue, striking extremes—weak or full—are unusual. The majority exhibit a typical strike.

Denver: See the comments for the 1937-P. THREE LEGGED VARIETY—Most are well struck considering the limitations imposed by the damaged die. Both weak strikes and full strikes are very rare.

San Francisco: These more often show a better strike than either the P or D issue, but, as with those, striking extremes are rare.

BUFFALO NICKEL RED BOOK VALUES

DATE	1937			1937-D			1937-S		
	FN	EF	MS60	FN	EF	MS60	FN	EF	MS60
1951	------	------	0.35	------	------	0.40	------	------	0.50
1955	------	------	0.35	------	------	0.40	------	------	0.60
1960	------	0.30	0.75	------	0.35	1.00	------	0.35	1.25
1965	0.20	0.60	3.00	0.20	0.60	3.50	0.30	0.75	4.00
1970	0.30	0.70	4.25	0.40	1.00	5.00	0.50	1.30	6.25
1975	0.30	0.70	6.50	0.40	1.00	6.50	0.50	1.30	7.50
1980	0.45	1.50	18.00	0.55	1.75	20.00	0.55	1.75	20.00
1985	0.45	1.50	20.00	0.55	1.75	25.00	0.55	1.75	25.00
1990	0.45	2.25	23.00	0.55	2.25	25.00	0.55	2.25	25.00
1995	1.00	2.00	18.00	1.00	2.00	19.00	1.00	2.00	19.00
2000	1.00	2.00	18.00	1.00	2.00	19.00	1.00	2.00	19.00
2005	1.75	3.00	15.00	1.75	3.00	30.00	1.75	3.50	30.00

1937 CERTIFIED POPULATIONS

NGC	Total	MS61	MS62	MS63	MS64	MS65	MS66	MS67	MS68	MS69
1937	5471	3	16	26	266	1369	3490	297	2	------
1937-D	2796	2	9	25	175	975	1502	77	1	------
1937-S	2199	0	9	28	217	1173	733	23	------	------

PCGS	Total	MS61	MS62	MS63	MS64	MS65	MS66	MS67	MS68	MS69
1937	7891	6	23	95	837	4145	2481	220	4	------
1937-D	4619	3	6	49	696	2598	1168	66	1	------
1937-S	4338	1	6	57	766	2490	931	70	------	------

1937-D 3 LEGS

NGC	Total	VG	F	VF	XF40	XF45	AU50	AU53	AU55	AU58
1937-D	3075	11	56	212	116	174	114	107	335	789
		MS60	MS61	MS62	MS63	MS64	MS65	MS66	MS67	------
		11	282	420	224	168	39	14	1	------

PCGS	Total	VG-VF	XF40	XF45	AU50	AU53	AU55	AU58	MS60	------
1937-D	3813	679	278	434	359	213	580	592	29	26
		MS62	MS63	MS64	MS65	MS66	------	------	------	------
		236	207	137	39	4	------	------	------	------

- WORLD HISTORY -

The German airship Hindenburg explodes when attempting to land in New Jersey. • India creates a constitution under the Government of India. • King George VI and Queen Elizabeth are crowned in Britain. • Neville Chamberlain becomes Prime Minister in Britain. • The Japanese occupy Beijing and bomb the Chinese Nationalist capital Nanjing. • Mexico takes over all U.S. and British oil companies in Mexico. • German bombers destroy the Basque town of Guernica. • Wallace Carothers creates nylon.

1938

BUSINESS STRIKE MINTAGES
Philadelphia: None
Denver: 7,020,000
San Francisco: None

PROOF MINTAGES
None

Images Courtesy of Heritage

DIE VARIETIES

One doubled die reverse is known on a 1938-D. Twelve RPMs are known for 1938-D. The nicest varieties for 1938 are the over mintmarks. Six OMMs were listed in the first edition of this book; two of these were delisted in this edition. OMM-001 is the most dramatic of these D/S varieties, but OMM-006 is easily the rarest.

SCARCITY

Denver: Exceedingly common in all but the very highest Mint State levels, many rolls of this issue were saved as the last of their kind—it's the Good and Very Good level coins that are rarities!

COMMENTS

Denver: Many are seen advertised as "Fully Struck," but the number of *true* full strikes is not appreciably greater, percentage wise, than most of the other typically well struck coins in the series. In most cases, these coins lack only the tiniest amount of full hair detail above the braid ribbon. A large majority of the issue shows a 90-95 percent full strike. Poorly struck and very late die state examples are almost unheard of.

BUFFALO NICKEL RED BOOK VALUES

	1938-D		
DATE	FN	EF	MS60
1951	------	------	0.25
1955	------	------	0.25
1960	------	0.25	0.75
1965	0.35	0.75	3.00
1970	0.45	1.25	4.75
1975	0.45	1.25	6.50
1980	0.55	1.75	17.50
1985	0.55	1.75	20.00
1990	0.65	2.25	23.00
1995	1.00	2.00	18.00
2000	1.00	2.00	18.00
2005	3.00	3.75	20.00

1938 CERTIFIED POPULATIONS

NGC	Total	MS61	MS62	MS63	MS64	MS65	MS66	MS67	MS68	MS69
1938-D	21956	4	5	35	439	4618	15418	1418	10	------
PCGS	Total	MS61	MS62	MS63	MS64	MS65	MS66	MS67	MS68	MS69
1938-D	40940	3	16	99	2571	18300	18810	1102	6	------

- WORLD HISTORY -

Sigmund Freud fleas Germany into Britain. • Austria joins Germany and Hitler's Reich. • German troops march into Czechoslovakia. • Anti-Jewish violence rises in Germany.

Chapter 2
Buffalo Nickel Proof and Brilliant Proof Issues

The "Proof" is in the Purpose

What are proof coins and how are they distinguishable from circulation strikes?

By definition, the term *proof* refers to the method of manufacture and not the condition of the coin.

Proof coins are made by the Mint for presentation, souvenir, exhibition, numismatic purposes, and to encourage coin collecting. They normally have mirror-like fields, sharp detailed designs, and high squared rims. In the eyes of the collector, proof coins represent the essence of beauty and the attainment of perfection in a coin. The sharp details of the design bring life to the images portrayed. The mirror surfaces create an aura around the figures, and the wire rims create the distinction between perfection and the rest.

All proof dies are made at Philadelphia. The working dies to be used for striking proofs are hand picked for their sharp details, and the dies are then cleaned and polished to create a mirror-like surface. The planchets to be used for proof coins are also polished. In the coining press, each coin was normally struck two or more times to produce sharper details and a wire edge rim. The coins, once struck, are handled by hand to prevent any contact marks. Almost all proofs until 1967 were struck at the Philadelphia Mint. All proofs struck after 1967 were stuck at the San Francisco Mint. The exact process of creating and treating the dies and planchets has changed over the course of the Mint's history.

Proof coinage was first struck by the U.S. Mint in the 1820s. Up until 1858, the Mint did not keep official records on how many proof coins were struck for a given year. Sometimes during this period, proof coins were struck for special occasions or foreign dignitaries. A clear example is in 1834, when the State Department requested a proof set for the King of Siam. This included the famous 1804 Dollar. In 1858, the Mint began publicly selling proof coins and sets. Hereafter, the proof mintages for most of the denominations is known. Some of these totals are not accurate as proof coins not sold for a given year were sometimes melted, sometimes held over for several years, and sometimes released with circulated coins.

During most of the 19th century, a proof coin was created through polishing of the face of the working die to give it mirror-like surfaces. In 1907, the curvature and texture of the fields of the new Saint-Gaudens twenty-dollar gold coins made it difficult to polish the dies. In 1908, and again between 1911 and 1915, a method called sandblasting was used on gold proofs. This method involved holding a coin under a stream of sand after it was struck. This created a dull, non-reflective surface which we know as a Matte Proof. Sandblasting was not used on silver coins before 1917, but it is believed to have been used on the Lincoln cents and Buffalo nickels. Some experts believe that for the Buffalo nickels, the dies were sandblasted, not the coins.

From 1917 through 1935, no proof coins were struck at the Mint. There is speculation that a handful of proof coins were struck in 1917, but no documentation has ever been found to back this up. In 1936, interest in coin collecting reappeared. Because the Mint had forgotten how to make Brilliant Proofs, the first proofs produced were "satin" like. Collectors complained about these coins, and the Mint struck Brilliant Proofs in the second half of 1936. These were produced until 1942.

With World War II, the production of proof coins at the Mint again was halted from 1943 through 1949. In 1950, proof coins were again struck. The techniques used in the preparation of the dies and planchets were improved. The dies were dipped in a solution of 5 percent nitric acid and 95 percent alcohol. This produced a light frosting over the entire die. After the fields of the coin were polished, the frosting was left on the design elements. This frosting, also known as a *Cameo*, was struck into the coin. After a few coins were struck, the frosting quickly wore off the dies, making these early Cameo proof coins rare. This process was refined up until 1970, when it was dramatically improved by sandblasting and chrome plating the dies. This new process etched the frosting deep into the dies and made the dies harder, thus retaining the Cameo effect after striking many coins.

Sometimes circulated strikes can have sharp details from being the first coins struck from a new die. These coins might even exhibit slightly mirror-like fields. *This does not make these coins proof.*

If the method of manufacture is not intended to create proofs, and if the Mint's intention was not to strike the coins as proofs, they cannot be classified as proofs.

For example, only 24 1894-S dimes were struck from a single set of working dies intended for circulated strikes. The coins exhibit sharp details as expected from new dies. This does not make them proofs. If we were to use the condition of a coin to determine if it is a proof, imagine the grey area that would be created: At what point would one determine that the sharp strike from new dies has been sufficiently diminished by wear and use to be classified as no longer proof or proof-like?

Defining a Difference: Cameo or Satin?

Methods of Minting Proofs

By Roger W. Burdette

Before 1907, all proof coins—gold, silver, copper-nickel and bronze—were made with polished fields and sometimes a dull, unpolished portrait and lettering. In 1907, the Saint-Gaudens designs were adopted for the eagle and double eagle. Due to die curvature and texture of the field (or "ground" as Mint engravers called it), polishing the dies to make brilliant proofs was not practical. To provide special coins for collectors, the Philadelphia Mint produced sandblast (called "dull" by Mint staff) proof coins for all four gold denominations in 1908.

To help understand the differences between each version of collectors' "proof" coin, the following presents a short description of how the pieces were manufactured.

Brilliant Proof, gold—Polished mirror-like surfaces on field and devices. Struck on a hydraulic press from new, carefully impressed dies. Dies and planchets usually polished. Standard minor "proof coin" sold to collectors from 1858 to 1909/1913; silver from 1858 to 1915; gold from 1858 to 1907. Standard for collectors' proof sets when modern series was begun in 1936. Very easily hairlined due to cleaning or rubbing with a cloth.

Cameo Proof, gold—Polished mirror-like fields with frosted devices (lettering and portrait). Struck on a hydraulic press from new, carefully impressed dies. Only field of dies polished; planchets usually polished. Seen on proof coins sold to collectors from 1858 to 1915 as consequence of incomplete die polishing. Highly prized today because of the visual contrast between portrait and field. Often encountered on modern proof coins made after 1936.

Sandblast Proof, gold—Dull, non-reflective surfaces. Struck on a hydraulic press from new, carefully impressed dies. Dies and planchets not polished although planchets selected for smooth surfaces. After striking, the coins were lightly sandblasted in a manner similar to medals. Standard gold proof coins sold to collectors 1908 and 1911-15. Correctly called sandblast proof since this describes how the pieces were made. Surface very delicate and easily marred. Sandblasting tends to exaggerate the color of the gold, particularly the greenish specimens (caused by excess silver in the alloy).

Satin Proof, gold—So-called Roman proof of 1909–1910. Lustrous non-mirror surfaces. Lacking mint frost commonly seen on normal circulation strikes. Produced on a hydraulic press from new, carefully impressed dies. Hubs were lightly buffed before annealing to remove stray burrs left from cutting the metal on the reducing lathe. Planchets not polished although planchets were selected for smooth surfaces. No post-strike treatment. Easily confused with early circulation strikes that were made the same way but on normal coining presses. Standard gold "proof coin" sold to collectors 1909 and 1910. Surface easily marred. Minimal visual distinction between these and ordinary circulation strikes. Analogous to satin proofs of later years.

Sandblast Proof, silver—Dull, non-reflective surfaces. Struck on a hydraulic press from new, carefully impressed dies. Dies and planchets not polished although planchets selected for smooth surfaces. After striking, the coins were lightly sandblasted in a manner similar to medals. Used on 1921 and 1922 Peace dollar proofs and some commemorative halves. Correctly called sandblast proof since this describes how the pieces were made. Surface very delicate and easily marred. Sandblasting tends to give silver a gray, pewter-like color.

Satin Proof, silver—Smooth, fine-grained, non-reflective surfaces with little "mint bloom" and only slight lustre. Struck on a hydraulic press from new, carefully impressed dies. Hubs not buffed, resulting in very fine texture. Dies were not treated; planchets not polished although planchets were usually selected for smooth surfaces. No post-strike treatment. Analogous process to "Roman" proofs as seen on gold coins 1909–1910. Seen on 1921–1922 Peace dollars and occasional later Saint-Gaudens gold coins. Also on some commemorative half dollars from the 1920s and '30s. This surface was called "bright" in contrast to "sandblast" by mint personnel in 1922. Easily confused with "first strikes" from new dies, since this is essentially what a satin proof is, except for the greater detail and square rims imparted by the hydraulic press. Not a standard mint "proof" surface until late 1980s when the U.S. Mint started calling them "Matte Proof." Surface easily marred.

Results of sandblasting and other techniques often varied from coin to coin and year to year, depending on which assistant did the work and whether procedures were followed carefully. The so-called Roman proofs typically look like perfect first strikes from new dies—which they were—and are similar to the 1907 Saint-Gaudens patterns which were not produced as deliberate proofs.

This excerpt originally appeared in *Renaissance of American Coinage 1905-1908*, by Roger W. Burdette, and is reprinted with permission.

Proof Overview: 1913-1916

One of the basic questions with the 1913 through 1916 Buffalo nickel proofs is what method was used to produce them?

No archive documents have been found to state what special measures were taken with the working dies or planchets. The coins do not exhibit the mirror-like fields found on Brilliant Proofs, such as those on the 1936 Type II and 1937 Brilliant Proof Buffalo nickels. Obviously the working dies and planchets were not polished. The coins display a granular, dull, non-reflective surface, also referred to as a matte-surface. Most experts believe these coins are the result of sandblasting.

One primary difference from the sandblast gold proofs of 1908 and 1911 through 1915 is that the gold proofs are the result of sandblasting the coins after the coins were struck. Many experts believe that Buffalo nickel working dies were sandblasted, not the individual coins. Another diagnostic that was presented by several experts is that the Buffalo nickel Matte Proofs exhibited mirrored edges. This is caused by the collar in the medal press and imparts a mirror or polished edge along with the square rim. If the coins were individually sandblasted, then it is very likely that many would show overrun from the sandblasting. For example, some of the edge would also appear sandblasted—yet that does not seem to be the case. It is a negative argument against each coin being sandblasted, as was done with the gold pieces.

Gold coins during this period were sandblasted after they were struck. But normally, there was only an average of 100 gold proofs of a given denomination. For minor proofs, there was normally over 1,000 proofs. Sandblasting the minor proof dies would be more practical to create this surface, rather than sandblasting each coin.

One point made by Roger Burdette is that sandblasting the dies should have created identical microscopic patterns of pits. If the dies were sandblasted then hardened, every coin made from the same dies would show the same pattern of tiny pits caused by quartz sand particles cutting the die's surface. This would be similar to a scratch on a die, which shows on hundreds of coins before it wears away. Thus, if two or more Buffalo nickels show identical micro-pit patterns, then they must have come from the same dies. This means they could not have been sandblasted individually. It also suggests that after a period of time, normal flow of die metal would wipe out much of the sandblast effect and the coins would look like well struck circulation pieces.

These Matte Proof coins did not have the brilliant surfaces of previous coins, making them harder to distinguish from well struck business strikes. As the coins were stored in yellow tissue paper by the mint, most coins also became toned. In most cases, Matte Proof nickels can be identified by their sharp, squared-off inner and outer rims, a soft, dull lustre, a slightly granular surface, and often, very fine die polish. Be careful when identifying these proofs because there are some deceptive circulated strikes.

Sales were low for these Matte Proof coins because collectors wanted the brilliant coins that stood out. Matte Proof production and sales steadily declined through 1916, with speculation that a few specimens were struck in 1917. But no documentation has ever been found to verify this. In James Rankin Young's book, *The United States Mint at Philadelphia* (1903), he describes the operations of the Mint, room by room. His description of the medal room supports the use of sandblasting in the production of Proof coins:

"In a single room in the southern end of the second floor of the building is the medal room, a department under the Coiner, though almost an independent mint in itself. All the "proof coins" [those given a particularly fine finish] and medals are made in this room. In one side of the room is a small furnace and a melting pot where melts can be made if necessary. In either side of the furnace is an annealing oven. In the center of the room is a large cutting press, which will cut dies up to four inches in diameter. Against the wall are two electrically driven hydraulic presses, capable respectively of a pressure of 400 and 300 tons to the square inch, and next to them the two hydraulic pumps.

In the basement this department has a huge press capable of giving 1100 tons pressure to the square inch. This is used on the largest dies, those four inches in diameter. Off in an out-of-the-way corner is the old-fashioned hand screw press, with its long arms and heavy weights.

The foreman, growing reminiscent, tells how, as a helper, he used to get these arms going around at such a gait that they would move the whole machine.

The proof sets of coins are made under the government supervision to be preserved for record, or sold to collectors. The face of the dies used in stamping these sets have been given an extra fine finish, and glisten as though they had been nickel-plated. The blanks for the coins are annealed and stamped by the hydraulic press. The operator then gives them a thorough acid bath, and polishes them singly with a handful of wet sand. If they are bronze pieces, they may be given the deep bronze finish or clouded over in the sandblast. The latter device is a small wooden box with glass slides. A pipe on the inside blows down a fine shower of sand. The operator, wearing a big pair of mitts to protect his hands, holds the coin under this stream of sand until the operation is finished, when it has a delicate frosted finish."

1913-1916 Buffalo Nickel Proof Counts

How many Buffalo nickel proof coins were struck between 1913 and 1916?

When trying to answer this question, it was discovered that some of the currently accepted totals are incorrect.

On the following pages is a year-by-year analysis. At the top of each page is the number documented in the *Red Book* that was first printed in 1951. These are the same as the totals in Breen's Proof book. Where did these totals come from? In 1947, a request was made to the Director of the Mint for these totals. The fiscal yearly totals were printed in the *Numismatic Scrapbook* in 1947, and these totals are the same as those in the Director of the Mint's Report. Proof counts for minor coins included Indians, Lincolns, Liberty nickels, and Buffalo nickels. How the yearly counts for each denomination were calculated from the fiscal totals is not known.

One question needs to be answered before the number of proofs is calculated. What should the total number of proofs reflect? The total number struck, the number delivered from the medal room to the Coiner, the number delivered from the Coiner to the Mint Superintendent, or the number sold? As most profits of proof coin sales are mixed in with other totals, especially for 20th century coinage, the number sold can not be used. Because specimens struck do not always meet standards to be called a proof, the total number struck should not be used.

The only logical conclusion would be to use the number delivered which were acceptable as proof coins. Most of the business strike totals reflect the number delivered from the Coiner to either the Superintendent or someone else. The same is true of the proof totals: they reflect the number delivered from the Coiner to the Superintendent.

Included is the number of proof coins from the Director of the Mint's Report for the fiscal year ending June 30th of each year. These totals are given for minor proof coins struck, including the Lincoln cents and Buffalo nickels.

When searching for answers at the National Archives, two books were found. These books show the number of proof coins struck, accepted and delivered to the Coiner Department from the medal room. Both were titled *Metal and Proof Coin Book*.

The first (called *Book 1*), showed the number of proof coins struck for a particular date and the number of those that were "acceptable." The second book (called *Book 2*), showed the number of specimens received by the Coiner. These totals were broken down into proof coins that were "good" and those that were "no good." The total number of proofs categorized as good specimens usually matched the number of struck that were acceptable. Proof coins were struck in the medal room and delivered to the Coiner.

It was assumed by some that proof coins were always struck in the beginning of the year. As the dates of the coins that were struck and delivered clearly show, proof coins were struck throughout the year. The number struck for that year cannot be established from the *Annual Mint Report*.

Both the "good" and "no good" proof coins were sent from the medal room to the Coiner, and there is no indication what the Coiner did with the "no good" proof coins. Were they melted, sold as proofs, or distributed with business strikes? If they were distributed with business strikes, would they have been mistaken as proofs by collectors? We must take a leap of faith that these coins were destroyed so that they would not be confused with genuine proofs.

For 1913 Variety I, the number of specimens that were struck and categorized as "accepted" and delivered to the Coiner as "good" matches the total count of Buffalo nickel proofs in the *Red Book* for that year. The totals for 1913 were obviously not all entered in these two books and therefore cannot be used.

For 1913 Variety II and 1914, the number accepted and the number delivered as "good" match up and is different than the number in the *Red Book*. The total number in the *Red Book* for 1913 Variety II should be changed to 1114. The total number in the *Red Book* for 1914 should be changed to 1275.

For 1915, the number struck and the number delivered do not match up. The number delivered and categorized as acceptable, however, matches the number listed in the *Red Book*.

1913
Variety I

STRUCK: 1,520

RED BOOK
Variety I: 1,520

BREEN PROOF BOOK
Variety I: 1,520

Images Courtesy of Heritage

Date-by-Date Analysis

REPORT OF THE DIRECTOR OF THE MINT - MINOR PROOFS MANUFACTURED FOR FISCAL YEAR 1913

Number of Pieces	Nominal Value
4,012	120.36

MEDAL AND PROOF BOOK FROM NATIONAL ARCHIVES (1906-1916), BOOK 1

Date Delivered	Number Struck	Number Accepted
Mar 3, 1913	1201	1000
Mar 20, 1913		300
May 1, 1913	250	220
TOTAL	1451	1520

MEDAL AND PROOF BOOK FROM NATIONAL ARCHIVES (1906-1916), BOOK 2, NUMBER DELIVERED FROM MEDAL ROOM TO COINER

Date Delivered	Number Delivered	Number Good	Number No Good
Mar 5, 1913	1000		
Mar 20, 1913	500	300	200
May 1, 1913	250	220	30
TOTAL	1760	520	230

1913 VARIETY I PROOF VALUES

Grade	PR63	PR64	PR65	PR66	PR67	PR68
Value	1250	2000	3000	3500	6000	30000

1913 VARIETY I PROOF CERTIFIED POPULATIONS

NGC	Total	PR63	PR64	PR65	PR66	PR67	PR68	PR69
1913	274	30	50	92	91	34	2	------

PCGS	Total	PR63	PR64	PR65	PR66	PR67	PR68	PR69
1913	280	10	57	95	78	37	2	------

COMMENTS

The 1913 Variety I is a little more frequently seen than the Variety II issue but priced higher because it's a one year variety. It, like the rest of the Matte Proofs, can be quite difficult to distinguish from a fully struck, early die state Mint State coin without the normal brilliant, cartwheel lustre.

The "textured" fields further complicate things. Look at the rims and edges: the rims will be wider and much sharper where they meet the fields than on a business strike and the edges will be even, with no beveling whatsoever where it meets the rim. The edge will be of even width around the entire circumference of the coin. They may appear "thicker" than a business strike (compare the edge of a modern proof cent or nickel with a business strike to better illustrate this).

It takes a good eye and a lot of practice to tell these by the surface characteristics. All the true Matte Proofs will show absolutely no "cartwheel" and no mint lustre. Well over 90 percent show a 100 percent full strike.

1913
Variety II

STRUCK: 1,114

RED BOOK
Variety II: 1,514

BREEN PROOF BOOK
Variety I: 1,514

Images Courtesy of Heritage

REPORT OF THE DIRECTOR OF THE MINT - MINOR PROOFS MANUFACTURED FOR FISCAL YEAR 1913

Number of Pieces	Nominal Value
4,012	120.36

MEDAL AND PROOF BOOK FROM NATIONAL ARCHIVES (1906-1916), BOOK 1

Date Delivered	Number Struck	Number Accepted
May 26, 1913	451	250
Oct 5, 1913	150	110
Nov 18, 1913	300	285
Nov 28, 1913	275	273
Dec 24, 1913	200	196
TOTAL	1376	1114

* The May 26th, 1913 entry, there is a notation "New Rev"

MEDAL AND PROOF BOOK FROM NATIONAL ARCHIVES (1906-1916), BOOK 2, NUMBER DELIVERED FROM MEDAL ROOM TO COINER

Date Delivered	Number Delivered	Number Good	Number No Good
May 26, 1913	451	250	201
Oct 13, 1913	150	110	40
Nov 19, 1913	300	285	15
Nov 29, 1913	275	273	2
Dec 24, 1913	200	196	4
TOTAL	1376	1114	262

1913 VARIETY II PROOF VALUES

Grade	PR63	PR64	PR65	PR66	PR67	PR68
Value	1200	1900	2800	3400	6000	30000

1913 VARIETY II PROOF CERTIFIED POPULATIONS

NGC	Total	PR63	PR64	PR65	PR66	PR67	PR68	PR69
1913	225	10	37	64	73	32	5	------
PCGS	Total	PR63	PR64	PR65	PR66	PR67	PR68	PR69
1913	279	11	61	86	74	40	4	------

COMMENTS

1913 Variety II is the scarcest of the Matte Proofs after the 1916. Slightly tougher than the 1915, but priced with the much more frequently encountered 1914. As a result, it seems to be somewhat undervalued. Some very deceptive early die state business strkes exist. Look for the same rim and edge characteristics as found on the Var I issue. Around 90 percent will be fully struck.

1914

STRUCK: 1,275

RED BOOK
1,325

BREEN PROOF BOOK
1,275

Images Courtesy of Heritage

REPORT OF THE DIRECTOR OF THE MINT - MINOR PROOFS MANUFACTURED FOR FISCAL YEAR 1914

Number of Pieces	Nominal Value
3,148	94.96

MEDAL AND PROOF BOOK FROM NATIONAL ARCHIVES (1906-1916), BOOK 1

Date Delivered	Number Struck	Number Accepted
Feb 7, 1914	400	390
Apr 6, 1914	250	250
Jul 30, 1914	200	185
Nov 18, 1914	250	200
Dec 23, 1914	300	250
TOTAL 1400		1275

MEDAL AND PROOF BOOK FROM NATIONAL ARCHIVES (1906-1916), BOOK 2, NUMBER DELIVERED FROM MEDAL ROOM TO COINER

Date Delivered	Number Delivered	Number Good	Number No Good
Feb 7, 1914	400	390	10
Apr 7, 1914	250	250	0
July 30, 1914	200	185	15
Nov 19, 1914	250	200	50
Dec 23, 1914	300	250	50
TOTAL 1400		1275	125

1914 PROOF VALUES

Grade	PR63	PR64	PR65	PR66	PR67	PR68
Value	1100	1600	2300	2900	4500	20000

1914 PROOF CERTIFIED POPULATIONS

NGC	Total	PR63	PR64	PR65	PR66	PR67	PR68	PR69
1914	377	10	73	118	111	56	7	------
PCGS	**Total**	**PR63**	**PR64**	**PR65**	**PR66**	**PR67**	**PR68**	**PR69**
1914	402	13	115	109	101	54	8	------

COMMENTS

1914 is the most frequently encountered of the Matte Proofs by a sizeable margin. It is a little more easily distinguished from an exceptional business strike because very few of the non-Proof coins will show a strike even close to the Proof issue. Approximately 90 percent show a complete, full strike, and when incompleteness is seen it is restricted to the hair detail immediately above the horizontal braid ribbon and the very bottom part of the diagonal hairline, just behind the upper part of the foreleg of the bison.

1915

STRUCK: 1,050

RED BOOK
1,050

BREEN PROOF BOOK
1,050

Images Courtesy of Heritage

REPORT OF THE DIRECTOR OF THE MINT - MINOR PROOFS MANUFACTURED FOR FISCAL YEAR 1915

Number of Pieces	Nominal Value
1,539	46.31

MEDAL AND PROOF BOOK FROM NATIONAL ARCHIVES (1906-1916), BOOK 1

Date Delivered	Number Struck	Number Accepted
Mar 23, 1915	250	200
Aug 11, 1915	300	200
Oct 25, 1915	400	300
Dec 4, 1915	300	250
Dec 22, 1915	300	200
TOTAL 1550		1150

MEDAL AND PROOF BOOK FROM NATIONAL ARCHIVES (1906-1916), BOOK 2, NUMBER DELIVERED FROM MEDAL ROOM TO COINER

Date Delivered	Number Delivered	Number Good	Number No Good
Mar 24, 1915	250	200	50
Aug 12, 1915	300	200	100
Oct 25, 1915	400	300	100
Dec 6, 1915	300	250	50
Dec 23, 1915	300	100	200
TOTAL 1550		1050	500

1915 PROOF VALUES

Grade	PR63	PR64	PR65	PR66	PR67	PR68
Value	1000	1400	2300	2750	4500	20000

1915 PROOF CERTIFIED POPULATIONS

NGC	Total	PR63	PR64	PR65	PR66	PR67	PR68	PR69
1915	303	12	64	98	89	32	3	1
PCGS	**Total**	**PR63**	**PR64**	**PR65**	**PR66**	**PR67**	**PR68**	**PR69**
1915	346	12	66	114	104	46	1	------

COMMENTS

The 1915 is about even in scarcity with the 1913 Variety I. Many exceptionally struck business strikes, showing as much detail as any proof, exist for this date; these can be easily confused with the Matte Proofs. As with the other Matte Proof issues, look at the rims and edges and the total lack of any mint lustre. It was a minor practice at one time to expose exceptional business strikes of all the 1913-1916 dates to cyanide to impart a matte surface to them to simulate proofs—a risky practice to say the least. Around 90 percent show a complete, full strike.

1916

STRUCK: 600

RED BOOK
600

BREEN PROOF BOOK
600

Images Courtesy of Heritage

REPORT OF THE DIRECTOR OF THE MINT - MINOR PROOFS MANUFACTURED FOR FISCAL YEAR 1916

Number of Pieces	Nominal Value
1,793	143.14

NOTE: For the 1913 through 1915 Director of the Mint's Report, it lists the coins manufactured for proofs. Starting in 1916, they list the number sold during the fiscal year.

MEDAL AND PROOF BOOK FROM NATIONAL ARCHIVES (1906-1916), BOOK 1

Date Delivered	Number Struck	Number Accepted
TOTAL	300	200

MEDAL AND PROOF BOOK FROM NATIONAL ARCHIVES (1906-1916), BOOK 2, NUMBER DELIVERED FROM MEDAL ROOM TO COINER

Date Delivered	Number Delivered	Number Good	Number No Good
Mar 25, 1916	200		
Oct 17, 1916	200		
Nov 28, 1916	200		
TOTAL	600		

1916 PROOF VALUES

Grade	PR63	PR64	PR65	PR66	PR67	PR68
Value	1400	2000	3200	4000	6000	30000

1916 PROOF CERTIFIED POPULATIONS

NGC	Total	PR63	PR64	PR65	PR66	PR67	PR68	PR69
1916	160	0	23	59	49	27	1	------
PCGS	**Total**	**PR63**	**PR64**	**PR65**	**PR66**	**PR67**	**PR68**	**PR69**
1916	209	1	40	56	74	29	7	------

COMMENTS

By far the toughest of the Matte Proof issues and one which seems to be significantly underpriced in any grade below PR65. It is thought that some of the issue was melted, making it even tougher than the already tiny mintage of 600 pieces would suggest. As with the other Matte Proofs, 90 percent or better will show a complete strike.

1917

RED BOOK
0

There are no official United States Mint records of proof coins struck in 1917. No records have been discovered at the National Archives stating that proof coins were struck in 1917. In the *Annual Report of the Director of the Mint* for the Fiscal Year Ended June 30, 1917, on page 31, it states "Minor Proof Coins ..... Pieces: 939, Nominal Value: 27.99." For the 1918 Fiscal Year *Director of the Mint's Report*, no proof coins are listed as struck.

In Walter Breen's *Encyclopedia of United States and Colonial Proof Coins, 1722-1989*, on page 219, under the chapter "The Clandestine Years, 1917-1935," Breen states under Five Cents:

Two seen, the broken die coin (break from rim through L into field) from the same set as the cent, the perfect die coin a later discovery. Both have matte finish, like 1916, with the same detail definition. Both have knife-rims in the same part of circumference.

A certification was issued by Walter Breen with one of the 1917 Buffalo nickels that Breen believed to be a Matte Proof. Breen compared the 1917 to an authenticated 1916 Buffalo nickel Matte Proof. Breen concluded that the striking quality was the same on both coins; that the 1917 had sharp inner and outer rims and had considerably more detail in the Indian's hair and on the Bison than on the 1916. The surfaces on both coins were identical.

In David Lange's book, *The Complete Guide to Buffalo Nickels*, Second Edition, David comments on page 178 that one of the specimens claimed by Breen to be a Matte Proof was submitted to NGC for certification as a proof. Dave concluded that the coin exhibited an extremely strong strike from unworn dies, but that the surfaces were of a slightly different texture. The NGC grading team concluded that the coin did not merit proof status.

Several characteristics of a proof coin include sharp details in the design elements and wire edge rims. It is possible that a coin struck from a new pair of working dies will show sharp design details and wire rims. What differentiates most proofs from circulation strikes is the surfaces on the fields. For Brilliant Proofs, the dies were polished as were the planchets, producing a mirror-like field. For the Matte Proofs, such as the Buffalo nickels, these coins exhibit a granular, dull, non-reflective surface. This makes differentiating Matte Proofs from strongly struck coins from new dies much more difficult. The only way to learn to tell the difference is to examine as many certified Matte Proofs as possible, comparing the surfaces to normal business strikes for the same year.

To date, no grading service has certified any 1917 coin of any denomination as proof. The legitimacy of the true proof status of this date is seriously doubted by most in the numismatic community, including most of the certification companies.

As proof coins are defined by the method of manufacture, (not the condition of the coin), there must exist some evidence that the United States Mint at Philadelphia intended to strike these coins as proofs. Absent this intent, or purpose, no 1917 coin of any denomination to be declared a proof. If the method of manufacture was not intended to create a proof, then these coins simply cannot be classified as proofs.

Brilliant Proof Overview: 1936 & 1937

In 1936, there was a growing resurgence of coin collecting. On April 28th, with the help of sympathetic politicians in Washington, Secretary of the Treasury Henry Morgenthau authorized the production of proof coinage. Henry's brother was a coin collector and numismatic columnist.

Although the first proofs struck in 1936 lacked mirror fields, they did have sharp designs and high rims. The fields are described as "satin-like." The techniques used to create brilliant proofs had been forgotten and had to be relearned. There was an outcry by the numismatic community and the Mint changed its process to create brilliant mirror fields. A Type II variety was created in 1936 in which the entire coin surface was brilliant. These were produced until 1942.

To create these brilliant proofs, working dies to be used for striking proofs were hand-picked for their sharp details. The dies were then cleaned and polished to create a mirror-like surface. The planchets to be used for proof coins were also polished. In the coining press, each coin was struck two or more times to produce sharper details and a wire edge rim.

Proof coin production ceased from 1943 through 1949. Again in 1950, proof coinage was resumed. At first, the coins were dull. This was quickly rectified by the Mint and the production of brilliant proofs was resumed. These dies were cleaned with a solvent to remove any oil or dirt. They were then dipped (also known as pickling) in a solution of five percent nitric acid and 95 percent alcohol. This pickling produced a light frosting over the entire die. This frosting is also known as a "Cameo." The die was then polished with a diamond dust compound. The incused design elements were not affected by this polishing and retained their frosting. The result

of the polishing were mirror fields. The frosting on the dies wore off quickly after striking a few coins, making Cameo proofs rare. Dies were cleaned about every 30 coins with cotton and alcohol. This sometimes left fibers of cotton on the die, which left a small incused impression in the coin.

The proof dies also were repolished after striking approximately 1,000 coins. The die was removed from the coining press. A wire brush was first used to polish the incused design elements with a diamond dust compound. This process recreated the frosted surfaces of these elements, but also left very fine scratches caused by the brush. The fields were polished to bring up the mirror surfaces.

Planchets used for proofs were put through a process called burnishing. The planchets were placed in a large stainless steel metal mixer with metal beads. This process created mirror-like surfaces on the planchets. The planchets were first annealed before they were struck.

In 1965, the production of proofs stopped as the Mint tried to meet the ever-increasing demand for coinage. Also, with the increased cost of silver, the dime, quarter, and half dollar were now being struck as "clad coinage," an outer layer of copper-nickel being bonded to an inner layer of pure copper. This required a great deal of attention by Mint employees. Instead of proof coinage, the Mint created Special Mint Sets from 1965 through 1967. These coins were struck twice from chosen dies, and the dies were replaced frequently, but no other attention was given besides placing the coins in a hard plastic holder.

In 1968, the production of proofs resumed. All denominations from the cent through the dollar were struck at the San Francisco Mint. Gold proofs were struck at West Point.

Around 1970, many improvements in die preparation and maintenance were made. The dies were first cleaned, then sandblasted to create the Cameo effect. The fields were then given an ultra mirror image, first through buffing with a wood buffing tip, and then with a hard felt tip. The fields were also treated with a diamond-impregnated compound.

Finally, the face of the die was chrome plated. The chrome plating strengthened the die and made the frosting stay on the die. A single frosted proof die could strike up to 3,000 flawless coins. Therefore, most proof coins produced after 1970 contain Cameo design elements and mirror fields.

In cleaning the dies during production, a lint-free cloth was used so that no fibers were left on the die. The brushes used in repolishing the dies were replaced with felt-tipped mandrils.

1936
Type I

STRUCK: 4,420

RED BOOK
4,420 (Type I & II)

Images Courtesy of Heritage

1936 TYPE I PROOF VALUES

Grade	PR63	PR64	PR65	PR66	PR67	PR68
Value	1100	1300	1900	2300	3000	12000

1936 TYPE I PROOF CERTIFIED POPULATIONS

NGC	Total	PR63	PR64	PR65	PR66	PR67	PR68	PR69
1936	538	9	52	108	207	140	19	------
PCGS	Total	PR63	PR64	PR65	PR66	PR67	PR68	PR69
1936	779	28	115	123	239	208	25	1

COMMENTS

Sometimes referred to as the "Type One" proof, this issue shows a finer, sometimes more brilliant surface than the 1913-1916 Matte issues. The line between Satin and Brilliant is very fine. Some of these coins that certify as Satin more closely resemble the Brilliant Proof coins struck later in the year and are aptly referred to as "Hybrids". It is the earliest die states that show the most "matte-like" finish. About equal in rarity to the fully Brilliant issue, the Satin Proofs typically only bring about two thirds of the price of the Brilliant issue, due mostly to the preference of the Brilliant coins by most collectors. Like the Matte Proofs, around 90 percent will show a complete, full strike.

1936
Type II

STRUCK: 4,420

RED BOOK
4,420 (Type I & II)

Images Courtesy of Heritage

1936 TYPE II PROOF VALUES

Grade	PR63	PR64	PR65	PR66	PR67	PR68
Value	1200	1500	2100	2600	3200	13000

1936 TYPE II PROOF CERTIFIED POPULATIONS

NGC	Total	PR63	PR64	PR65	PR66	PR67	PR68	PR69
1936	447	12	73	101	164	77	11	------
PCGS	**Total**	**PR63**	**PR64**	**PR65**	**PR66**	**PR67**	**PR68**	**PR69**
1936	817	26	158	254	264	105	5	1

COMMENTS

Referred to as the "Type Two" proof, these coins are preferred by most collectors and list at higher values. A significant portion (around 30 percent) will show minor to moderate incompleteness of strike on the braid above the horizontal part of the braid ribbon on the obverse and the lower part of the diagonal hairline on the bison on the reverse.

1937

STRUCK: 5,769

RED BOOK
5,769

Images Courtesy of Heritage

1937 PROOF VALUES

Grade	PR63	PR64	PR65	PR66	PR67	PR68
Value	1000	1400	1700	2000	2600	4500

1937 PROOF CERTIFIED POPULATIONS

NGC	Total	PR63	PR64	PR65	PR66	PR67	PR68	PR69
1937	1251	34	174	320	414	274	32	------
PCGS	**Total**	**PR63**	**PR64**	**PR65**	**PR66**	**PR67**	**PR68**	**PR69**
1937	2113	66	374	607	699	347	9	1

COMMENTS

The most common of all the Proof Buffalo nickels. A majority show incompleteness of the strike in the areas mentioned above for the 1936 Brilliant issue, with a few showing considerable weakness, especially on the obverse. Only around 30 percent show a complete, full strike. A handful of Cameos exist; these bring multiples of fully Brilliant coins.

Chapter 3
Die Varieties Explained

Die Making Process

In order to better understand what a die variety is, it is important to first understand the die making process. The techniques and equipment used have changed over the years. The following is a detailed analysis of this process and equipment used.

With the Act of April 2, 1792, Congress authorized the first coinage of the United States. The following were required to be on each coin:

1. The year of the coinage

2. The words UNITED STATES OF AMERICA

3. The word LIBERTY

4. The denomination of the piece

Hand Engraved Dies: 1792-1836

Sketches of the obverse and reverse designs were made by the engraver and then approved by the Director of the Mint. Once approved, the main design of the coin was engraved directly onto the face of a master die from the original sketch. Inscriptions, dates or stars were not applied to the master die, but were added to the working die. This accounts for the many positional varieties during this period.

For the master die, sections of steel were cut from a bar or ingot and forged into a cylindrical die body. One face of the die body was then machined to slight convexity and lapped smooth. The body was then thoroughly cleaned and given to the engraver.

The engraver covered the die face with a thin layer of transfer wax and carefully placed a drawing of the intended design face down on the wax. The engraver then traced the design, impressing each line into the wax. The drawing was removed and the engraver touched up any details as necessary.

Using gravers, scorpers and other tools, the engraver cut the design into the face of the master die using the wax image as a guide. He periodically checked his work by pressing the master die into soft wax or clay. When finished, the master die contained an incuse image of only the main or central device. The die was then hardened by heating to a cherry red and quickly quenching in water. The die, now very hard, but too brittle for use, was tempered by heating to a straw color and allowing to cool slowly. The master die was now ready to be used in a screw press to make working hubs.

For the working hub, a die body was forged and one face was machined to a shallow cone. The master die and die body were then placed in a large screw press with the master die in the hammer position and the die body was given a few blows.

As the steel was deformed, it consequently hardened. Since it normally took more than one hubbing to get a good impression, the working hub was removed from the press, annealed to soften it, and then thoroughly cleaned. The working hub was impressed again, and this process repeated until the detail was fully imparted. The engraver then touched up any details as necessary. The working hub was then hardened and used to hub working dies in a like manner. The peripheral design elements—stars, lettering, or numerals—were then hand punched or cut into each working die.

While other researchers have offered many reasons why the peripheral features were not added to the master die, numismatic historian Craig Sholley has shown through research in the Mint records from the National Archives that the sole reason for this laborious process was the Mint lacked the proper hubbing process.

Edge dies were used to discourage "shaving" of coins for their metal content. The blank planchet was placed in this die and struck with the obverse and reverse working dies. The pressure of the obverse and reverse dies squeezed the edge of the coin planchet into the design. A few types of edges were applied, such as reeded, starred and lettered.

The die production process was plagued with problems and was too slow to meet the growing demand for more coins. In 1836, this changed with a device that quickened the production of dies.

The French Portrait Lathe: 1836-1867

Franklin Peale was sent by Mint Director Moore to Europe in May of 1833 to learn the techniques and machinery used in their mints and refineries. Peale spent two years there and, upon returning, introduced many valuable improvements.

The most important development to the production of dies was the new hubbing process. This process was a little different than previously used. The sole difference was the periodic machining away of the disturbed metal pushed to the periphery of the die during hubbing. This little trick had kept the Mint from hubbing full dies for nearly 40 years.

Peale also returned with word of another improvement for die making, namely, the reducing pantograph or portrait lathe that Peale had seen at the Paris Mint. The French portrait lathe revolutionized die creation by eliminating the need for the engraver to cut the design into the master die. Instead, the engraver created a wax or clay model of the main design elements, such as the head or wreath. The model could be up to approximately six inches in diameter. From this, a mold was made that was used to make a metal casting, which was a duplicate of the original model. The metal casting was put in the portrait lathe to make a master hub.

The portrait lathe is composed of a pivot bar with a tracer attached to one end and a sharp cutting tool on the other. The tracer is applied to the center of the metal casting, while the cutting tool is applied to the center of a steel blank hub the size of a coin. The models are rotated in an equal counterclockwise motion. As the tracer follows the design on the metal casting, the cutting tool engraves the design into the steel blank in a smaller ratio. After each rotation, the cutting tools are adjusted toward the rim. After it is completed, the steel hub is a positive or raised image of the design and is known as the master hub. The engraver hand-finishes any final details that were not transferred in the process.

Once finished, the master hub was used to create a master die in the hubbing press by the same method of hubbing described previously. After the main design elements were impressed into the master die, the engraver touched up any details lost in the hubbing process. In many cases, the master die was then annealed and the lettering or other elements were punched into the master die. The master die was then used to make working hubs. Working hubs were used to make working dies into which the date and mintmarks were added. A screw press was used in the hubbing operation until 1893, when it was replaced by a hydraulic press.

Then Mint Director Robert Patterson wrote to an agent in Paris, Mr. Samuel Fisher, about purchasing one of these lathes. Officials at the French Mint informed Fisher that the lathe had been made by a Mssr. Contamin, and Patterson ordered a lathe through Fisher. In a letter dated November 1836, Contamin wrote directly to Patterson to inform him of improvements to the lathe and a slight increase in price.

The lathe arrived March 20th, 1837 and, according to a letter dated June 20th, 1837 from Mint

Director Patterson to Secretary of the Treasury Levi Woodbury, it was first used to reduce the design for the Seated Half Dime and Dimes.

Observation:

I have had for a long time the intention to improve the portrait lathe, this improvement I have succeeded in making in the lathe which I showed you. I will not make to you a detailed statement of the changes which I have made in my lathe. I should have too much to say, but there is not a single part which has not had a more or less improvement, I will mention only that which has been changed and not that which has been merely modified.

The port marked P which carries the axis of the bar. The piece which carries the group... holding the revolving conductor of the bar.

The tool holder. You will observe on the back part of the tool carriage, a governing keg (marked B), which screws to advance or withdraw the tool by being placed within the neck of the adjusting screw. As it sometimes happens the cutter should be dulled, by the aid of this keg the carriage may be withdrawn and a touch of oil given to the tool and it may be replaced without the necessity of recutting.

The tracer carriage. The small panel at the extremity of the bar containing the small cylinders. The bar, instead of being made of iron, is made of cast steel, and has a rack almost its whole length which moves the cutter and tracer from right to left, and from left to right. On the said small panel is a set screw, marked A, which is adjusted to prevent the tracer from falling in too deep, and for making tables or planes.

The spring lever carrying a ball (which is raised according to the desired pressure) serves to draw the bar. This arrangement is exceedingly good by the springs, the breaking ... and other injuries is avoided ... augments, when the tool sinks deeper and cuts more, and decreases when the tool has less to cut. This permits heavier cuts to be made, and yet saves the model from injury by the pressure of the tracer. All the circular movements are made on pivots which make my kind of lathe run very light.

It is important that a portrait lathe should have solidity and perfect exactitude (the absence of which is the fault of all lathes) this one possesses these qualities. I have made reductions of three millimeters almost at right angle, with the greatest attention and have not perceived the slightest spring. I have also reduced exceedingly small and have obtained all possible sensitivity.

All the adjustments susceptible to wear, are provided for by tightening screws, so my kind of lathe will necessarily become better by use. Because the changes produced by wear can be restored. All my adjustments are ... of ports N and O have a collar behind carrying a set screw in order to compensate for the wear of the ... in the boxes. These screws should not be tightened unnecessarily, it would render the lathe too heavy and if any play is left in the boxes by the screws, the work will be good for nothing, it is important that the whole should be well set, to be that it is necessary to take hold of the brass wheels with both hands and shall then forcefully paying attention to the collars, if the oil which is upon then moves, tighten them one 20th to 30th of a turn of the end in set screw marked M.

To reduce the head well, it is requisite to cut in front of the profile and ... at the back of the head, for instances of you have to reduce the head which looks to the right, turn .... direction of the arrows ... at part A, in order to reach the center B you will cut in rising, and if your head looks to the left, start from the center B in order to terminate your cut at the exterior A and turn in the contrary direction you will cut in descending. If you have a strong reduction to make, always make in sketch or roughing out for the latter always turn in the direction opposite to the arrows, for all reduction in general for roughing out only, and to finish proceed according to my direction as above it may be made with one or two cuts at most without turning backwards, unless it should be required by the profile.

It is of the utmost consequence to center the tracer well with the model, by the aid of the wrench with the ivory handle. Which raises and depresses the bar, and when once centered, do not touch it again. In order to center the cutter, if it is too high, turn the screw which is under the back part of the cutter carriage, if it is too low, unscrew that which is below and screw that which is above.

If it desired to remove the large chunk, from the mandrill, take care to remove the small screw which prevents the mandrill from unscrewing when you turn against the direction of the screw. You will also remove the small piece which is attached. The shoulder base of the mandrill E, is a piece of brass, furnished with two pointed screws, when this is moved to the right, the depth is diminished and when moved to the left it is incused to the piece of iron F containing the little conical holes is attached to part H by two screws. If it is desired to change the relief, the screws are changed to the other holes by sliding the piece F on H from one side to the other. The part N should never be changed from its place. The part O can be slid from left to right according to the reduction that is desired to be made. This part has at its base an index which coincides with a ....of reduction on the cast iron plates and permits reduction from one 6th to 8/10 1/2.

The tracer with the cutter F has been employed to make the reduction which accompanies the lathe. This tracer F is to make rough cuts and not to finish, the tracer T is for bolder reductions than that which is sent. The cutters V and T are prepared to cut in rising, others should to be made for use and then retained as models (supposing that you do not form which the cutter ought to have). The

accompanying reduction was made with a draft upon a bar of about one pound or one half kilo.

You will acknowledge sir, that I have worked more like an artist than a mechanic. In order to avoid all surprises in case you should order another, I inform you in advance that I could not make one for less than 4000 francs, also declaring on my word as an artist that I have gained nothing on this piece. I have agreed that it is true with Mr. Fisher for the price of 3000 francs, but I did not promise to double the work, but in the execution we are led on and I was not willing to leave out the smallest thing and that which I have added deceived me as to the price.

If you think it proper sir, that an artist should not lose in working for you. I propose to you to send me through Mr. Fisher the sum of 500 francs, to indemnify me for the additional work that I have put upon the lathe. I hope to receive a satisfactory answer after your careful examination.

I have the honor to be your entirely devoted

Contamin

The following was printed in Q. David Bowers' *Flying Eagle and Indian Cent* book and is an excerpt from *"Making Money: The Mint at Philadelphia"* by Waldo Abbot, in *Harper's New Monthly Magazine*, March 1861.

We visit the Die Room to learn how the dies are made.

A coin has an impression on both sides, requiring, of course, a die for each. These are made with extreme care, to be of the finest workmanship, and all exactly alike. Their manufacture is one of the most important operations in the Mint.

Look at the bas-relief of Liberty on one side of a coin. It would be exceedingly difficult to design this in hard steel and of so small a size,

The photos (above from left to right) are the original bronze cast from a model by Christian Gobrecht after a design from Titian Peale used on a 1838 Half Dollar Pattern, a reduction made from the Contamin portrait lathe, and a trial impression.

so they first make the design in wax, probably six times as large as the coin, by which means the beautiful proportions can be obtained. From this a brass cast is taken, and reduced on steel to the size of the coin by a transfer or reducing lathe. This ingenious instrument was introduced from France by Mr. Peale, who also operated it for some time.

The brass cast is fastened to the large wheel at the right-hand side of the lathe. On the small wheel to the left of the cast is fastened a piece of soft steel, on which the design is to be engraved. Both of these wheels revolve in the same way and at the same speed. There is a long iron bar or lever fastened by a joint to an iron support at the extreme left, which runs in front of the two wheels. A spring at the upper end draws it toward the wheels. Fastened to the lever is a pointed steel stub, which touches the cast. A very sharp "graver" is fastened to the lever below, which touches the steel. The wheels revolve, and the stub when it is pushed back by the heavy relief of the cast, forces back the lever, which draws back the graver and prevents it from cutting the

steel. So where there is a raised place in the cast the graver is prevented from cutting into the steel, but where there is a depression in the cast the graver cuts the same in the steel.

As the lever is jointed at the left, the nearer the graver is placed to that end, the less motion it will have. The distance of the steel from the joint regulates the proportion of the reduction from the cast.

After the graver has cut one small shaving around the steel, a screw is turned, which lowers the right end of the lever slightly, just enough to allow the graver to cut another shaving and the stub to touch the cast a very little further from the centre. Thus the graver cuts a very little at a time; but the work is cut over several times, until the design is sufficiently blocked out. This machine will not finish off the die perfect enough to use, but it reduces the design in perfect proportion, and performs most of the rough work. The original dies for coins being now all made, the lathe is used mostly for medals, of which a great many are struck, by order of

Congress, for various purposes. A very fine one was presented to the Japanese while they were in this country. There is now on the machine a cast of Washington's bust, merely to show how the cast is placed.

After the die comes from the lathe it is carefully finished off by hand, and when all polished is a beautiful piece of work. It is still very soft, requiring to be hardened before it can be used, which is done by heating it very hot, and holding it under a stream of water until cold. The relief is exactly like the coin—that is, the device is raised as in the coin. It will not do to use this stamping, as it would reverse the appearance on the coin. Therefore this "hub," or "male die," as it is named, is used only to make other dies.

Rounded pieces of very soft steel, a little larger than the die, are smoothed off on the top, the centre being brought to a point a little higher than the sides. It is placed on a solid bed, under a very powerful screw press, and the hub placed on top of it—the centre of the hub on the point of the steel, like a seal on sealing wax. The screw is turned with great force by several men, and presses the hub a little into the steel. It is necessary to have the steel higher in the centre, as if the centre impression is not taken first, it can not be brought out sharp and distinct. The steel is softened again by being heated and allowed to cool slowly, and the operation is repeated. This is done several times, until the whole impression is full and distinct. If there is any little defect it is rectified with the engraver's tool. The surplus steel around the edge is cut off, and the date put in by hand, when it is hardened and ready for use.

The date is not cut on the hub or on the first die—which is called a "female,"—as perhaps the hub will last for two years, and the date can not be altered. This die is never used to stamp with, but preserved, so that if the hub breaks it can be used to make another. The dies for use are prepared in the same way. About 1,300 a year are made for the various branch mints, and those for the New Orleans Mint were sent on just before the state seceded, which the authorities have not yet had time to return. Sometimes a die will wear for a couple of days and again it will break while stamping the first coin. Steel is treacherous, and no dependence can be placed in its strength. As nearly as can be ascertained their cost is $16 a pair.

The Hill Reducing Lathe: 1867-1907

Chief Engraver James B. Longacre wrote Mint Director Millward on November 30, 1866, regarding an improved reducing lathe by C.J. Hill of London. Mr. Longacre was very impressed with samples sent by Mr. Hill. The quality of the dies produced was far better than what was produced with the French portrait lathe. The Mint bought a Hill portrait lathe in September of 1867 and began using it in 1868.

This portrait lathe was bought to greatly improve the quality of the reproduction of the design elements to the master hub. On the Indian cents, the obverse rim letters were still struck into the master die until around 1886, when they were placed on the master hub. Most coins of this time period did not have the date punched into the master die. Consequently, the same master die could be used over many years. As the reducing lathe was used to make a master hub from a Galvano, this would not have been necessary for a series that already had a working master die. Thus, one would not see an improvement in the detail of the design in 1867.

The following is the letter from Longacre to Millward concerning the Hill reducing lathe:

Dear Sir

The matter referred to me in the letter of B.F. Stevens to the Secretary of the Treasury is one of importance to the operations of the mint.

My attention was called to the Reducing Machine to which it refers, about four years ago from specimens sent to the mint by the inventor, C.J. Hill of London, purporting to be produced by the operations of his machine, which were so much superior to any other machine reductions I had seen, as to create some doubt with regard to the accuracy of the representations of the process by which they were produced. I was induced to open a correspondence with an artist friend residing then in London, on whose judgment I could only rely, to make further inquiries; his reply satisfied me of the value of the invention, but Mr. Hill would not then agree to construct and furnish the machine, preferring to keep it in his own hands, and take orders for the work produced by it. He has since however, as I have learned, parted with his interest in the invention to the Messrs. Wyon, the parties referred to in the letter before me, and who it seems now propose to furnish the machine.

The work produced by this machine judging, from the specimens before me, is so far superior to that of our present machine (which was constructed in Paris many years ago) or any other in existence of which I have knowledge, that I consider it exceedingly desirable the Mint should possess it, if it can be obtained on fair terms and guaranteed to produce work equal to the specimens now submitted.

It is scarcely possible to overrate the value of such a machine in its relations to the work required for the coinage, provided the Mint can have the entire and absolute control of its operation, without restrictions from the patentee.

Very Respectfully Your Obt. Servt,

James Longacre

From 1836 through about 1880, the pattern for the reducing lathe was made from the original model as previously described. Sometime after this, electroplating was used to create the electrotype or "galvano." As before, this process began with the creation of a large model with the raised design features of the obverse or reverse of the coin in plastilene (modeling wax or clay). Once finished and approved, the model was coated with graphite, which conducts electricity, and a copper coating was applied through immersing the model in a copper bath and applying electricity. When cooled, the copper shell was removed from the model and given a backing to make it stronger. The design elements of the copper shell were incused and made a mirror image of the model. The copper shell was then filled with a plaster and allowed to set. When removed from the copper shell, the plaster model was an exact duplicate of the original model and was called the Galvano. Any flaws were cleaned up by the engraver and the Galvano was used to make the master hub in the reducing lathe.

The following was printed in Q. David Bowers' *Flying Eagle and Indian Cent* book and is an excerpt from the *Manufacture of Dies* by Chief Engraver Charles E. Barber, 1896:

After a design for the coin or medal is decided upon, the engraver prepares a model in wax, or any material he may prefer to use, of the design selected, or as much of it as he may think most desirable for the medal or coin. The model is generally made three, four, or five times as large as the finished work is intended to be. When the model is finished an electrotype [a.k.a. Galvano] is made. This electrotype when sufficiently strong is prepared for the reducing lathe, and a reduced copy is made the size required for the coin or medal, as the case may be.

The reducing lathe is a machine, working somewhat upon the principle of the pantograph, only in this case the one point traces or follows the form of the model, while another and much smaller point made in the form of a drill cuts away the material and thus produces a reduction of the model. This process of reducing the design from the model is necessarily a very slow operation, as the accuracy of the reduction depends upon the slow motion of the machine and delicate handling of the operator. While it is not in the power of the operator or machine to improve the model, it is quite an easy matter, if not properly managed, for the machine to distort or the operator to lose the delicacy of the model.

The reducing machine can work either from a model in relief or intaglio, though the relief is more often used and is considered the better way.

In describing the process, I have said the engraver makes a model of the design he wishes to produce, or as much as he thinks desirable. To explain more fully, I would say some designs or parts of a design are not calculated for reducing by machine, and therefore the engraver only reduces so much of the design as he knows from experience will give the desired effect; the rest he cuts in...namely with gravers and chisels. [Dates, letters, ornaments, wreath elements such as berries, etc., were often added by the use of punches or gravers.]

When the reduction is made by the machine from the model it is then taken by the engraver and worked over and finished in all the detail and delicate parts, as the machine does not produce an entirely finished work. When finished by the engraver it is hardened and tempered. If the reduction has been made intaglio [cut into the die, rather than in relief], when hardened it is completed and is called a [master] die, and coins or medals can be struck from it; but if in relief, it is called a hub, and the process of making a die from it commences, which is done as follows:

The hub or relief being made hard, a piece of steel is prepared in the following manner to receive the impression of the hard hub: Take a block of steel sufficiently large to make your die, and carefully anneal it until it is quite soft. This is done by heating the steel to a bright red and allowing it to cool very gradually, being careful to exclude the air by packing the steel in carbon. The steel being soft, turn off the surface of the block of steel [by using a lathe] and smooth it before you commence the process called hubbing, which is as follows:

Place the block of soft steel under the plunger of a strong screw press; then put the hard relief or hub on top of the soft steel, and bring down your plunger with a good sharp blow. This will give you an impression upon the soft steel. In order to make a proper impression, the process of annealing the steel just described, called hubbing, must be repeated many times, until you have a perfect impression of the hub. This being obtained, you have a die which only requires being hardened and tempered to be ready for use...

To harden the steel dies, they are packed in cast-iron boxes filled with carbon to exclude the air, and when heated to bright red are cooled suddenly with water. As this would leave them too hard, and liable to crack and break on the edges, the temper is technically what is drawn, which is done by gently heating until you notice a color appearing upon the surface of the steel. A light straw color is a good color for cutting tools [such as letter punches fabricated at the Mint], but dies are generally brought to a deeper color, and in some cases to a blue.

This is the first time that it is mentioned that a reducing lathe could make a master die from a model which is in intaglio. Almost always the master hub is made from the Galvano in the reducing lathe.

The Janvier Lathe: 1907 to Present

In 1907, the Janvier lathe replaced the Hill reducing lathe. The Janvier's prime feature over the Hill lathe was that it could work in different heights of relief. The model could also be much larger.

The date was no longer punched into the working die, but the first two digits were sculpted into the original model. The final two digits were punched into the master die. Mintmarks were punched into the working die as required.

Around 1908, a Galvano was made with only two digits in the date (19). This way, when a master hub was made, it could be used for years. The master hub would make a master die, and the second two digits would be punched into the master die. This method was used until the mid-1980s. This was confirmed by Frank Gasparro, who was the Chief Engraver until he retired in 1981. After that, a new master hub was made each year from a Galvano with all four digits. In 1960, a problem occurred when a new master die was made. Three digits were punched in, and the master die was used to make working hubs. The master die cracked, and a new master die was created with a larger set of 3 digits (960), producing two types of working hubs, large date and small date. Because working dies have to be hubbed more than once to get a good impression, some working dies were hubbed from both the large and small date hub, producing large/small date and small/large date varieties.

In the mid-1980s, the method of making the Galvano from the original model was also improved. The following is a statement from the Department of the Treasury on the "preparation of working dies from the original design."

The sculptor-engraver prepares a plastilene model (modeling wax) in bas-relief from the approved sketch of the design from a coin, keeping in mind the depth of relief suitable for coining. This model is generally made from three to twelve times larger than the size of the finished coin.

A plaster of Paris negative is cast from the plastilene model, incorporating detail work and refining. After suitable preparation, a plaster positive is made from this negative. The plaster positive is then submitted to Mint Headquarters and interested parties for approval.

When final approval is received, a negative rubber mold is made and epoxy is poured into this mold. This produces a positive epoxy model which has an extremely hard surface.

The completed epoxy model then is mounted on a Janvier transfer engraving machine. This machine works on the same principles as a pantograph. A tracing tool at one end of the machine traces the large epoxy model while at the other end a stylus cuts the design into a soft tool steel blank directly to the size of the finished coin or medal, producing a positive replica, or hub. This hub is then heat-treated to harden it, and is used on a hydraulic press to prepare a master die. The master die, in turn, is hardened, and by the cold forging process a working hub is extracted. This working hub is used to produce working dies. The original hub is carefully stored in a safe place to insure against loss of the original reduction. Today, the Mint produces about 140,000 dies a year. Up to now all dies were created at the Philadelphia Mint. Beginning in May of 1996, an auxiliary die making shop will be opened in Denver. With all of the improvements in equipment at the Mint, the one tool that has remained constant at the Philadelphia Mint since 1907 is the Janiver reducing lathe. A few of the original machines are still used at the Philadelphia Mint.

Using the Die Variety Section

The following provides a description of the component parts used for each die variety. Each component part is a piece of the puzzle, which is used in the identification of the variety. Used together, distinguishing varieties is made simple.

Reference System

The Reference System used in the following chapters is very basic.

1. Each reference number starts with a three letter abbreviation, which describes the type of variety.

> DDO - Doubled Die Obverse
>
> DDR - Doubled Die Reverse
>
> OVD - Overdate
>
> OMM - Over Mintmark
>
> RPM - Repunched Mintmark

2. Reference number: Sequential numbers are used starting with 001 for each year, mintmark, and type of variety.

Example: 1935 DDO-002—This is the second doubled die listed for the 1935 Buffalo nickel.

Identifying Characteristics

Description: All characteristics of the doubling, overdate, over mintmark, or repunched mintmark are given in detail.

Photographs: Using microphotography, all parts of the doubling, overdate, over mintmarks, or repunched mintmark are shown. As the date was part of the Galvano during the Buffalo nickel series, the date is not shown unless it shows part of the variety.

Diagnostics: To help distinguish between some varieties, other features or die markers of the coin must be examined. In the creation of the working die and during its life in the coining press, sometimes the die will become damaged. The die could become cracked due to stress, scratched when polished, chipped due to being mishandled or having a weakness in its metal. Sometimes these flaws grow due to more stress or other factors. On 19th century coinage, these flaws are common. On 20th century coinage, they happen much less frequently. These flaws are used to help identify one particular die variety from another and are also used to study the die stages of a variety (Early, Mid, Late, Very Late Die States).

Universal Rarity Scale

Notation	Description
URS-0	None known
URS-1	1 known, unique
URS-2	2 known
URS-3	3 or 4 known
URS-4	5 to 8 known
URS-5	9 to 16 known
URS-6	17 to 32 known
URS-7	33 to 64 known
URS-8	65 to 125 known
URS-9	126 to 250 known
URS-10	251 to 500 known
URS-11	501 to 1,000 known

Overall Rarity: This represents the aggregate or average rarity as estimated over all grades.

For the Buffalo nickel varieties, a few of the more popular varieties, such as the 1916 doubled die, the 1918/7-D, and the 1935 doubled die reverse have been known about and collected for years. For these and a few of the other published die varieties, the rarity and interest level have already been established.

For many of the Buffalo nickel doubled dies and repunched mintmarks, this is the first time the varieties are being published with photographs. It will take a few years to establish the true rarity for these.

Interest Level

The interest level is the amount of demand from numismatists for a particular variety. The greatest factor used to determine interest is the degree of the doubling, repunching, or clashing. The more dramatic a variety, the more interest, and vice versa. Another factor that contributes to the interest level is the rarity. Some varieties that receive a large amount of numismatic press are sometimes rocketed in the spotlight and highly sought after.

The following terms are used to indicate interest: *Low, Moderate, High, Very High, Extremely High.* When a variety is between two levels, it is expressed as *Moderate to High* or *High to Very High.*

Pricing

The most current sales totals for each variety was used to calculate the prices given. For many varieties, there have been no sales recorded for a particular grade. For some varieties, no sales have been recorded at all. For these, the prices were calculated from varieties which were similar in the type and degree of the variety.

Note: The prices given are from the best possible information. As rarity and interest change, as more specimens are found, or as more people become interested in a variety, the premium factor and price of a variety will change. Supply and demand greatly shapes the value of these varieties. Publicity of a variety also affects the price. The author and publisher are not responsible for gains or losses because of prices listed in this book. Each collector needs to research the market before they buy a coin.

Cross Reference Numbers

Some of the varieties are listed in other books. A cross reference is given so that varieties can easily be identified. The following are books that varieties in this book are also listed in:

1. **FS**: Fivaz/Stanton Numbers used in the third edition of *The Cherry Pickers Guide to Rare Die Varieties.*

2. **Breen**: Numbers used in Walter Breen's *The Complete Encyclopedia of U.S. and Colonial Coins.*

3. **RPM**: Numbers used in John Wexler and Tom Miller's *The RPM Book.*

Chapter 4
Buffalo Nickel Doubled Dies (Hub Doubling)

Doubled Die Overview

A hub doubled die is created when a working die receives multiple images from a working hub in the hubbing press. Other forms of doubling are not the result of the hubbing process. These include mechanical doubling, abrasion doubling, re-engraved dies, and die deterioration doubling.

Hubbing is the process of transferring the image of a hub into a steel blank. To get a good impression into the steel blank, the working die must be hubbed several times. The steel blank is annealed between hubbings. Annealing softens the die by heating it so that a deeper impression can be made into the die.

If the images of the working die from previous hubbings are not aligned properly with the images of the working hub, a second image will be impressed into the die.

Another problem might occur if the images of the hub was modified or taken from a working hub of a different design. If the working die was not annealed properly, the design elements might become distorted. Either of these would cause the die to be impressed with an image that is different from the original image impressed from the previous hubbing. There are several classes of doubled dies that are defined by how the doubling occurred.

John Wexler greatly expanded, clarified, and classified the hub doubling theory, which members of CONE and NECA, (notably LeRoy Van Allen, Bill Fivaz, and Alan Herbert), put forward. In this system, Wexler classifies doubled dies by how the doubling was created in the die.

Since this system was created, research has proved that the cause of doubling in at least one of these classes is different from what was originally suspected. There is an additional class of doubling that has been discovered. There are also some doubled dies that have been attributed to a wrong class of doubling, probably caused by hybrid doubling, These facts and others will be covered in this chapter.

Determining how a die was doubled is not an exact science. We can examine the current Mint procedures to help us learn how doubling occurs on modern day doubled dies. Unfortunately, there is very little documentation on the Mint procedures of 19th century die production. For some classes of doubling, it is easy to determine the cause of doubling because the diagnostics lead to a singular conclusion, such as if the die is rotated about the center in reference to the hub in the hubbing press. However, the cause of some other types of doubling is tougher to determine because the diagnostics of the doubling do not lead to an obvious conclusion. For example, if the doubling is distorted, the distortion was probably caused during the annealing process. There might also have been equipment or procedures that were used for which we have no information.

A problem in determining the class in which a doubled die belongs occurs when a doubled die exhibits characteristics of more than one class of doubling, such as when a working die is rotated and tilted in reference to the working hub. This type of hybrid doubling is often misclassified as Class III (Design Hub Doubling).

The most reliable way to determine the class that a doubled die falls under is by reproducing the doubling using clay models, transparencies, or other methods to simulate the hubbing process. This methodology shows how the die was misaligned (rotated, offset, etc.) to the hub. Although it is possible that the same misalignment could be caused by a simple movement (the die was pivoted about the rim in reference to the hub), or a complex movement, (the die was first rotated about the center, then offset in reference to the hub), it is far easier to believe that the dies were aligned with a simple movement rather than a complex one, because a complex movement would probably bring the alignment under suspicion.

The objective in classifying a doubled die is to evaluate all of the evidence of doubling. Sometimes there is very little evidence. A good example is the 1873 Indian Open 3, where only the L of LIBERTY is doubled. In cases like this, it is probably better to classify these types of doubled dies as "undetermined."

On the following pages is a summation of the causes and diagnostics of the eight classes of Hub Doubling.

Classes of Hub Doubling

Class I, Rotated Hub Doubling:

Rotated hub doubling occurs when a die being rehubbed is rotated near the center of the die in the hubbing press from a position it had been in a previous hubbing.

DIAGNOSTICS:

Doubling will show on all design elements about the rim.

The spread of the doubling will increase as you move outward from the pivot point. The strongest spread of doubling is usually observed on the design elements near the rim.

The doubling on all design elements about the rim will be in the same direction from the primary design elements, either CW or CCW.

Class II, Distorted Hub Doubling:

Distorted hub doubling occurs when the design images on the die or hub become distorted during the annealing or tempering process, causing a misalignment of the images when returned to the hubbing press.

DIAGNOSTICS:

The doubling usually occurs on the design elements near the rim.

The images that are doubled are usually distorted.

The doubling is toward the center or toward the rim.

Class III, Design Hub Doubling:

Design hub doubling occurs when working hubs bearing two different designs are used to hub a die. The two hubs were created from two different master dies, which had differences in designs. The doubling in this class will depend on the differences between the two hubs that were used to make the impressions. This difference could be of one letter or the whole design.

DIAGNOSTICS:

Each impression should show the characteristics of the design of that hub.

The doubling is equal to differences between the design elements of the hubs.

Class IV, Offset Hub Doubling:

Offset hub doubling occurs when a die being rehubbed is off center in the hubbing press from a position it had been on a previous hubbing. When this occurs, the doubling will be in the direction in which the die was offset from the first hubbing to the second. All of the doubling will be going in the same direction and will have the same spread across the die.

DIAGNOSTICS:

The doubling is all in one direction.

The degree of doubling is constant.

Class V, Pivoted Hub Doubling:

Pivoted hub doubling occurs when a die is pivoted about a point near the rim during rehubbing. Because the point of pivot is near the rim, the spread of doubling will be the strongest at the point directly opposite the pivot point and will decrease as you move away from that point. The point closest to the pivot point on the rim will show little or no doubling. The doubling will be fan shaped, with the direction of doubling going one way.

DIAGNOSTICS:

There is little or no doubling on one side of the coin. The strongest doubling is opposite the pivot point and decreases from there.

The doubling is fan shaped.

Class VI, Distended Hub Doubling:

Distended hub doubling occurs when the images on the hub become flattened or thickened from use, producing thick letters or a design into the working die. This could happen to the working hub from being too soft, or the working die from being too hard, causing wear in the form of expansion of the images on the working hub.

DIAGNOSTICS:

Separation of images usually not seen.

Doubling takes the form of extra thickness of the letters, digits, or other design elements.

Class VII, Modified Hub Doubling:

Modified hub doubling occurs when a die being hubbed is impressed with a normal hub and a hub that has been modified. An unwanted element of the hub could have been ground off.

DIAGNOSTICS:

The doubling shows as the difference between a normal hub and the modified hub.

Class VIII, Tilted Hub Doubling:

Tilted hub doubling occurs when the top of the die being hubbed is not parallel to that of the hub. This will cause one side of the hub and die to make contact before the other side. Depending on the degree of tilt, the impression made from the hub into the die will be off center. Also one side of the die will be impressed with a greater depth of the design (the side that made contact with the hub first).

DIAGNOSTICS:

One side of the coin will have a stronger impression of the design.

The doubling is in one direction and is strongest at the point where the hub and die made contact first.

The doubling decreases in spread from the strongest point and usually only shows on half the coin.

Class I, Rotated Hub Doubling

With Class I, Rotated Hub Doubling, the die is rotated in the hubbing press with respect to its position in a prior hubbing. The pivot point of the rotation is normally near the center of the die, but for a Class I, it can be between the center of the die and the outer design elements of the die. The degree of rotation determines the strength of doubling. The strength of the impression of the design elements produced in the second hubbing will normally be stronger than the first. The direction of doubling, either clockwise (CW) or counter-clockwise (CCW) is determined by the direction of the second hubbing with respect to the first hubbing.

In a pure Class I, the pivot point is at the center, and the spread of doubling will be constant at points the same distance from the center. If the pivot point is moved from the center toward the rim, the doubling will be stronger at the point farthest from the pivot. As you move the pivot point close to the rim, the design elements closest to the rim show little or no doubling. A pivot at the rim is a Class V. Also, the doubling on a Class V will be fan-shaped. It will not be CW or CCW consistently all the way around the rim.

What happens, then, if the pivot point is between the rim and center? Should it be called a Class I or V? And is there a point between the center and rim where a pivot point makes a doubled die change from a Class I to V? Many doubled dies have been classified as Class V, because they did not exhibit the "pure Class I" diagnostics. This means the doubling was not equal at points the same distance from the rim. In other words, the doubling on one side of the coin was stronger than that on the other.

The distinguishing feature between a Class I and a Class V is that for a Class I the doubling is CW or CCW for all elements around the rim of the coin.

For a Class V, the doubling is fan-shaped. A perfect example of this is the 1917 Lincoln cent DDO 1-0-V, shown on the next page. Notice that the doubling on LIBERTY is very weak, whereas the doubling on the date and IN GOD WE TRUST is very strong. But the doubling on LIBERTY is CCW as is the doubling on the other design elements about the rim. The pivot point was between the center and the date.

There are three features of rotated hub doubling:

1. Doubling will show on all design elements about the rim.

2. The spread of the doubling will increase as you move outward from the pivot point. The strongest spread of doubling is usually observed on the design elements near the rim.

3. The doubling on all design elements about the rim will be in the same direction from the primary design elements, either CW or CCW.

All working dies produced at the U.S. Mint are hubbed at least twice to get a strong image of the design impressed into the die. Given that today the hubbing press is hydraulic and uses a constant pressure, the image produced during the first hubbing will usually be weaker than subsequent hubbings. This is because of the metal's natural resistance to compression and pressure. It is one way to help identify which image was produced from the first hubbing. Another way to identify which image was produced first is to look to see which image is on top. Looking at the 1955 Lincoln cent doubled die on the top of the next page, both primary and secondary images are very close to strength in the design elements, but examining the E of WE and the S of TRUST, it is obvious that the second hubbing is CCW.

The photos above are of the 1955 Lincoln Doubled Die Obverse. Because the L of LIBERTY is closer to the rim, the spread of doubling is much greater than that on the Y. The spread of doubling on the legend IN GOD WE TRUST is constant because they are the same distance from the center. The doubling is CCW.

These photos are of the 1917 Lincoln DDO 1-0-1. This variety was originally classified as a Class V, probably because the doubling on one side of the coin is stronger than that of the other. Because the pivot point was between the center and the L of LIBERTY, this variety is being reclassified as a Class I. The doubling on all of the design elements about the rim is CCW.

Exception: If the doubling only shows on the center of a doubled die, but the pivot point is on or about the center with all doubling either CW or CCW, and if the degree of doubling is constant for all points the same distance from the pivot point, then this variety would fall under Class I. This diagnostic was the result of a partial hubbing during the first hubbing. Because a screw press was used to hub dies before 1893, the pressure was not constant. If the impression was not great enough, only the center of the design would have been incused into the working die.

Class II, Distorted Hub Doubling

Distorted hub doubling occurs when the design images on the die or hub become distorted during the annealing or tempering process, causing a misalignment of the images when returned to the hubbing press.

There are three distinct features of distorted hub doubling:

1. The doubling usually occurs on the design elements near the rim.

2. The images that are doubled are usually distorted.

3. The doubling is toward the center or toward the rim.

A working die must be hubbed several times to get a deep impression of the hub into the die. Between hubbings, the die is annealed, or softened. As the die steel is annealed, the steel expands during the heat treatment and contracts as it is cooled. If the die is heated or cooled too slowly or too quickly, the images on the die may not return to their previous position. This will become most apparent in the areas of greatest stress, which are usually near the perimeter of the face of the die. Another possibility is that the dies are composed of different metals that might expand and contract at a different rate, creating a change in the shape of the design. Such a change could range from minute to dramatic, depending on the composition of the die steel, heat applied, and/or time taken to cool. When the die is returned to the hydraulic press, its design is different from the hub from which it was originally hubbed, and a second image is created. Because the amount of distortion that might occur to a die during annealing, it is dependent on many factors, such as heat and steel composition. The amount and place of distortion are usually not predictable or common among doubled dies in this class. Note that when a working hub is made from a master die, it could also become distorted during the annealing process.

It was originally believed that the cause of distorted hub doubling was that the dies were hubbed with an old hub, then rehubbed with a new working hub or vice versa. The old hub was flattened out because of use, which resulted in an outward displacement of the design elements on the hub. After the die was hubbed with this old hub, it was then annealed and brought back to a new working hub in the hubbing press that had a more centralized design. The result was a "small over large" design. The problem with this theory is that the design elements on the working hub are raised and that they bare the brunt of the hubbing stress. Thus if anything would flare, it would be the raised design elements, which would distend in all directions. The distance from the center of the radius of the design elements would not change to any significant degree. In other words, if a working hub became "flattened" due to overuse, then the design elements on the working hub would become thicker and would show up as Class VI, distended hub doubling.

Before being used in the hubbing press, the working hub is hardened, and the working dies are softened through annealing. It is less likely that the working hub became worn, especially during the 19th century, when only a small number of dies were needed for each denomination. Yet in many series where only a small number of working dies were created each year, we find examples of distorted hub doubling.

Another common 19th century scenario where only a limited number of dies were created at the beginning of each year occurred if a working hub was used to hub 20 working dies, which were then annealed and brought back to a different working hub in the hubbing press (this working hub being

worn). All 20 working dies should then display the same doubling. Most of the doubled dies in this Class were not caused by a worn working hub, but by the images on the working die that became distorted during the annealing process between hubbings.

There are many doubled dies in the Two cent series that have the Class II doubling. But there were not a great number of working dies hubbed for each year in this series. In 1864, there were probably less than 100 obverse working dies. In 1872, there were probably only 4 obverse working dies hubbed.

One of the easiest ways of classifying a variety as a Class II, is when the doubling of all rim elements is either all toward the center or all toward the rim. On most Class II doubled dies, the doubling is toward the center, above is the 1971 Lincoln cent DDO-001 where the doubling is toward the rim.

How then could the working hub, which is normally used to impress hundreds of working dies, wear so quickly?

A good example of this is that only one working die was created for the 1864 Small Motto business strikes; yet this die exhibits diagnostics of Class II doubling. Even though it is possible, it is extremely unlikely that the Small Motto working hub became worn or expanded after two or three hubbings with one working die. The Small Motto two cent piece is believed to be a pattern die that slipped in with the production dies. With only four obverse working dies made in 1872, how could only one of these exhibit very dramatic Class II doubling on TRUST, but no other 1872 dies show any doubling?

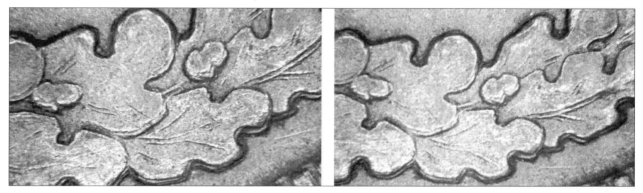

Above is the 1891 Indian cent DDR-001 with a very strong Class II doubled die reverse. Doubling is seen on both the left and right wreathes going toward the center.

Above are photos of a 1890 Indian cent quadrupled die obverse, one might speculate as to the odds of a die shrinking or expanding four or five times if it is hubbed and annealed five times. Most Indian cent dies were hubbed only twice. This is a rare example of a working die being hubbed and annealed five times. But in the Trade Dollar series, all of the working dies were hubbed five or six times. More than 30 different specimens of Trade Dollars have been examined from different dies that exhibited this "step doubling" with four or five "steps."

Class III, Design Hub Doubling

Design hub doubling occurs when working hubs bearing two different designs are used to hub a die. The two hubs were created from two different master dies that had differences in design. A good example of this type of doubling is the 1943/2 Jefferson nickel. The die first received an impression from a hub with a 1942 date, then hubbed with a hub containing the 1943 date. The doubling in this class will depend on the differences between the two hubs that were used to make the impressions. This difference could be of one letter or the whole design. The doubling will not follow the constant spread of the Class I or IV or the gradual increase or decrease of doubling of the Class V.

There are two features of design hub doubling:

1. Each impression should show the characteristics of the design of that hub.

2. The doubling is equal to differences between the design elements of the hubs.

Note: As the images on the working hub are raised, you can only remove or modify them, not add to them. If the differences in the two hubs used were caused by one of the hubs being modified by the removal or altering of one of the design elements, then that doubled die would fall under the Class VII, modified hub doubling. For a doubled die to fall into this category, there must be proof that a master die with a different design was used during the course of a year or between years, and the doubled die must show the diagnostics of both designs.

Many doubled dies have been misclassified in this class because, using the initial definition, it was explained that this class of doubled die usually exhibits erratic doubling. The problem is many hybrid doubled dies (doubled dies of more than one class) that could not be classified were, by default, called a Class III, even though there was no known design changes to the master hub for a particular year. As more research is done on each denomination and design changes are more thoroughly documented,

The photos above are examples of Class III Doubled Dies. The top photo is a 1878 Morgan Dollar VAM-41 8/7 tail feathers. A number of Morgan Dollar reverse dies were modified by impressing the 7 tail feather design over the 8. The photo on the bottom right is a 1960 Lincoln cent proof Small Date/Large Date. In early 1960, a Lincoln cent master die was made with a small date, but when it broke a new master die was made with a large date. The photo on the bottom left is a 1943/2 Jefferson nickel. A working die was struck from a working hub with the 1942 date, then a second time from a working hub with a 1943 date.

we will more readily be able to recognize Class III doubled dies.

One side effect of using a screw press to hub dies up until 1893 has been to cause many misidentifications of the correct class. If not enough pressure was applied in the hubbing press, only part of the design from the working hub was incused into the working die. As the working die started with a cone-shaped top, the center of the working die would have received the design first. If on the second hubbing the working die was misaligned, only the center of the working die would have the doubling. This is very common among Shield nickels. Doubling only shows on the center as offset or pivot, but because no doubling shows on the rim design elements, these were incorrectly classified as Class III. Refer to the "Other Factors To Consider When Classifying Doubled Dies" section for a complete description of this problem.

Class IV, Offset Hub Doubling

Offset hub doubling occurs when a die being rehubbed is off center in the hubbing press from a position it had been in on a previous hubbing. When this occurs, the doubling will be in the direction that the die was offset from the first hubbing to the

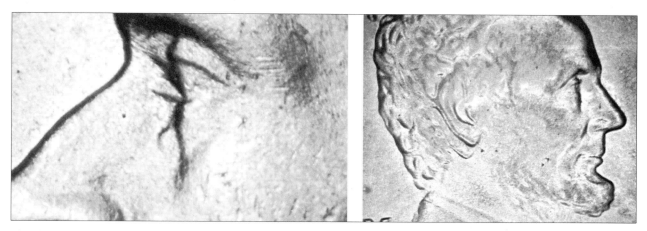

The above left photo is the 1943 Jefferson Nickel doubled eye where the second hubbing was offset to the northeast. The above right photo is the 1984 Lincoln cent DDO-001 with very strong Class VI doubling seen on the ear and beard. Both of these doubled dies do not show doubling on the rim elements.

Above are photos of the 1983 Lincoln cent DDR-001, which shows very strong Class IV doubling north on the entire reverse.

second. All of the doubling will be going in the same direction and will have the same spread across the die.

There are two features of offset hub doubling:

1. The doubling is all in one direction.

2. The degree of doubling is constant.

Exception: If the doubling only shows on the center of a doubled die, but it is in one direction and the degree of doubling is constant, then this variety falls under Class IV. This diagnostic is the result of a partial hubbing during the first hubbing. As a screw press was used to hub dies before 1893, the pressure was not constant. If the impression was not great enough, only the center of the design would have been incused into the working die. A complete explanation is presented in the "Other Factors To Consider When Classifying Doubled Dies" section.

Class V, Pivoted Hub Doubling

Pivoted hub doubling occurs when a die is pivoted about a point near the rim during rehubbing. Because the point of pivot is near the rim, the spread of doubling will be the strongest at the point directly opposite the pivot point and will decrease as you move away from that point. The point closest to the pivot point will show little or no doubling. The doubling will be fan shaped.

Many Class I doubled dies are called Class V because the doubling on the design elements on one side of the coin is stronger than that on the other. This is because the pivot point is off center. But if the pivot point is between design elements closest to the rim and the center, then all the design elements about the rim are "rotated" about that point and that doubled die would be classified as a Class I. If the pivot point is on or near the rim, the die was "pivoted" about that point on the rim and the doubling will be fan shaped from that pivot point.

An easy way to distinguish whether a doubled die is a Class I or V is to recreate how the working hub was pivoted in the hubbing press. Use a picture of the obverse or reverse of the denomination in question. Enlarge it using a photo copier, make a copy on a transparency. Placing the transparency over top of the original, match the design images of the transparency to those of the secondary images or doubling.

From here, you should be able to determine the pivot point. Holding your finger on the transparency, find the pivot point, so that when you rotate the transparency, the design images of the transparency overlay the design images of the original. If the pivot point is between the design images nearest the rim and the center, all of the design elements about the rim were rotated about that pivot point to produce the doubling and it would fall under Class I. If the pivot point is between the design elements closest to the rim, then the working die was pivoted at about that point to produce the doubling.

Above are photos of the 1995 Lincoln cent DDO-001, with strong Class V doubling seen on LIBERTY and IN GOD WE TRUST. The pivot point is about 2:30 on the rim. No doubling is seen on the date.

There are two features of pivot hub doubling:

1. There is little or no doubling on one side of the coin. The strongest doubling is opposite that point and decreases from there.

2. The doubling is fan shaped.

Exception: If the doubling only shows on the center of a doubled die, but the doubling is fan shaped and no pivot point can be assigned near the center, then this variety falls under Class V. This diagnostic is the result of a partial hubbing during the first hubbing. Because a screw press was used to hub dies before 1893, the pressure was not constant. If the impression was not great enough, only the center of the design would have been incused into the working die. A complete explanation is presented in the "Other Factors To Consider When Classifying Doubled Dies" section.

Class VI, Distended Hub Doubling

With each of the other classes of doubling, a clear separation is seen between the primary and secondary images. Distended hub doubling does not show any separation lines. This class of doubling occurs when the design images on the working hub become flattened and thickened from use in the hubbing press, producing thick letters or designs into the working die. This could happen to the working hub from being too soft or the working die being too hard, causing wear in the form of expansion of the images on the working hub.

There are two features of distended hub doubling:

1. No separation of any image shows.

2. Doubling takes the form of extra thickness of the letters, digits, or other design elements.

The design elements on the working hub are raised. They bear the brunt of the hubbing stress. Thus, if anything flared, it would be the raised design elements, which would distend in all directions. The distance from the center of the radius of the design elements would not change to any significant degree. In other words, if a working hub became "flattened" from overuse, then the design elements on the working hub would become thicker.

The above photos are of a 1943 Lincoln cent doubled die reverse. Notice the Class VI extreme thickness in the letters E PLURIBUS UNUM and the dots.

If a die were hubbed with a flattened hub, annealed, then brought back to the hubbing press with a normal hub with a centralized design, the centralized design elements of the hub would be impressed into the already thicker design elements of the working die and not be seen as doubling.

The working hub is hardened before being used, and the working dies are softened through annealing before being hubbed. It is less likely that the working hub became worn, especially during the 19th century, when only a small number of dies were needed for each denomination. But in the 20th century, in series with high die productions, this type of doubling is more common; such is the case with the Lincoln cent series, where "extra thickening" can be found on many coins.

Class VII, Modified Hub Doubling

Modified Hub Doubling is caused when a working die is struck by a working hub that had a modification done to part of the coin design. If the working die is struck by a normal working hub and this modified hub, then the differences caused by the modification will show on the working die. The

design elements on the working hub are raised and could have been ground off. A good example of this type of doubling occurred in 1970 in the Lincoln cent series, when the date on two different hubs was at different levels.

There is one key feature of modified hub doubling:

1. The doubling shows as the difference between a normal hub and the modified hub.

Because a single working hub can be used to make many working dies, a large number of working dies can display the same doubling. If the master hub was modified, then the doubling will show on a large number of working dies.

Class VIII, Tilted Hub Doubling

Tilted hub doubling occurs when the top of the die being hubbed is not parallel to that of the hub. This could occur when:

1. The bottom of the die is not cut parallel.

2. A foreign object, such as a scrap of metal, is caught below the die in the hubbing press.

3. The hub is tilted.

The above photo is of a 1970-S Lincoln cent doubled die obverse. It is a good example of a Class VII. This working die was struck with a working hub with the date slightly lower than that of the working hub used in the second hubbing.

4. The hubbing press is loose, bent, or tilted.

If the top of the die is tilted with respect to the hub, one side of the hub and die will make contact before the other side. Because of the tilt, the impression made from the hub into the die will be off center. Also, one side of the die will be impressed with greater depth of the design (the side that made contact with the hub first).

Dramatic tilts would probably be caught and fixed. Even though this class is rarely found, it is possible that when combined with another class of doubling, such as Class IV, that doubling could be

Shown above is the 1867 Two cent DDO-001 with extreme doubling seen on IN GOD WE TRUST and other portions of the top of the coin. No doubling is seen on the bottom of the coin. The design elements on the bottom of the coin are weaker than those on top. Also, on the doubled images, which are from the first hubbing, the design elements are strongest at the top and decrease as you move toward the middle. These factors indicate that on the first hubbing the working die was tilted where the top of the coin was struck first by the working hub.

Looking to the left of the center of the obverse, the doubling seen on the shield and leaves is going directly north, looking on the right side, the doubling is seen going south. This leads to the conclusion that the pivot point was at the center like a Class I. Using overlays, it was easy to calculate that the pivot point was slightly off center, a little above and to the right. This variety is a Class I + VIII, Rotated and Tilted Hub Doubling.

seen on three fourths of the coin going in the same direction but no doubling on the final one fourth of the coin. This form of hybrid doubling does happen, so when you are trying to classify a doubled die, do not just consider one category.

Class IX, God Only Knows

This class of doubling is for doubled dies that are simply unexplainable. It is for those extremely few doubled dies that defy logic and common sense. The physical evidence simply does not support a reasonable conclusion on how the working die was hubbed to produce the secondary images. This is the reason for the title, "God Only Knows"—varieties in this class of doubling cannot be explained by human logic. The doubled die that brought attention to problems like this is the 1870 Shield nickel doubled die reverse. This doubled die was shown to several experts, and each came to the same conclusion: they could not determine the class of doubling.

As discussed throughout this chapter, a doubled die is a working die that has design images which are doubled in some manner. The doubling is usually created in the hubbing process. Up until about 1998, working dies required multiple hubbings in order to create a deeper image of the design.

Many classes of doubled dies are caused if on multiple hubbings, the working die is not lined up with images struck during previous hubbings. In most cases, how the working die is misaligned, determines the class of doubling. If there is a pivot point around the center, the doubling is called Class I. If offset in one direction, it is Class IV. There are other causes of doubled dies, such as Class II, which is caused during the annealing process, and Class III, which is caused by two working hubs with different a design.

For most doubled dies, it is easy to determine the class of doubling. There are characteristics of each class of doubling that make it easy to separate. Some doubled dies are more difficult to classify. One method used to logically classify a doubled die is to determine which classes of doubled dies can be ruled out. This method narrows the choices and helps select from the remainder.

In looking at the doubled die example on the following pages, it becomes clear that there is no logical pattern. Looking first at UNITED, on UN, the doubling is counter-clockwise and no doubling is seen on I. On TED and on the two stars below, strong doubling is seen clockwise and towards the rim. These are in the opposite direction of UN. Some of the letters on STATES and the stars below show doubling consistent with TED of UNITED. Using the stars below STATES OF, the doubling from left to right decreases in strength, which leads towards tilt hub doubling combined with another class of doubling. No doubling is seen on OF or the star below OF. Dramatic doubling is seen on the stars below AMERICA. Doubling on AMERICA is very unusual. The first A of AMERICA shows doubling clockwise and towards the rim. The M shows dramatic doubling counter-clockwise and towards the center, and is also in the opposite direction of TED of UNITED. Doubling is strongest on the M and decreases in depth of strike from left to right. The two stars below MER show doubling clockwise, which is opposite from MER. On CENTS, the doubling is counter-clockwise and towards the rim on CENT, decreasing in spread from left to right. On the S, the doubling is clockwise and towards the rim. No doubling is seen on the star above the E, and strong doubling is seen on the star above the T counter-clockwise.

Class I can be ruled out because there is no consistent doubling around the design elements around the rim in the same direction. Class II can also be rule out as almost all of the doubling shows pivoting. The doubling does not display any characteristics of being from a distended (Class VI) or modified hub (Class VII). Offset doubling (Class IV) can be ruled out as the doubling is not consistent in direction or strength. Pivot doubling (Class V) can be ruled out as the doubling is not in a consistent direction, and design elements right next to each other are in the opposite direction and different strength.

When ruling out Class III, we must examine the different hubs used in the Shield nickel series. Pages 25 through 27 of Edward Fletcher's book on Shield nickels, published in 1994 states that the "Rays" reverse hub was used in 1866 and 1867. Obviously, this reverse could not have been the result of a "Rays" reverse hub. There were three different "No Rays" reverse hubs designs that were used between 1867 and 1883. On the Type I "No Rays" reverse, (which is the same as the "Rays" reverse without the rays), the stars are larger and very close to the letters around the rim. In addition, the stars are in a different relative location to the outside letters.

For example, using the star below AM of AMERICA, on the Type I, the tip of the star is pointing between AM. On the reverse of Type II and III, it points to the left upright of the M of AMERICA. Type I reverse is found on reverses from 1867 through 1869. Obviously, this is not the result of a Type I "No Rays" reverse design because the stars are not close to the letters or in the relative position to the letters. The Type II "No Rays" reverse was used in 1868, and the Type III "No Rays" reverse was used from 1869 through 1883. The stars on the Type II and Type III are the same distance from the outside letters, but the relative location on some of the stars is different. On OF, the Type II star points to F, and the Type III points between OF. On ES of STATES, the Type II points to the left side of the second S, and the Type III points to the right side of

the E. Using this information, a conclusion can be drawn that this reverse was only the result of a Type III "No Rays" reverse. There are no stars that are in the Type II position.

Sometimes you have to use your imagination and think outside the box. For example, imagine what would happen if you combined a Class IV (offset) and V (pivot). An easy way to visualize this is to use a stamp that has a round image. Strike the stamp once on a piece of paper, lift the stamp over the image, offset in one direction, then pivot your hand and strike the stamp again. You can see how these two classes could be combined. The motions you use to change from the primary to secondary images is the same motion that the engraver used when placing the working die into the hubbing press opposite the working hub.

On this doubled die, even combining classes of doubling does not help. For example, on the S of CENTS, the doubling is clockwise and towards the rim. On the star above the T of CENT, the doubling is counter-clockwise. The same is true with the doubling on AMER of AMERICA and the stars below: the doubling is in the opposite direction.

One point to consider is all rules cannot always be applied. For example, we normally conclude that the secondary hubbing would create a deeper hubbing and therefore a more prominent image. On the first strike, we have a cone-shaped working die being pushed into the working hub (hubbing). Between hubbings, the working die is annealed, which softens it. The second hubbing created a deeper image from the working hub. What if less pressure was used in the hubbing press in the second hubbing? The image produced in the secondary hubbing might be weaker than the first. Also, what if the metal used to make the working die was inferior? What might occur?

Doubled dies like these are fun to examine and theorize. It pushes our minds to contemplate all of the possibilities. It would be good to hear any theories on how this doubled die was created.

Other Factors To Consider

1. Hybrid of classes of doubling in a single hubbing—Classes of hub doubled dies are defined by how the doubling occurred. Working dies are hubbed multiple times to get a detailed impression incused into the die. If upon subsequent hubbings, the images of the working die are not lined up with the images of the working hub, a second image will be produced. The alignment of the working hub and die in the hubbing press is manual, and the motion used to produce this misalignment of the die to the hub defines the class of doubling. There are four classes of hub doubling caused by a misalignment in the hubbing press: rotated, offset, pivot, and tilt

hub doubling. Each is defined by the relative motion of the working die to the hub in the hubbing press.

Because the alignment is a manual process, it is possible to have a combination of motions producing a "hybrid" of two or more classes of doubling occurring during a single hubbing.

For example: if a working die is rotated and offset relative to the working hub in the hubbing press, it will not have diagnostic features of either class of doubling but a combination of both. The classifying of these types of doubled dies is no easy art. The easiest way to understand how the doubling was created is to try to simulate the doubling with transparencies, clay, or anything else where you can produce the same results as that of the doubled image.

2. Hybrid of classes of doubling in multiple hubbings—Working dies normally are hubbed more than two times. There are many examples of tripled dies, quadrupled dies, and so on. Many of these display different classes of doubling, with each class produced during a different hubbing. Many of these doubled dies were called Class III, because they could not be classified under one class.

3. Partial hubbing due to lack of pressure in the hubbing press—If not enough pressure is used in the hubbing press, only the central design elements of the working hub will be incused into the working die. This happened more in the 19th century because a screw press was used up to 1893 to hub dies. After 1893, a hydraulic press was used.

To prepare a working die to be hubbed, a die blank was prepared and annealed to reduce its resistance to pressure. The die blank had a neck with the same diameter as that of the working hub. The die blank also had a cone-shaped top to allow metal to properly disperse and fill the die cavity of the master die without disturbing the surface below the periphery point. This also allowed additional metal to form up greater detail on the first hubbing. The working hub die was put in the upper portion of a large screw press and brought down with great force onto the die blank. As pressure was applied to the die blank, the steel within hardened from the pressure and became brittle. This was caused by the compression of the molecules of steel.

If not enough pressure was used in the hubbing press, only the central design elements would have been incused into the working die. This is because of the cone-shaped top of the die blank. The center of the cone is pressed by the center of the working hub first and thus the central design elements are incused first into the working die.

If upon subsequent hubbings the images are lined up correctly, no doubling will occur; only weak design elements about the rim. If there is a misalignment, then a secondary image of the design elements only will occur in the center of the working die because the design elements around the rim have only received one impression. This happened many times on Shield nickels and these varieties were incorrectly classified as Class III, Design Hub Doubling. In the Indian cent series, there are approximately 15 doubled die obverses between 1864 and 1886, and only one of these shows doubling on design elements around the rim.

The common diagnostic for this occurrence is a weak strike of the design elements around the rim, with stronger design elements near the center.

Overdates

An overdate occurs when a coin exhibits dates of different years. This can occur when the date is punched or hubbed into a die for one year and the date of another year is punched or hubbed over one or more of the digits of that working die. This might have happened intentionally for a number of reasons:

1. If there was a shortage of dies or die steel, old dies could be reused with a new date.

2. If too many dies were produced for a given year, unused dies could be restruck with a new date.

3. Dies which had low usage could be reused with a new date.

4. On the second hubbings of a working die, a new working hub with a different date was used.

In the 18th and 19th centuries at the Mint, the date was punched into the working die by hand. During the early 19th century, it was acceptable to reuse working dies if they were new or only had been slightly used. The date of the working die could be removed with an abrasive by the die sinker, then the die sinker would strike the new date over the old. If remnants of the digits of the previous year were left showing on the die, dates of two different years would be on the same die producing an overdate

Overdates could also have been produced by accident at the mint. If, at the end of a year, punches for more than one year are present, the die sinker could have used the current date punch, then upon deciding to restrike the date into the die, picked up the date for the next year. This type of accident is extremely unlikely, but possible if dates of different years were kept in the same room as dies were being hubbed around the New Year.

Overdates after 1908 might have also been caused by accident if a die was hubbed at the end of the year. To get a deeper impression, dies are hubbed more than once. If on the first hubbing, a

working hub of one date is used, then on the second hubbing, a working hub of a different date is used. This happened for the 1918 over 1917 Buffalo nickel and the 1942 over 1941 Mercury dime.

Other Forms of Doubling

There are other forms of doubled images that can show on a coin that are not doubled dies and command no premium. A double die is created during the die making process and exhibits raised rounded secondary images, most of the time with splitting on the serifs. Not all doubled dies have split serifs, some only show extra thickness.

Strike doubling (also called mechanical, machine, or ejection doubling) occurs during the striking of the coins in the coining press. This type of variety exhibits flat shelf-like secondary images with no splitting of the serifs. Also seen is metal flow from the primary to the secondary images. Strike doubling is caused by the die or part of the

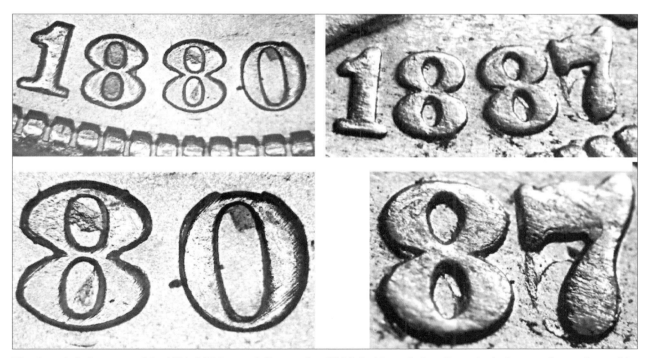

The above left photos are of the 1880-CC Morgan dollar overdate VAM-6 with an obvious 7 seen in the lower and upper loop of the second 8. The two photos on the above right are of the 1887 three cent nickel 8/7, which is found on both proof coins and business strikes. This variety is especially nice because it also has 4 digits in the denticles.

machinery being loose. If the die is loose as the hammer comes down and strikes the blank planchet with tons of pressure, it will have a tendency to twist across the face of the planchet at the point of greatest pressure. This movement will cause some of the metal of the design that was raised on the planchet to be smeared across the face of the planchet, resulting in a flat shelf-like outline created by the die. Because the pressure in the coining press is constant, the strike doubling should be the same for all coins struck from that die unless the degree of looseness changes.

If the hammer die twists in the coining press, it will most likely rotate about the center. This effect will cause a greater movement of the outer elements of the die and a greater spread of the strike doubling to show on the outer elements of the coin, which is the case most of the time. It will also show on most of the outer elements of the coin. Before 1984, the mintmark was struck into each working die by hand. If a pre-1984 mintmark shows the same doubling as seen on the other parts of the coin, it is most likely strike doubling. The same is true of the date before 1909. Before this year, the date was struck into each die by hand. The date was not on the die during the hubbing of the die and could not have become doubled like the design elements on doubled dies.

Another type of doubled image that occurred on some 19th century series displayed a secondary image around the edges of the lettering. This type of variety is sometimes called "outline images" or "shoulder doubling." From about 1836 to 1886, for some series, the main design elements were put onto a Galvano and transferred through a reducing lathe to the master hub. The master hub was then used to create a master die which design elements are incused. A ring punch was then used to punch the outer design elements into the master die.

The ring punch was a circular metal bar with raised letters or numerals on it. If the engraver wanted to trim the letters, he might sheer metal from the sides, which could cause a build up of metal at the base of the letters. If struck hard enough, the extra metal at the base of each letter would be incused into the master die. With improvements to the reducing lathe and hubbing press in the later part of the 19th century, all images except for the date and mintmark were made part of the Galvano. After this period, there are no more occurrences of outline images.

The above left photo is of a 1969-S Lincoln cent that shows strike doubling. The above right photo is of a 1995 Lincoln cent that exhibits strike doubling. On the '69-S, notice that the S mintmark is doubled the same as the date. Notice on the '95, there are no serifs, the outline of the secondary images are flat, and do not have the shape or contour of the normal digits.

Date-by-Date Analysis

1913 Variety I

DDO-001

CLASS VI
Offset & Tilted Hub Doubling

Cross Reference	FS-14.8, WDDO-001
Overall Rarity	URS-07
Interest Level	Moderate

GRADE	VF	XF	AU	MS60	MS63	MS65
VALUE	50	85	135	225	260	425

DESCRIPTION

A moderate thickness seen on the date, and, to a slightly lesser degree on LIBERTY. Distortion can also be seen at the top of the head, feathers, and the nostril.

DIE MARKERS

Obverse: Stage A - No clashing present. Stage B - Strong EPU clash under the chin. Stage C - EPU clash is polished away. LIBERTY and date have a mushy appearance.

Reverse: None

COMMENTS

Though this is not a major doubled die, it is nevertheless a scarce variety from what was probably a problem die that saw limited use. Given the tendency for the rapid wearing of the date and inherent weakness of LIBERTY on all 1913 coins, it could be difficult to identify in any grade below Fine or VF. It remains a tough variety to locate. Sales records are few and far between. The photos below are of a Mint State LDS coin.

1913 Variety I   DDR-001

CLASS II
Distorted Hub Doubling

Cross Reference	FS-014.86, WDDR-001
Overall Rarity	URS-09
Interest Level	Moderate

GRADE	VF	XF	AU	MS60	MS63	MS65
VALUE	35	65	85	125	200	450

DESCRIPTION

Significant doubling seen on FIVE CENTS, UNITED STATES OF AMERICA, and the dots. EDS specimens will show additional doubling at the back edge of the left rear leg and in the details within the fur at the top of the back. This variety shows multiple hubbings.

DIE MARKERS

Obverse: Heavy die clashing.

Reverse: Heavy die clashing. Die scratches evident through and below UNITED. Circular die scratch from the chin to field.

COMMENTS

Late die states have the appearance of a Class VI doubled die, that is, thickness of the lettering but without separation lines. This variety is relatively easy to locate, even in Mint State, though it is more difficult to find that DDR-002. As with most doubled dies, it is much tougher in an early state of dies.

1913 Variety I

DDR-002

Cross Reference	WDDR-002
Overall Rarity	URS-11
Interest Level	Moderate

CLASS II
Distorted Hub Doubling

GRADE	VF	XF	AU	MS60	MS63	MS65
VALUE	35	55	75	100	150	400

DESCRIPTION

A moderate spread seen on FIVE CENTS, UNITED STATES OF AMERICA, and the dots.

DIE MARKERS

Obverse: None noted.

Reverse: None noted.

COMMENTS

Similar to DDR-001, but only shows one extra hubbing, whereas DDR-001 shows multiple hubbings. It is relatively easy to find.

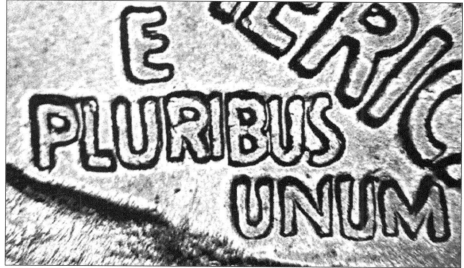

1913 Variety II

DDO-001

Cross Reference	WDDO-001
Overall Rarity	Unknown
Interest Level	Moderate

CLASS IV
Offset Hub Doubling

GRADE	VF	XF	AU	MS60	MS63	MS65
VALUE	35	55	75	95	150	450

DESCRIPTION

A minor to moderate spread can be seen on the eyelid, nose nostril, and braid.

DIE MARKERS

Obverse: None noted.

Reverse: None noted.

COMMENTS

As the photos show, the doubling seems to be restricted to the central elements of the design. This is characteristic of many of the Class IV doubled dies and is probably the result of the conical nature of the dies themselves, where the central parts of the design hub up first. This phenomenon is seen over and over on the Class IV varieties listed here throughout the series. This is a newly reported variety, so value and rarity have yet to be accurately determined.

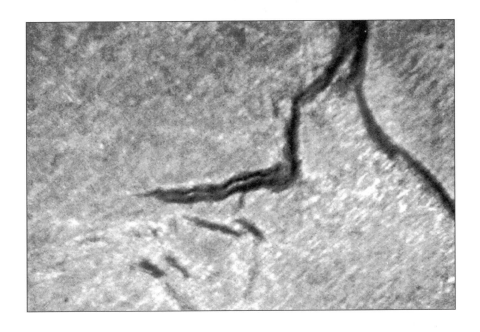

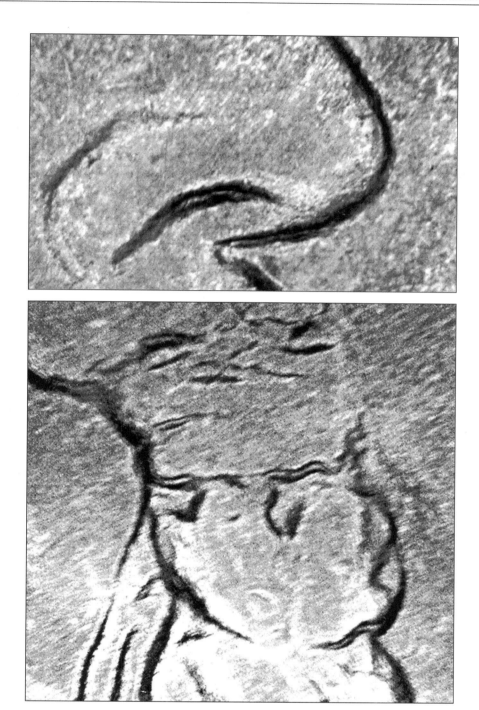

1914/3

DDO-001
(OVD-001)

Cross Reference	FS-014.87, WDDO-001
Overall Rarity	URS-10
Interest Level	Very High

CLASS III
Design Hub Doubling

GRADE	VF	XF	AU	MS60	MS63	MS65
VALUE	400	500	850	1250	2500	27,500

DESCRIPTION

Clear portions of a 3 are seen underneath the 4 in the date. The top horizontal bar of the 3 is seen to the left of the top of the 4. The top right corner is seen to the right of the top of the 4. The bottom curve of the 3 is seen below the extreme right of the crossbar of the 4.

DIE MARKERS

Obverse: Strike doubling seen on date, upper feathers, and braid. A strong, angled EPU die clash is seen under the chin.

Reverse: Strike doubling seen on cents. Die clashing seen to left of EPU.

COMMENTS

Without question, these overdates are working hub doubled dies. At last count, five different dies (a couple have been de-listed), some with only a trace of the crossbar showing, have been discovered, along with similar coins for both Denver and San Francisco Mint coins. Many have turned up since the first edition of this book with a corresponding sharp drop in values. The first two dies have been slabbed by the major certification companies, and only these first two dies are worth the premiums commonly listed for the variety.

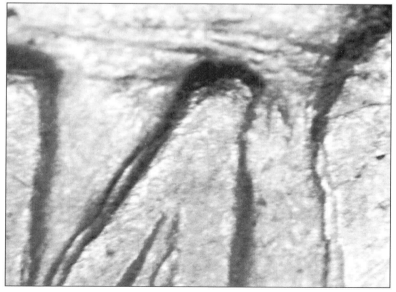

1914/3

DDO-002
(OVD-002)

Cross Reference	FS-014.87, WDDO-002
Overall Rarity	URS-10
Interest Level	Very High

CLASS III
Design Hub Doubling

GRADE	VF	XF	AU	MS60	MS63	MS65
VALUE	400	500	650	1250	2500	27,500

DESCRIPTION

Clear portions of a 3 are seen underneath the 4 in the date. The top horizontal bar of the 3 is seen to the left of the top of the 4. The top right corner is seen to the right of the top of the 4. On this die, the curve of the 3 below the crossbar shows only faintly, if at all.

DIE MARKERS

Obverse: No strike doubling seen on obverse.

Reverse: None noted.

COMMENTS

The underdigit is very nearly as strong as it is on DDO-001, and it should bring identical premiums. Clearly, a vigorous attempt to remove as much of the 3 as possible was made, as heavy die polish lines are quite visible above and around the top of the 4. Many of these, too, have been found since the first edition was published in 1999.

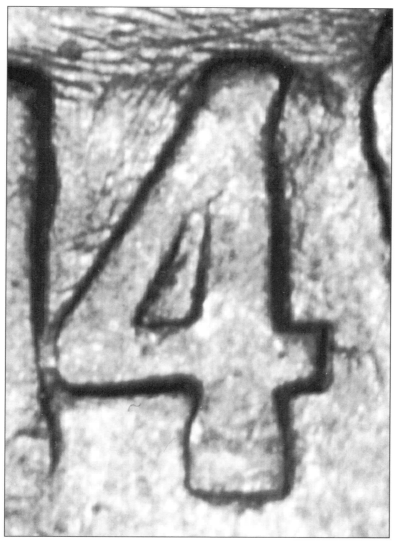

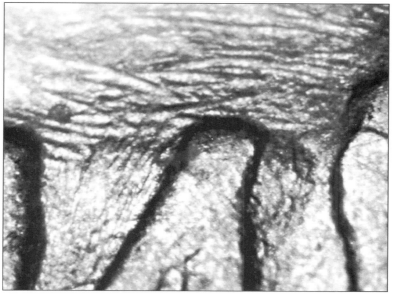

1914/3 DDO-001

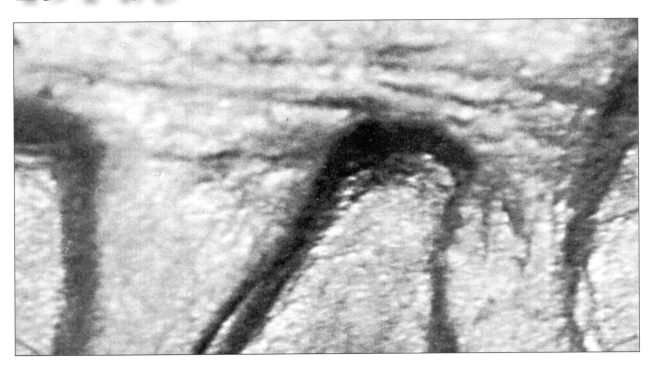

1914/3 DDO-002

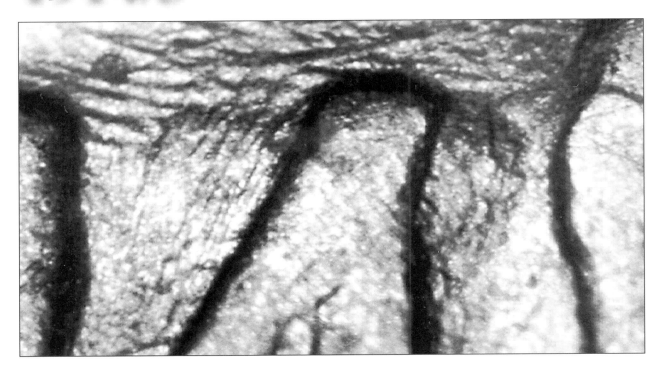

1914/3

DDO-003
(OVD-003)

Cross Reference	WDDO-003
Overall Rarity	Unknown
Interest Level	Very High

CLASS III
Design Hub Doubling

GRADE	VF	XF	AU	MS60	MS63	MS65
VALUE	225	350	500	------	------	------

DESCRIPTION

A fairly clear crossbar of the 3 is visible to the left and right of the top of the 4. The top horizontal bar is seen to the left of the top of the 4. The top right corner of the 3 is seen to the right of the top of the 4.

DIE MARKERS

Obverse: Strike doubling is seen at the tops of the date digits. Strong polish lines above and around the top of the 4 are seen, but in a different pattern that on DDO-002. There is an EPU clash under the chin.

Reverse: None noted.

COMMENTS

The crossbar here is not as clearly visible as it is on DDO-001 and DDO-002, but this die has likely been slabbed as an overdate by the major slabbing companies, possibly as a "late die state." The premium for DDO-003 should not be quite as high as for the first two dies, however. Few sales have been recorded, therefore the rarity is not clearly known at this time.

1914/3

DELISTED

CLASS III
Design Hub Doubling

Cross Reference	Old WDDO-004
Overall Rarity	Unknown
Interest Level	None

GRADE	VF	XF	AU	MS60	MS63	MS65
VALUE	------	------	------	------	------	------

DESCRIPTION

This variety has been delisted. It is no longer considered an overdate.

DIE MARKERS

Obverse: No strike doubling seen on obverse.

Reverse: None noted.

COMMENTS

A higher grade specimen showed that this was not an overdate.

1914/3

DELISTED

Cross Reference	Old WDDO-005
Overall Rarity	Unknown
Interest Level	None

CLASS III
Design Hub Doubling

GRADE	VF	XF	AU	MS60	MS63	MS65
VALUE	------	------	------	------	------	------

DESCRIPTION

This variety has been delisted. It is no longer considered an overdate.

DIE MARKERS

Obverse: No strike doubling seen on obverse.

Reverse: None noted.

COMMENTS

A higher grade specimen showed that this was not an overdate.

1914/3

DDO-006
(OVD-006)

Cross Reference	None
Overall Rarity	Unknown
Interest Level	High

CLASS III
Design Hub Doubling

GRADE	VF	XF	AU	MS60	MS63	MS65
VALUE	400	500	650	1250	2500	27,500

DESCRIPTION

A clear crossbar of the 3 is visible to the left of the top of the 4, with a very noticeable 'bump.' The top right corner of the 3 is seen to the right of the top of the 4.

DIE MARKERS

Obverse: Strong die polish lines above and around the top of the 4 as on DDO-002 and DDO-003. It appears that this effacement attempt was at least partially successful in removing some of the crossbar to the left of the 4. Die clashing seen below the chin.

Reverse: Heavy die clashing is seen under E PLURIBUS UNUM.

COMMENTS

This appears to be the third best of the overdates for 1914, very close in strength to DDO-001 and DDO-002. There is a very prominent 'bump' to the right of the 4 with a weaker but still visible crossbar to the left. This is a very significant overdate die and should certainly be worth very close to what the first two dies are. It's probable that this die has been slabbed as an overdate along with DDO-001 and DDO-002.

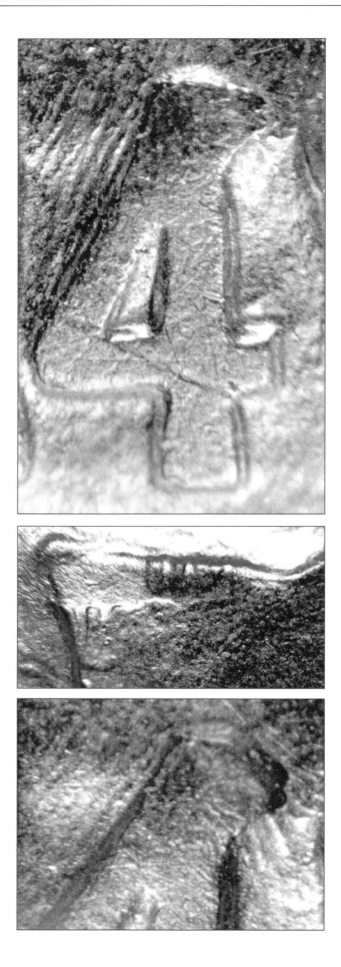

1914/3

DDO-007
(OVD-007)

Cross Reference	None
Overall Rarity	Unknown
Interest Level	Moderate

CLASS III
Design Hub Doubling

GRADE	VF	XF	AU	MS60	MS63	MS65
VALUE	75	150	225	325	475	------

DESCRIPTION

Portions of a weak crossbar is visible to both sides of the 4. This can be seen best by viewing the date sideways instead of the normal vertical view.

DIE MARKERS

Obverse: None noted. No die polishing seen above 4.

Reverse: None noted.

COMMENTS

This is a weak overdate and the first where there is no evidence of attempted effacement of the underdigit. By the time this die was hubbed, the erroneous '3' has been worn down to near invisibility by repeated hubbings. It should bring only a fraction of the price of the better overdates. Low grade coins (Good through Fine) are probably impossible to attribute with any certainty.

1915

DDO-001

Cross Reference	FS-14.9, WDDO-001
Overall Rarity	URS-07
Interest Level	High

CLASS IV
Offset Hub Doubling

GRADE	VF	XF	AU	MS60	MS63	MS65
VALUE	350	500	750	1000	1500	2500

DESCRIPTION

Strong doubling seen on the eyelid, nostril, eyebrow, chin, lips, braid, and some of the interior hair details. Minor doubling seen on LIBERTY.

DIE MARKERS

Obverse: None noted.

Reverse: None noted.

COMMENTS

This remains a very rare coin. Very few additional specimens have been found since the publication of the first addition of this book—few, in fact, since its discovery. It is very similar in appearance to the 1930 DDO-002. Values have increased substantially since the first edition based on the sale of several at very high prices. An article on this variety appeared in the September 21, 1998 issue of *Coin World*.

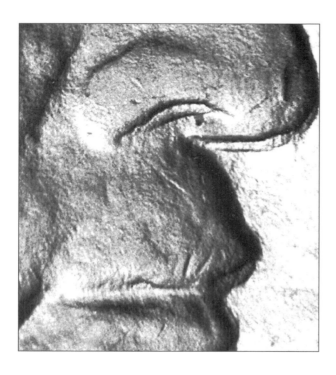

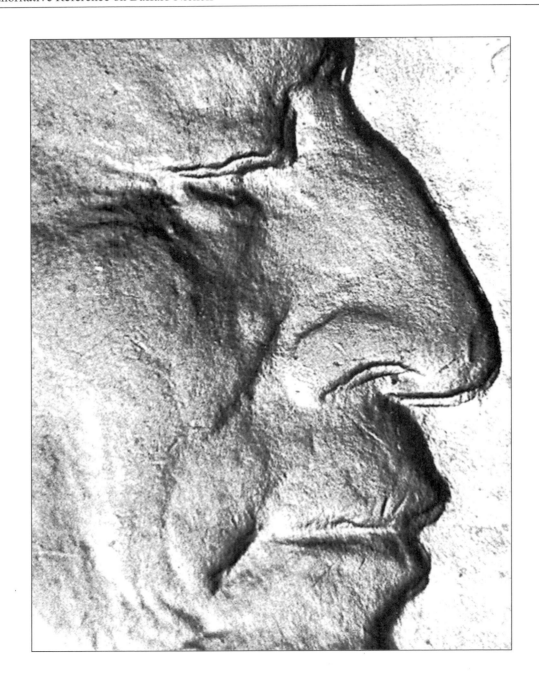

1916

DDO-001

CLASS V
Pivot Hub Doubling

Cross Reference	FS-16, 1-O-V, WDDO-001
Overall Rarity	URS-09
Interest Level	Very High

GRADE	G4	VG	F12	VF	XF	AU	MS60	MS63	MS65
VALUE	3000	5000	7500	10,000	17,500	40,000	85,000	300,000	n/a

DESCRIPTION

Extreme doubling on date and ribbon ties. Strong doubling on feather tips, neck, chin, braid, lips, and nose from a pivot point at or near 2 o'clock. The doubling on the date is further accentuated by the thinness of the numerals.

DIE MARKERS

Obverse: None noted.

Reverse: None noted.

COMMENTS

The undisputed "Chief" of the Buffalo nickels. It actually has a wider spread on the date than the 1955 Lincoln cent doubled die obverse. This defective die must have been seen and pulled from production very early in the die run, explaining its continued rarity in spite of its well known status and object of intense search for the last 25 years. It has established itself as the premier and most expensive coin in a very popular series. An MS65 has yet to be certified, but if one ever makes it, there's no telling how high in value it could go.

The current finest known, an MS64, sold for nearly $300,000 at auction in 2004 and a 'lowly' MS62 brought $115,000 during the same year. Dateless coins can still be easily identified by the obvious doubling on the feather tips and ribbon ties. Demand is so high that even these (and acid date coins) are worth several hundred dollars. This is currently the most expensive 20th century non-gold U.S. coin in the higher grade levels.

1917

DDR-001

Cross Reference	FS-16.4, WDDR-001
Overall Rarity	URS-07
Interest Level	Very High

CLASS IV
Offset Hub Doubling

GRADE	VF	XF	AU	MS60	MS63	MS65
VALUE	650	850	1250	3000	7500	25,000

DESCRIPTION

Dramatic doubling seen on E PLURIBUS UNUM, with a strong spread evident on all of the buffalo's hair details, face details, legs—especially the back edge of the left rear leg, base of the mound, and VE of FIVE and CE of CENTS. Second hubbing offset to northwest.

DIE MARKERS

Obverse: None noted.

Reverse: None noted.

COMMENTS

This surprisingly rare coin has remained that way since its discovery in 1992. A number have surfaced, but certainly not enough to explain its rarity. It shows no severe clashing, die cracks or other problems that may have contributed to a short-ended die life, so this rarity continues to be a mystery. While it is very tough in all grades, it becomes extremely rare (possibly unique) in Mint State. For some reason, a sizeable percentage of the ones that are known have problems of one type or another such as scratches or harsh cleaning, which make a problem-free coin all that much more desirable. A number have sold for very high prices in the last few years, prompting an increase in the values listed here. The finest currently known is the discovery coin, an MS64. This may be the only Mint State piece known, though population reports list two in this grade. This outstanding variety is one of those coins that deserves a listing in the *Red Book*. A PCGS slabbed MS64 was sold for $10,925 in January 2007. It is, without question, one of the best half dozen doubled dies of the series.

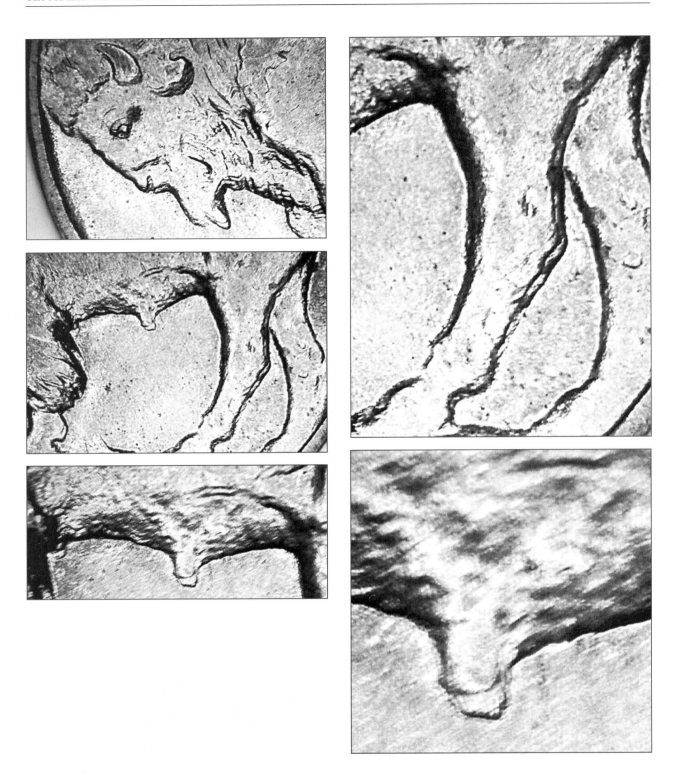

1917

DDR-002

Cross Reference	WDDR-002
Overall Rarity	Unknown
Interest Level	Moderate

CLASS IV
Offset Hub Doubling

GRADE	VF	XF	AU	MS60	MS63	MS65
VALUE	50	100	175	250	325	500

DESCRIPTION

Nice doubling on E PLURIBUS UNUM and UNITED STATES OF AMERICA.

DIE MARKERS

Obverse: Strike doubling is seen on the date. Die clashing is seen under the chin.

Reverse: None noted.

COMMENTS

Not nearly as dramatic as, and overshadowed by, DDR-001. At the same time, its popularity and value are probably enhanced by the existence of DDR-001. It is a worthwhile variety and seems to be quite rare, at least at the present time.

1918

DDR-001

Cross Reference	FS-016.45, WDDR-001
Overall Rarity	URS-09
Interest Level	Moderate

CLASS II
Distorted Hub Doubling

GRADE	VF	XF	AU	MS60	MS63	MS65
VALUE	100	150	225	500	------	------

DESCRIPTION

Moderate doubling on E PLURIBUS UNUM. Slight doubling seen on UNITED STATES OF AMERICA.

DIE MARKERS

Obverse: None noted.

Reverse: Stage A - None. Stage B - Heavy die crack from tail to rim.

COMMENTS

It's uncertain if any of this variety have turned up lacking the die crack, but such coins must certainly exist. The doubling is easily seen on EPU, even on low grade coins. Numerous examples have been found in the last several years, necessitating a change in the rarity rating and a decrease in the listed values. This frequently happens with recently discovered varieties such as this one as they become known and searched for. Immediately after this coin's discovery, an MS63 sold for $3,000. It's very doubtful that a similar coin would bring anything close to this today. This is another characteristic of a newly discovered variety—high prices at the beginning that tend to level off as more turn up and the novelty of a new variety wears off.

1918-D

DDO-001
(OVD-001)

Cross Reference	FS-16.5, 1-O-III, WDDO-001
Overall Rarity	URS-12
Interest Level	Very High

CLASS III
Design Hub Doubling

GRADE	G4	VG	F12	VF	XF	AU	MS60	MS63	MS65
VALUE	1000	1750	3250	7500	10,000	15,000	35,000	75,000	350,000

DESCRIPTION

A distinct bold 7 is seen beneath the 8 in the date.

DIE MARKERS

Obverse: Stage A - none. Stage B - Die crack from braid ribbon to jaw.

Reverse: None noted.

COMMENTS

Second only to the three legged coin in popularity among Buffalo varieties, it is readily available in the grades AG through VG but becomes much more difficult in properly graded Fine and VF. Better than this, it is quite rare, with Mint State specimens considered to be major rarities. A total of four MS65 coins have been encapsulated by the leading certification companies, but it is generally believed that this number is artificially high due to re-submissions. Very late die state examples are seen with some frequency, which would indicate that the die ran its full life span of 200,000 or more coins. The overdate feature is clearly visible even on an About Good coin. An MS65 sold last year (2004) at auction for $287,500. Value has increased tremendously for this coin in the last year or two in all grades. It was not recognized as an overdate until 1931, a primary reason for its rarity in Mint State.

1919

DDO-001

Cross Reference	WDDO-001
Overall Rarity	Unknown
Interest Level	Low

CLASS VI
Distended Hub Doubling

GRADE	VF	XF	AU	MS60	MS63	MS65
VALUE	15	25	40	75	125	825

DESCRIPTION

Moderate extra thickness on LIBERTY and the date.

DIE MARKERS

Obverse: None noted.

Reverse: Small die scratch seen above AM of AMERICA.

COMMENTS

Minor to moderate extra thickness is most apparent at the base of the L and top of the TY in LIBERTY. Accurate rarity levels and values for this, as well as most of the other minor doubled dies listed in this book are very difficult to determine because of the very infrequent sales of these varieties.

1919   DDR-001

CLASS IV + VIII
Offset & Tilted Hub Doubling

Cross Reference	WDDO-001
Overall Rarity	Unknown
Interest Level	Low

GRADE	VF	XF	AU	MS60	MS63	MS65
VALUE	20	35	50	85	135	850

DESCRIPTION

Minor spread seen on the right side of E PLURIBUS UNUM.

DIE MARKERS

Obverse: None noted.

Reverse: None noted.

COMMENTS

This appears to be a Class IV+VIII doubled die. A higher grade specimen must be examined to verify both the class of doubling as well as any die markers that may be present. Like so many other doubled die Buffalo nickels of this class of doubling, the spread is clearest on the motto, most likely due to an incomplete first hubbing.

1921

DDO-001

Cross Reference	WDDO-001
Overall Rarity	Unknown
Interest Level	Moderate

CLASS IV
Offset Hub Doubling

GRADE	VF	XF	AU	MS60	MS63	MS65
VALUE	40	65	100	150	400	875

DESCRIPTION

Moderate doubling seen on the nostrils, eye, upper lip, left side of the ribbon, and possibly on the date.

DIE MARKERS

Obverse: Die clash mark at the throat.

Reverse: Die clash marks below EPU. Die scratch from the upper T to E and the upper E to S of STATES.

COMMENTS

The doubling on this coin is very much like some of the 1930 DDOs, specifically DDO-001 and DDO-002 but not quite as strong as on those coins. This is another fairly recent discovery, so rarity has not been established and values are a rough estimate based more on the "eye appeal" of the coin than anything else. Due to the limited number of dies used in 1921, it should not be too difficult to find. Of note concerning ALL 1921 Buffalos, both P and S mint coins: the 1921 could be considered a minor variety as the hair details directly above the braid ribbon is of a distinct type unique to this year only. It is totally different than any other year in the series. This variety was the subject of an article on the October 18, 1998 issue of *Coin World* and was discovered by Tony Boccuti.

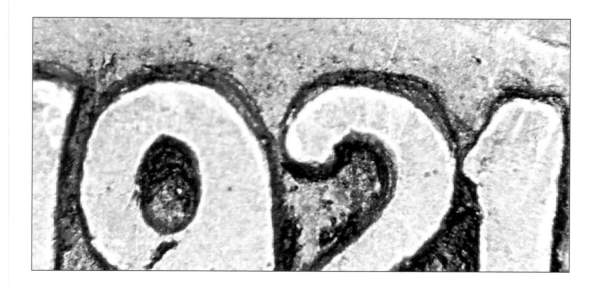

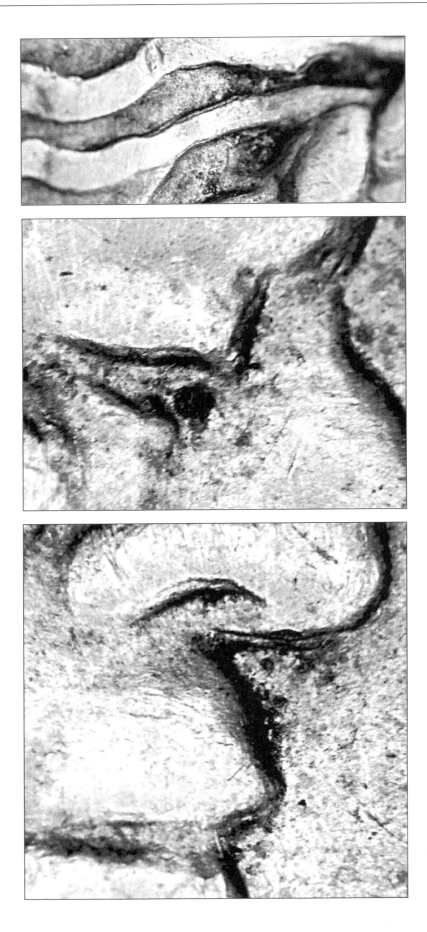

1923

DDO-001

CLASS IV
Offset Hub Doubling

Cross Reference	WDDO-001
Overall Rarity	Unknown
Interest Level	Low

GRADE	VF	XF	AU	MS60	MS63	MS65
VALUE	10	20	35	65	200	850

DESCRIPTION

Minor doubling seen on 23 in the date.

DIE MARKERS

Obverse: None noted.

Reverse: None noted.

COMMENTS

Slight, probable Class IV doubling can be seen at the top of the last two numerals of the date. Yet another recent discovery and it is too new to accurately determine the true rarity or value. As with most relatively minor doubled dies the premium over a normal coin would be nominal and would decrease as the grade increase. This has been taken into account in estimating a value for all such varieties listed in this book.

1923

DDO-002

Cross Reference	None
Overall Rarity	Unknown
Interest Level	Low

CLASS VI
Distended Hub Doubling

GRADE	VF	XF	AU	MS60	MS63	MS65
VALUE	10	20	35	65	200	850

DESCRIPTION

Fairly obvious Class VI spread at the bottom of the date.

DIE MARKERS

Obverse: None noted.

Reverse: None noted.

COMMENTS

Very similar to the better known S mint coin that follows. Probably the product of a doubled working hub.

1923-S

DDO-001

CLASS VI
Distended Hub Doubling

Cross Reference	WDDO-001
Overall Rarity	URS-08
Interest Level	Moderate

GRADE	VF	XF	AU	MS60	MS63	MS65
VALUE	175	325	400	575	1150	16500

DESCRIPTION

Extra thickness seen on the date and LIBERTY.

DIE MARKERS

Obverse: None noted.

Reverse: None noted.

COMMENTS

Quite noticeable extra thickness can be seen at the base of the date. It is a little stronger than the previous P mint coin. It is not a very difficult coin to find, except in the higher grades (as is true with the normal coins for this date and mintmark). The high value listed for this variety are a direct result of the high values that are listed for the normal date and mint. The increase in values over the first edition are due to increases for the regular issue.

1925 PDS DDO-001

Cross Reference	WDDO-001
Overall Rarity	URS-15
Interest Level	Very Low

CLASS VI
Distended Hub Doubling

GRADE	VF	XF	AU	MS60	MS63	MS65
VALUE	------	------	------	------	------	------

DESCRIPTION

Master die doubling seen on the left side of the ribbon and on the lower hair braid.

DIE MARKERS

Obverse: None noted. Master die.

Reverse: None noted. Master die.

COMMENTS

Master die doubling found on all coins from all three mints. No premium is indicated. Priced as normal die.

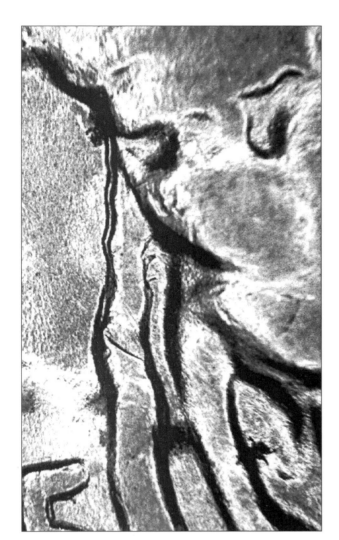

1926

DDO-001

Cross Reference	WDDO-001
Overall Rarity	URS-09
Interest Level	Low

CLASS VI
Distended Hub Doubling

GRADE	VF	XF	AU	MS60	MS63	MS65
VALUE	15	25	35	50	125	200

DESCRIPTION

Significant extra thickness on the date; less so on LIBERTY.

DIE MARKERS

Obverse: None noted.

Reverse: None noted.

COMMENTS

Fairly easy to locate with a little searching. A somewhat better variety than most of the other minor Class VI varieties in this series. Note the nice doubling at the top of LIBERTY.

1927

DDO-001

Cross Reference	WDDO-001
Overall Rarity	URS-08
Interest Level	Low

CLASS IV
Offset Hub Doubling

GRADE	VF	XF	AU	MS60	MS63	MS65
VALUE	15	25	35	75	125	350

DESCRIPTION

Moderate doubling on the lips, nose nostrils, chin. Minor doubling seen on the eyelid. Second hubbing offset to the northwest.

DIE MARKERS

Obverse: None noted.

Reverse: None noted.

COMMENTS

The first hubbing may have been incomplete to begin with and many of the details of the first hubbing may have been obliterated by any subsequent hubbing(s), so the doubling shows only in a few selected places, mainly on the nose and lips.

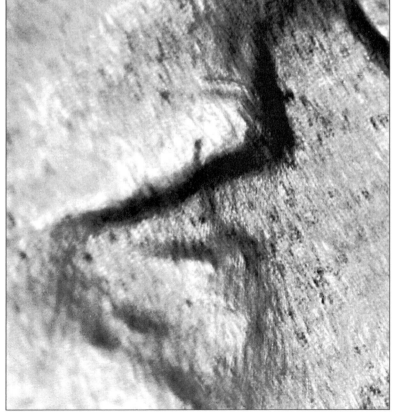

1927-D

DDO-001

CLASS V
Pivoted Hub Doubling

Cross Reference	None
Overall Rarity	Unknown
Interest Level	Moderate

GRADE	VF	XF	AU	MS60	MS63	MS65
VALUE	45	150	175	275	------	------

DESCRIPTION

A minor to moderate spread can be seen on the inner edge of the large feather, bottom of the small feather, the date, and the ribbon ties.

DIE MARKERS

Obverse: A large, irregular die crack, almost a retained cud, runs from the bottom of the neck, through the date, and to the bottom of the large feather almost to the rim.

Reverse: None noted.

COMMENTS

This recently discovered variety is nearly identical to the following 1927-S, but the doubling, especially on the date, seems to be a little less clear. It was discovered by the late Norm Talbert. Norm was a true Buffalo nickel specialist, and was one of the "good guys" in the hobby. This could turn out to be a very rare variety, not the large die crack through the date. The coin examined is not a late die state, so this may have severely limited the production from this die due to early die failure.

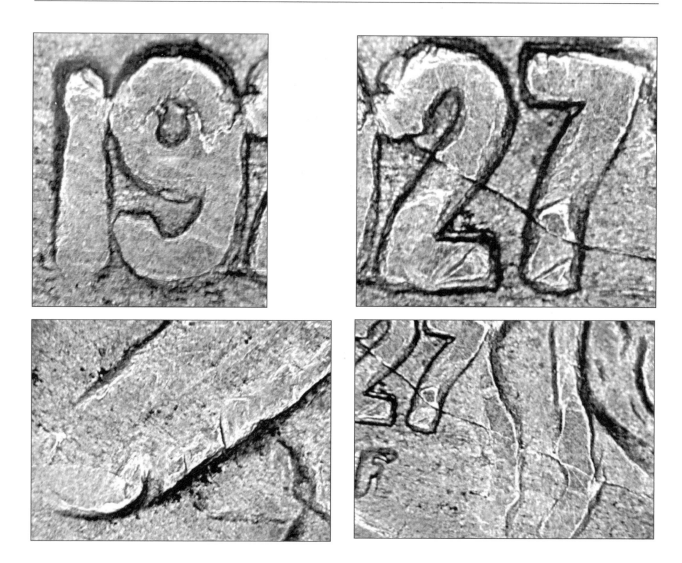

1927-S

DDO-001

Cross Reference	Breen 2630, WDDO-001
Overall Rarity	URS-09
Interest Level	Moderate

CLASS V
Pivoted Hub Doubling

GRADE	VF	XF	AU	MS60	MS63	MS65
VALUE	85	175	350	750	------	------

DESCRIPTION

Moderate doubling on the date, ribbon ties, braid, and the small feather at the back of the neck. Clockwise doubling with a pivot point at or near 1 o'clock.

DIE MARKERS

Obverse: Stage A - None. Stage B - Heavy die polishing under chin and in front of neck.

Reverse: None noted.

COMMENTS

Fairly popular in spite of the less than dramatic spread, probably due to its listing in the Breen reference book on U.S. coinage (with its own number). The doubling is also on the best place it can be on a coin, the date, which helps too. It does not seem to be overly difficult to find, but EDS high grade coins are much tougher.

1927-S

DDR-001

Cross Reference	WDDR-001
Overall Rarity	Unknown
Interest Level	Moderate

CLASS IV
Offset Hub Doubling

GRADE	VF	XF	AU	MS60	MS63	MS65
VALUE	50	125	------	------	------	------

DESCRIPTION

Moderate doubling seen on the buffalo's left and right front leg. Similar to but not as obvious as the 1930 DDR-001. Second hubbing is offset to the southwest.

DIE MARKERS

Obverse: None noted.

Reverse: None noted.

COMMENTS

This "Six Legged" variety was first reported by Tom Arch. As perviously mentioned, the doubling is not as pronounced on this coin as it is on the 1930 'Five' legger. The first hubbing was weak and may be difficult to see on low grade coins or where dirt obscures the area between the front legs, but the doubling should be still visible on the right front leg under these circumstances.

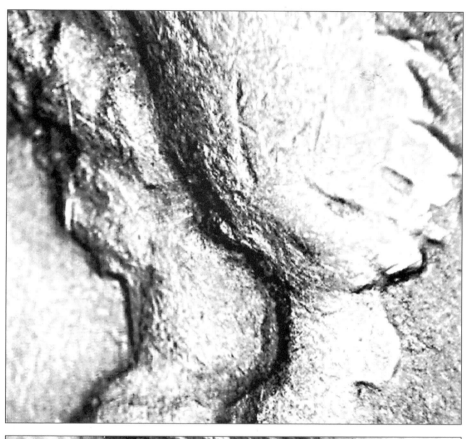

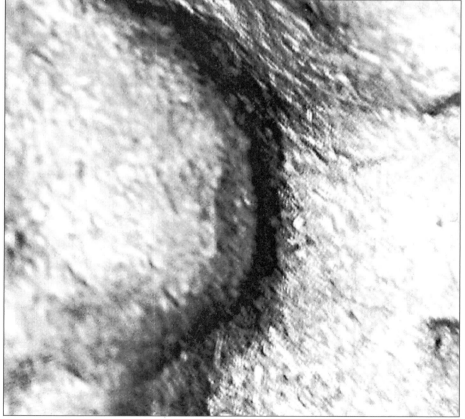

1929

DDO-001

Cross Reference	FS-16.8, WDDO-001
Overall Rarity	URS-06
Interest Level	Moderate

CLASS V
Distorted Hub Doubling

GRADE	VF	XF	AU	MS60	MS63	MS65
VALUE	50	65	100	135	175	400

DESCRIPTION

Moderate doubling seen on the date, ribbon ties, and braid. Minor doubling seen on the lips, neck, the feathers and chin.

DIE MARKERS

Obverse: None noted.

Reverse: None noted.

COMMENTS

The doubling is clear on the date and ribbon ties. The fact that the doubling is clearest on the date enhances its desirability. The doubling can be seen even on low grade pieces. A similar S mint coin has been reported.

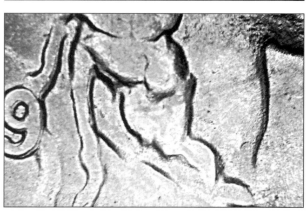

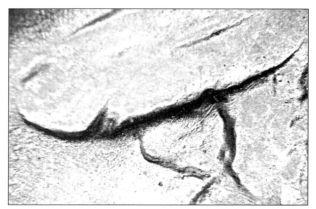

1929

DDR-001

Cross Reference	WDDR-001
Overall Rarity	Not known
Interest Level	Moderate

CLASS I
Rotated Hub Doubling

GRADE	VF	XF	AU	MS60	MS63	MS65
VALUE	15	25	35	50	115	525

DESCRIPTION

Moderate doubling seen on E PLURIBUS UNUM, with less noticeable doubling on UNITED STATES OF AMERICA and FIVE CENTS. Clockwise rotation.

DIE MARKERS

Obverse: None noted.

Reverse: None noted.

COMMENTS

The doubling on the minor side, but this variety is significant because it is the only Class I doubled die in the series as of this date. Most easily seen on the motto and consisting of division lines near the center of the letters, it may be difficult to see in grades less than Fine. Like so many of the infrequently seen and attributed doubled die varieties listed here, rarity is uncertain at this time.

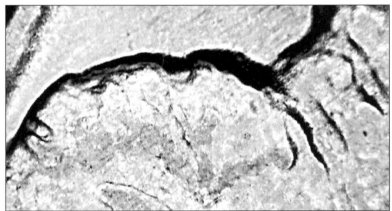

1930

DDO-001

Cross Reference	FS-17, WDDO-001
Overall Rarity	URS-10
Interest Level	High

CLASS IV
Offset Hub Doubling

GRADE	VF	XF	AU	MS60	MS63	MS65
VALUE	50	85	100	150	200	350

DESCRIPTION

Significant doubling seen on the upper eyelid, nostril, both feathers, and on EDS coins LIBERTY. The second hubbing is offset to the northwest.

DIE MARKERS

Obverse: Die crack from the rim at 10 o'clock through the back of the head to the rim at 12 o'clock.

Reverse: None noted.

COMMENTS

The best known, though not the strongest of the 1930 DDO's. This is the one listed in the Breen reference. EDS coins with the doubling clear on LIBERTY are especially desirable. These can be very impressive, the coin pictured is such a die state. Compare this image with the mushed MDS or LDS usually seen. This perfectly illustrates how important die state is when dealing with ALL doubled dies and why the die state should accompany the grade.

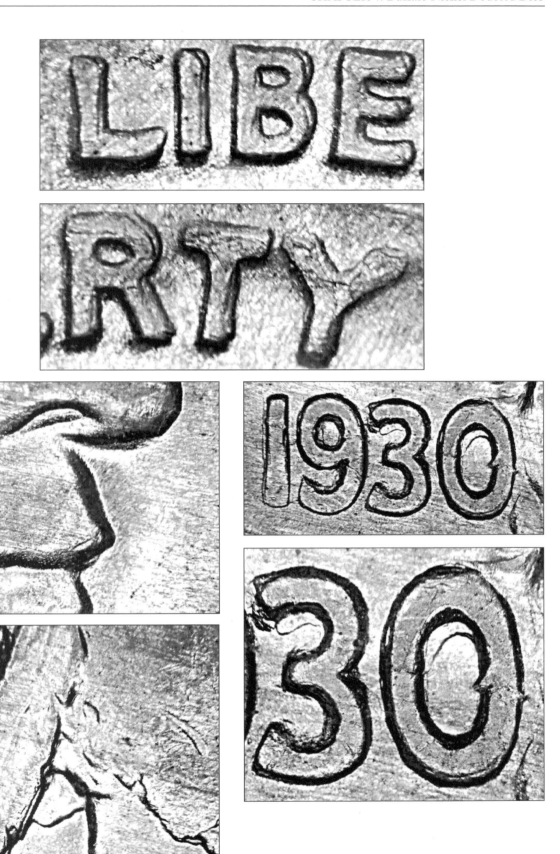

1930

DDO-002

CLASS IV
Offset Hub Doubling

Cross Reference	WDDO-002
Overall Rarity	URS-08
Interest Level	Moderate

GRADE	VF	XF	AU	MS60	MS63	MS65
VALUE	35	85	100	125	150	300

DESCRIPTION

Moderate doubling on the upper eyelid, nostril, tip of nose, and upper lip. Some doubling is also seen on the large feather. Second hubbing offset to the northwest.

DIE MARKERS

Obverse: None noted.

Reverse: A small raised lump of metal seen in front of the Buffalo's ear. Die scratch from the field through UR of PLURIBUS.

COMMENTS

Not as strong as, but somewhat scarcer than DDO-001. Only slight doubling shows on the date. One of the better doubled dies for the date.

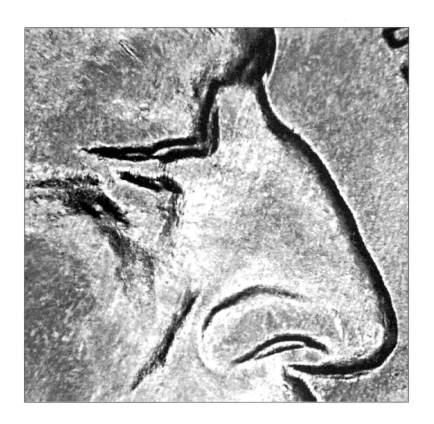

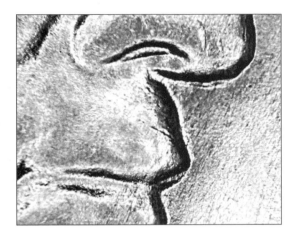

1930

DDO-003

Cross Reference	WDDO-003
Overall Rarity	Unknown
Interest Level	Low

CLASS IV
Offset Hub Doubling

GRADE	VF	XF	AU	MS60	MS63	MS65
VALUE	10	20	30	50	100	300

DESCRIPTION

Minor doubling on left side of 1 and 9, and on the inside of 9 and 3.

DIE MARKERS

Obverse: None noted.

Reverse: Machine doubling on E PLURIBUS UNUM.

COMMENTS

Rarity has yet to be accurately determined for this variety. Unlike most other DDOs for the year, this one shows doubling only on the date. It may be rather tough to see on lower grade coins.

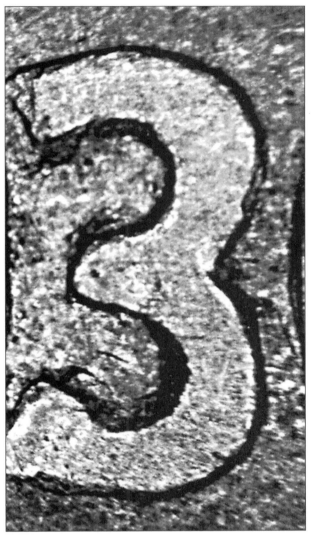

1930

DDO-004

Cross Reference	WDDO-004
Overall Rarity	URS-08
Interest Level	Moderate

CLASS IV
Offset Hub Doubling

GRADE	VF	XF	AU	MS60	MS63	MS65
VALUE	35	65	85	100	175	300

DESCRIPTION

Strong doubling seen on the eyelid and large feather. Doubling also seen on the lower lip.

DIE MARKERS

Obverse: Small die scratches between the two ribbons.

Reverse: Small die scratch from the E to the P of PLURIBUS.

COMMENTS

Somewhat similar to 1930 DDO-001, but the doubling on the eyelid is lower and has a slightly greater spread.

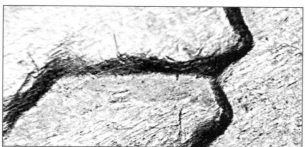

1930

DDO-005

Cross Reference	WDDO-005
Overall Rarity	Unknown
Interest Level	Low

CLASS IV
Offset Hub Doubling

GRADE	VF	XF	AU	MS60	MS63	MS65
VALUE	12	20	30	50	85	280

DESCRIPTION

Moderate doubling seen on the top of the 3 and the 0 in the date.

DIE MARKERS

Obverse: None noted.

Reverse: Die crack through the base of the mound.

COMMENTS

As with DDO-003, the doubling is restricted to the date only, but it is a little stronger on this die than on DDO-003. The spread shows best on the inside of the 0.

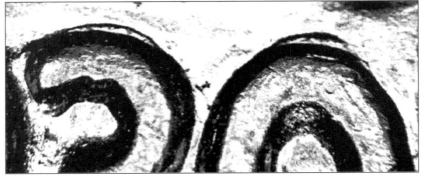

1930

DDO-006

Cross Reference	WDDO-006
Overall Rarity	URS-10
Interest Level	High

CLASS IV
Offset Hub Doubling

GRADE	VF	XF	AU	MS60	MS63	MS65
VALUE	50	75	125	150	200	350

DESCRIPTION

Very strong doubling seen on the upper eyelid, brow, and large feather. Moderate doubling seen on the tip of the nose and date. The second hubbing is offset to the northwest.

DIE MARKERS

Obverse: Strike doubling seen on ribbon.

Reverse: Die crack through the base of the mound.

COMMENTS

This is the strongest and most frequently encountered of all the doubled die obverses for the year. Even higher grade pieces are not overly difficult to find, though it is scarce in Mint State. It is one of the most visible doubled dies in the series, as it can easily be seen with the naked eye. Even though it is relatively common, it should be considered as one of the top 10 doubled die Buffalo nickels.

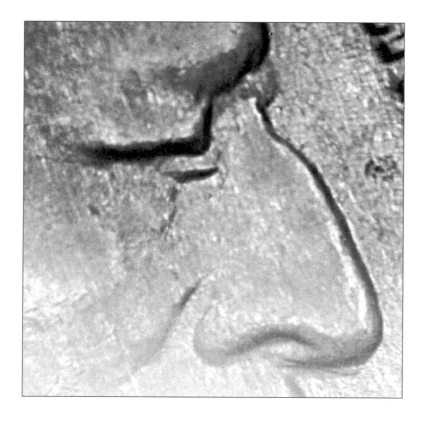

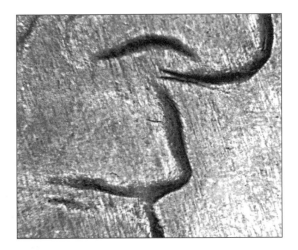

1930

DDO-007

CLASS IV
Offset Hub Doubling

Cross Reference	WDDO-007
Overall Rarity	Unknown
Interest Level	Moderate

GRADE	VF	XF	AU	MS60	MS63	MS65
VALUE	35	65	85	100	200	300

DESCRIPTION

Strong doubling on the upper eyelid. Minor doubling is seen on the large feather and the date. Second hubbing offset to the north.

DIE MARKERS

Obverse: Strike doubling seen on the date and ribbons. Die clashing seen under the chin.

Reverse: Die deterioration doubling seen on FIVE CENTS, UNITED OF. Die clashing seen below UNUM.

COMMENTS

This die can be easily confused with DDO-004, but note the very slight difference in the location of the doubled eyelid. The spread on the date is also just a little bit stronger here. Values should be very close to those for DDO-004, since the two are so similar. Currently, at least 12 distinctly different doubled dies are known for the 1930 obverse dies alone. It would be quite a challenge to put together a complete set of them.

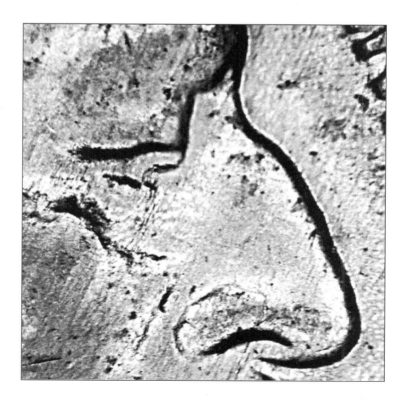

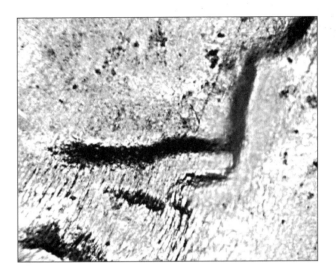

1930

DDR-001

Cross Reference	1-R-III, FS-17.5, WDDR-001
Overall Rarity	URS-12
Interest Level	High

CLASS IV
Offset Hub Doubling

GRADE	VF	XF	AU	MS60	MS63	MS65
VALUE	65	100	125	175	300	750

DESCRIPTION

Moderate doubling on the buffalo's left front leg and neck with slight doubling on the right front leg and FIVE CENTS. Second hubbing is offset to the southeast.

DIE MARKERS

Obverse: None noted.

Reverse: Stage A - Raised lump of metal on the lower left rear leg. Stage B - Triangular die chip next to the T of CENTS. Stage C - Die chip joins the front of the bison's head to the rim.

COMMENTS

This is the famous "5 Legged" variety. It has proved to be very common in low to all grades short of Mint State. About three quarters of those seen have the characteristic die chip found on Stage C. Both rarity and values have been firmly established for this coin. It is very frequently seen for sale.

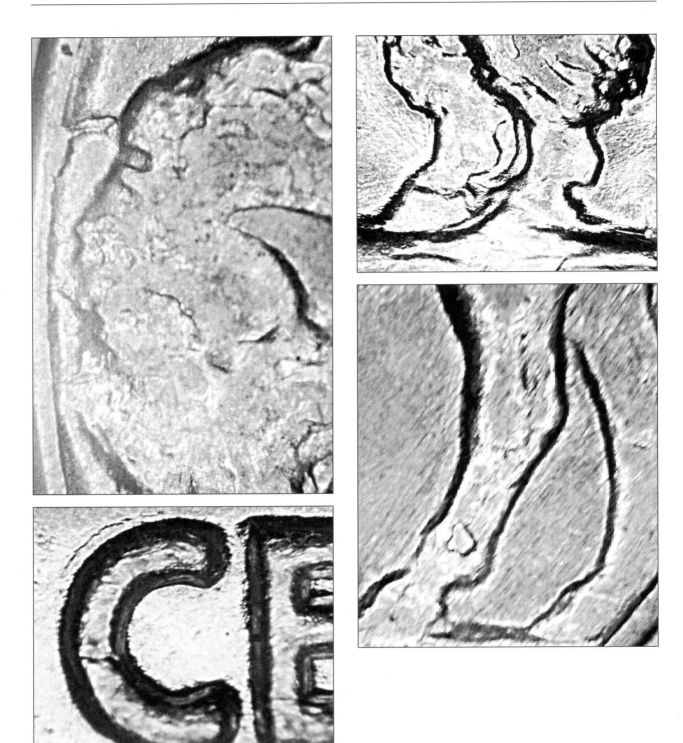

1930

DDR-002

Cross Reference	WDDR-002
Overall Rarity	URS-08
Interest Level	Moderate

CLASS IV
Offset Hub Doubling

GRADE	VF	XF	AU	MS60	MS63	MS65
VALUE	50	85	115	150	225	450

DESCRIPTION

Strong doubling on PL of PLURIBUS and UN of UNUM. Doubling is also evident within the folds of the buffalo's neck. Second hubbing offset to the east.

DIE MARKERS

Obverse: None noted.

Reverse: None noted.

COMMENTS

It is unfortunate that this doubled die did not hub up better at the periphery of the design. Had it done so, it would have been a major doubled die, at least as strong as the 1917 DDR-001. This is a *much* scarcer coin than the previous. Since it is not as popular or well known as DDR-001, it unjustifiably brings a smaller premium. It is a nicer doubled die, but has no 'leg' involvement, which limits its value.

1930

DDR-003

Cross Reference	WDDR-003
Overall Rarity	URS-09
Interest Level	Moderate

CLASS IV
Offset Hub Doubling

GRADE	VF	XF	AU	MS60	MS63	MS65
VALUE	35	50	75	100	150	300

DESCRIPTION

Significant doubling seen on PLUR of PLURIBUS and UN of UNUM. Doubling is visible under the belly and at the rear edge of the left rear leg. Second hubbing offset to the west.

DIE MARKERS

Obverse: None noted.

Reverse: None noted.

COMMENTS

Similar to the previous variety but with the doubling in the opposite direction. It is scarcer than DDR-001 but more findable than DDR-002.

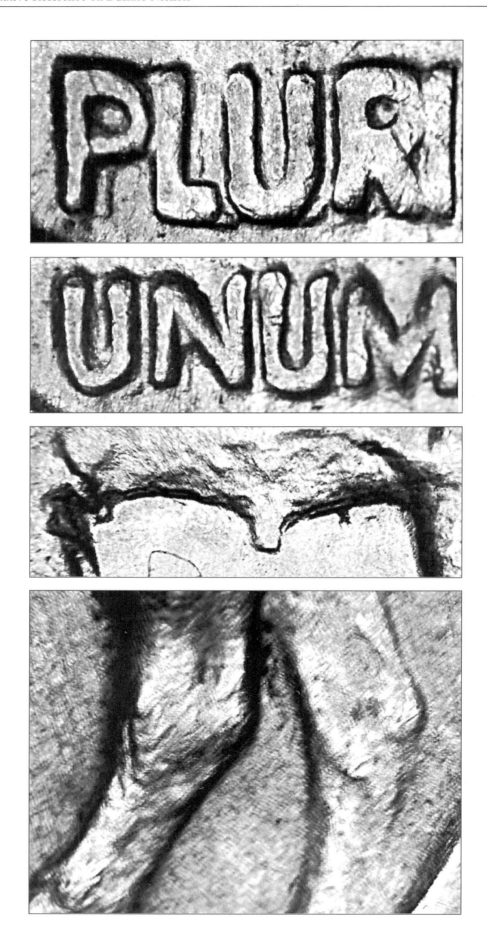

1930

DDR-004

Cross Reference	WDDR-004
Overall Rarity	URS-07
Interest Level	Low

CLASS IV
Offset Hub Doubling

GRADE	VF	XF	AU	MS60	MS63	MS65
VALUE	20	35	45	65	125	250

DESCRIPTION

Moderate doubling along the bottom edge of the E and L of PLURIBUS. Minor doubling seen E of FIVE and CE of CENTS. Doubling also seen behind the left rear leg and on the bottom fur on the left front leg. Second hubbing to north.

DIE MARKERS

Obverse: None noted.

Reverse: None noted.

COMMENTS

The doubling on the motto is not nearly as strong on this variety as on the previous two.

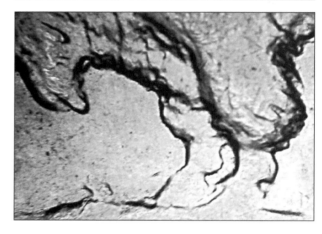

1930

DDR-005

CLASS IV
Offset Hub Doubling

Cross Reference	WDDR-005
Overall Rarity	Not known
Interest Level	Low

GRADE	VF	XF	AU	MS60	MS63	MS65
VALUE	10	15	25	50	85	250

DESCRIPTION

Minor doubling seen on the right side of most of PLURIBUS, with the L showing the strongest doubling. Second hubbing is to the west.

DIE MARKERS

Obverse: None noted.

Reverse: None noted.

COMMENTS

This is one of the more minor reverse doubled dies for this year and more than likely can not be seen on low grade coins. It is still collectable, especially to someone who is trying to put a complete set of 1930 doubled dies together (currently consisting of at least 19 coins). A collection of only these doubled dies would make an impressive display by itself.

1930

DDR-006

CLASS IV
Offset Hub Doubling

Cross Reference	WDDR-006
Overall Rarity	Not known
Interest Level	Low

GRADE	VF	XF	AU	MS60	MS63	MS65
VALUE	15	20	35	60	85	250

DESCRIPTION

Moderate doubling seen on the E PLURIBUS UNUM, UNITED STATES OF AMERICA and the center of the left rear leg.

DIE MARKERS

Obverse: Strike doubling seen on the date and parts of LIBERTY.

Reverse: Die scratch seen above the tail.

COMMENTS

Another of the more minor doubled dies for the year, but this one is unusual because it also shows a spread on USA in addition to the motto.

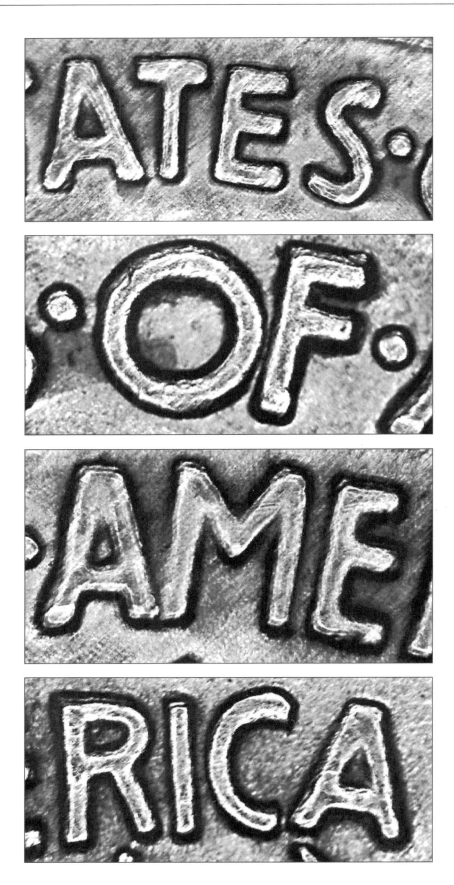

1930

DDR-007

CLASS IV
Offset Hub Doubling

Cross Reference	WDDR-007
Overall Rarity	Not known
Interest Level	Low

GRADE	VF	XF	AU	MS60	MS63	MS65
VALUE	15	25	45	65	95	275

DESCRIPTION

Moderate doubling seen on NTS of CENTS, IV of FIVE, the back of the rear leg, and very slightly on some of the letters of E PLURIBUS UNUM.

DIE MARKERS

Obverse: Strike doubling seen on the date.

Reverse: None noted.

COMMENTS

This variety is distinctive because it is the only Class V doubled die for the year. As a fairly recent discovery, its rarity has not yet been established.

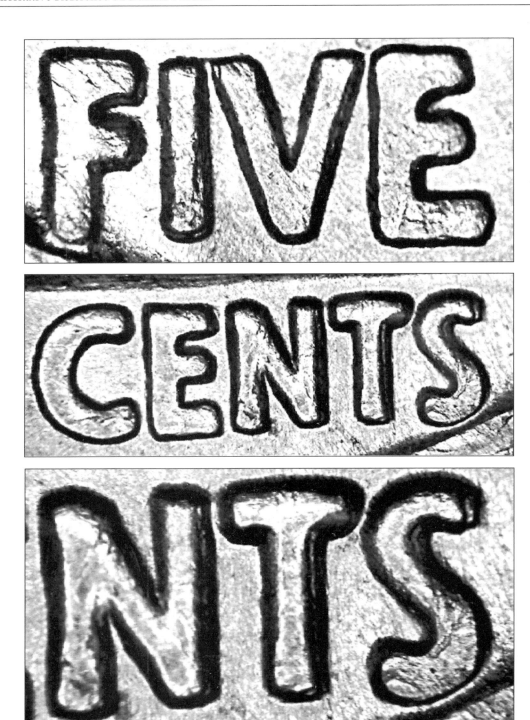

1930-S

DDO-001

Cross Reference	WDDO-001
Overall Rarity	URS-09
Interest Level	Moderate

CLASS VI
Distended Hub Doubling

GRADE	VF	XF	AU	MS60	MS63	MS65
VALUE	35	50	75	100	175	925

DESCRIPTION

Dramatic extra thickness seen on LIBERTY, with weaker extra thickness on the date.

DIE MARKERS

Obverse: None noted.

Reverse: None noted.

COMMENTS

A very nice Class VI doubled die, not as strong as the 1936 DDO-001, but still quite easy to see. Note the additional machine or strike doubling on the left side of LIBERTY visible on the coin pictured.

1931-S

DDR-001

Cross Reference	WDDR-001
Overall Rarity	URS-09
Interest Level	Moderate

CLASS VI
Distended Hub Doubling

GRADE	VF	XF	AU	MS60	MS63	MS65
VALUE	30	45	65	100	150	500

DESCRIPTION

Strong extra thickness seen on E PLURIBUS and UNITED STATES OF AMERICA.

DIE MARKERS

Obverse: None noted.

Reverse: Die crack from the forehead to the U of UNITED.

COMMENTS

This is a Class VI of moderate strength, showing especially well on the dots between USA, where they are nearly twice their normal size. It is also evident on the crossbars of the T's of STATES. It seems to be scarcer than DDR-002. Value increases for this, as well as for the other 1931-S varieties from the first edition, are more the result of price increases in the normal date than for the varieties themselves.

1931-S

DDR-002

CLASS IV
Offset Hub Doubling

Cross Reference	WDDR-002
Overall Rarity	URS-09
Interest Level	Moderate

GRADE	VF	XF	AU	MS60	MS63	MS65
VALUE	30	45	75	135	175	500

DESCRIPTION

Significant doubling can be seen on the fur at the back of the Buffalo's front leg. Doubling is also present below the neck and on the left rear leg.

DIE MARKERS

Obverse: Numerous die scratches seen at the top of the Indian's head.

Reverse: Die crack through the top of the head to the U of UNITED.

COMMENTS

The hubbings are close in strength, but it should be naked eye visible on the left front leg, at least to those with good eyesight. It is not to difficult to find in any grade.

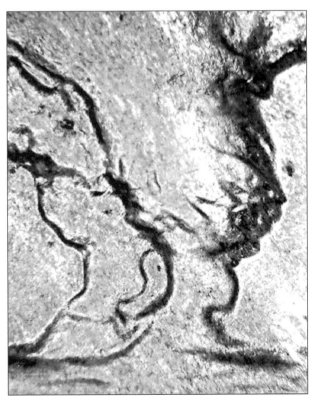

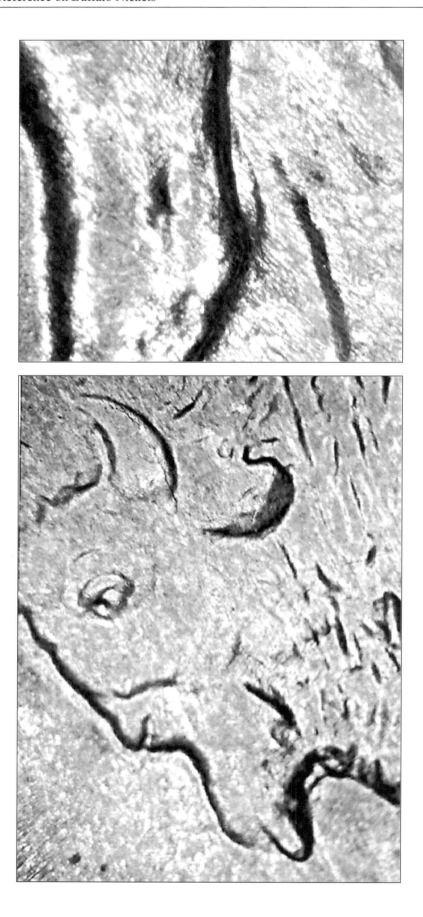

1931-S DDR-003

Cross Reference	WDDR-003
Overall Rarity	URS-08
Interest Level	Moderate

CLASS IV
Offset Hub Doubling

GRADE	VF	XF	AU	MS60	MS63	MS65
VALUE	50	65	85	165	240	500

DESCRIPTION

Tripling seen on the PL of PLURIBUS, first U of UNUM, and the fur on top of the back. Doubling seen on the UR of PLURIBUS, fur on the shoulder, the front of the left front leg, and the front of the left rear leg.

DIE MARKERS

Obverse: None noted.

Reverse: None noted.

COMMENTS

A tripled die and also another "six legged" Buffalo, somewhat like the 1927-S previously listed. Like the rest of the 1931-S varieties, it is not overly difficult to find. This is a result of the limited number of dies used for the year. Locating a coin from any one particular die should not be a problem, unless, for some reason, a certain die had a short run due to die failure. (Of course, this would be true of any low mintage date or date/mint combination.)

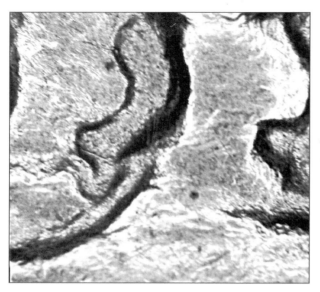
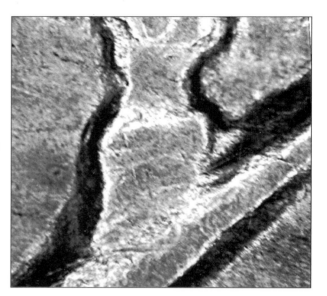
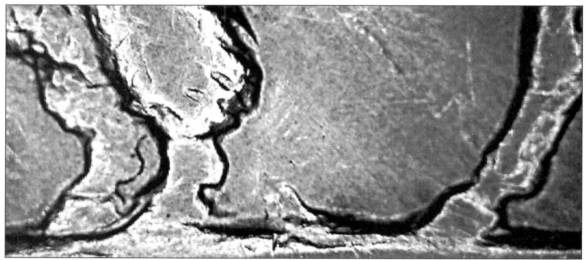
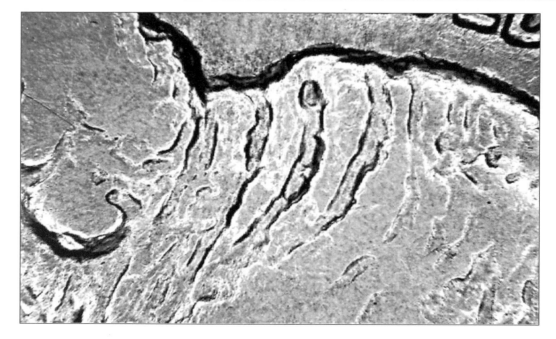

1934

DDO-001

Cross Reference	WDDO-001
Overall Rarity	Unknown
Interest Level	Low

CLASS ?
Unknown Doubling

GRADE	VF	XF	AU	MS60	MS63	MS65
VALUE	8	15	25	65	85	450

DESCRIPTION

Very minor doubling seen on the right side of the 4 in the date.

DIE MARKERS

Obverse: None noted.

Reverse: None noted.

COMMENTS

The only doubled die obverse for the date so far reported. Very minor doubling shows on the date. Probably worth a premium only in high grade. Value increases shown here are the result of increases for the 1934 in general, not for the variety.

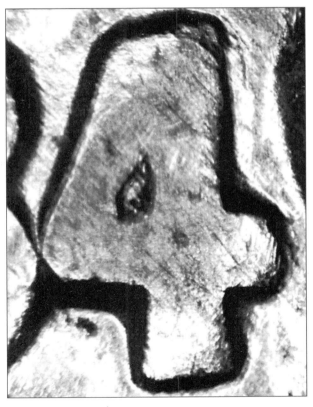

1934

DDR-001

Cross Reference	WDDR-001
Overall Rarity	Unknown
Interest Level	Low

CLASS II
Distorted Hub Doubling

GRADE	VF	XF	AU	MS60	MS63	MS65
VALUE	8	15	25	65	135	450

DESCRIPTION

Moderate doubling seen on the back top left rear leg, under the neck, and the back of left front leg at the bottom of the hair.

DIE MARKERS

Obverse: None noted.

Reverse: None noted.

COMMENTS

Compare with the almost identical 1934-D DDR-002. This could possibly be a doubled working hub.

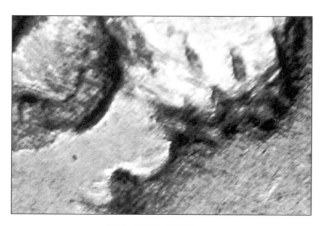
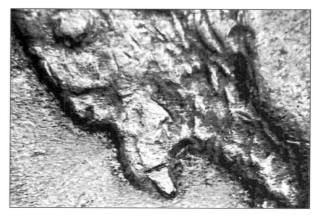
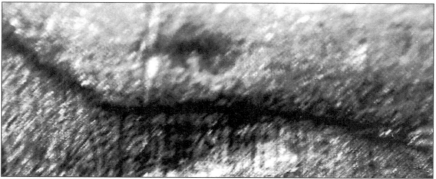

1934

DDR-002

CLASS VI
Distended Hub Doubling

Cross Reference	WDDR-002
Overall Rarity	R-6
Interest Level	Moderate

GRADE	VF	XF	AU	MS60	MS63	MS65
VALUE	20	35	50	75	125	475

DESCRIPTION

Strong extra thickness seen on UNITED STATES OF AMERICA, the dots and FIVE CENTS.

DIE MARKERS

Obverse: None noted.

Reverse: None noted.

COMMENTS

Typical Class VI doubling can be seen on the peripheral lettering. The sample show here is a little stronger than most. It would be interesting to research why Class VI doubled dies are common in some years and rare in others. It is probably the result of new personnel working the annealing furnace and heating and cooling the dies too quickly.

1934

DDR-003

CLASS II
Distorted Hub Doubling

Cross Reference	WDDR-003
Overall Rarity	Unknown
Interest Level	Low

GRADE	VF	XF	AU	MS60	MS63	MS65
VALUE	8	15	25	65	100	450

DESCRIPTION

Moderate doubling seen on the back of left front leg at the bottom of the hair and below the neck.

DIE MARKERS

Obverse: Strike doubling seen on the date, feathers, and braid. Die clashing of the EPU seen in front of face, below chin.

Reverse: Die crack from the head up through the U of UNITED.

COMMENTS

Similar to 1934-P DDR-001 in many ways, but definitely from a different die. It would be very easy to confuse the two dies, especially on low grade coins. As with DDR-001, this would command a premium only in higher grades.

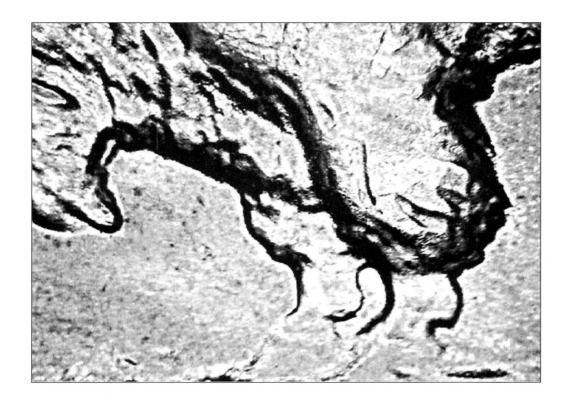

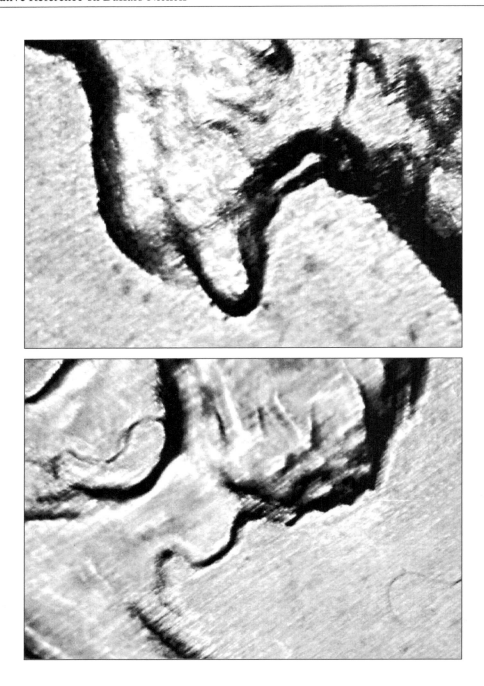

1934-D

DDO-001

CLASS II
Distorted Hub Doubling

Cross Reference	WDDO-001
Overall Rarity	Unknown
Interest Level	Low

GRADE	VF	XF	AU	MS60	MS63	MS65
VALUE	15	25	55	90	125	450

DESCRIPTION

Minor doubling seen on the 19 of the date.

DIE MARKERS

Obverse: Several die scratches to the left of the 1. Die scratch below the 934.

Reverse: Strike doubling above D mintmark.

COMMENTS

The precise class of doubling for this coin, as on the nearly identical 1934-P, is difficult to determine. It could just as well be as Class II or Class V as a Class IV.

1934-D

DDR-001

CLASS II
Distorted Hub Doubling

Cross Reference	WDDR-001
Overall Rarity	Unknown
Interest Level	Low

GRADE	VF	XF	AU	MS60	MS63	MS65
VALUE	15	25	35	65	125	1,100

DESCRIPTION

Moderate doubling seen on E PLURIBUS UNUM, the left rear leg, and the tail.

DIE MARKERS

Obverse: None noted.

Reverse: None noted.

COMMENTS

As with most of the other minor doubled dies listed, many of the value increases from the first edition are the result of an increase in the value of the regular die coins and not the varieties themselves.

1934-D

DDR-002

Cross Reference	WDDR-002
Overall Rarity	URS-6
Interest Level	Low

CLASS II
Distorted Hub Doubling

GRADE	VF	XF	AU	MS60	MS63	MS65
VALUE	15	25	35	65	115	1,100

DESCRIPTION

Doubling seen on the back of the rear left leg, the bottom of the fur on the left front leg, and below neck.

DIE MARKERS

Obverse: None noted.

Reverse: Reverse is rotated 15 degrees.

COMMENTS

See the previously listed 1934 DDR-001. This coin is almost, if not exactly identical to the P mint. It is likely to carry a premium only in fine or better grades.

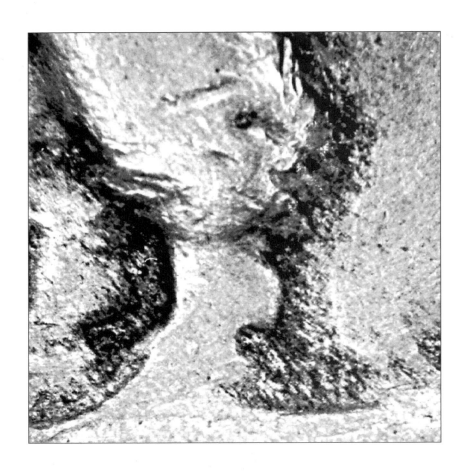

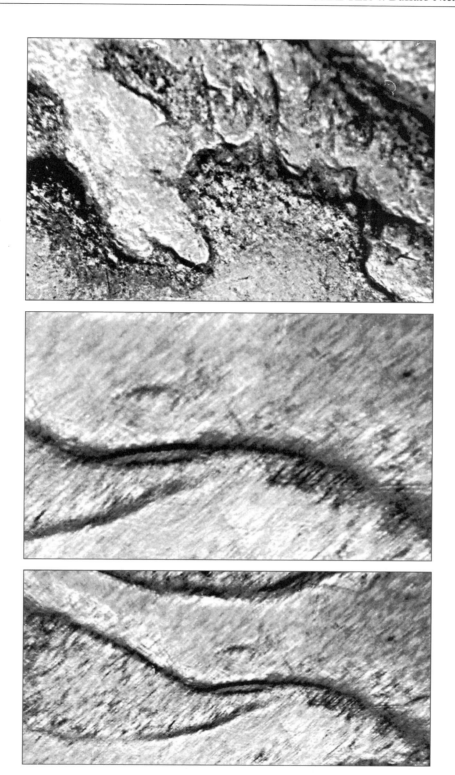

1935

DDO-001

CLASS VI
Distended Hub Doubling

Cross Reference	WDDO-001
Overall Rarity	Unknown
Interest Level	High

GRADE	VF	XF	AU	MS60	MS63	MS65
VALUE	100	175	200	250	300	375

DESCRIPTION

Very strong extra thickness seen on LIBERTY and the date.

DIE MARKERS

Obverse: Short horizontal die scratch in hair above feathers. Slanted die gouge in front of neck.

Reverse: Two horizontal die scratches through ME of AMERICA. Many die scratches through UNITED STATES. Many die scratches between the front and back legs just above the ground.

COMMENTS

This variety is a recent discovery, so rarity and values are not yet established with any certainty. However, it appears to be *much* rarer than the 1936 DDO-001, and it should carry a high premium in just about any grade. The above values are an estimate based on apparent rarity and the strength of the spread.

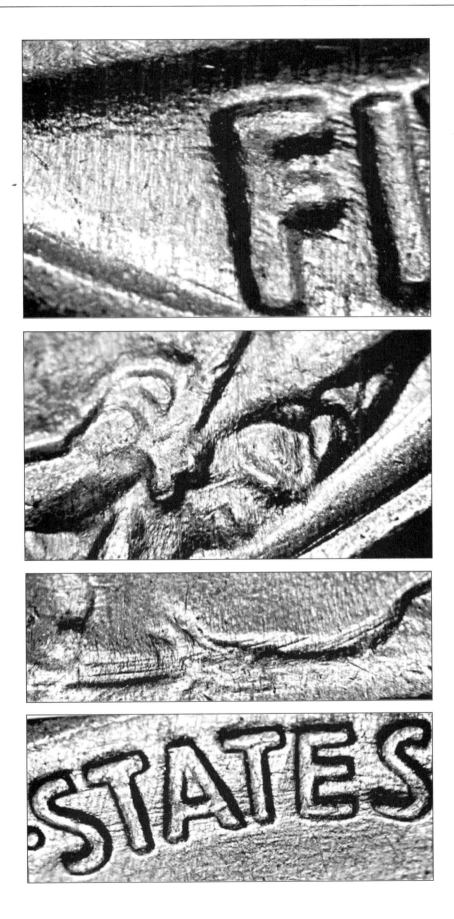

1935

DDR-001

Cross Reference	1-R-III, FS-18, WDDR-001
Overall Rarity	URS-12
Interest Level	Very High

CLASS IV
Offset Hub Doubling

GRADE	G4	VG	F12	VF	XF	AU	MS60	MS63	MS65
VALUE	35	45	85	250	400	1250	5000	10,000	32,500

DESCRIPTION

Strong doubling shows on just about every reverse detail—all lettering and the entire Buffalo, where it shows most clearly on the horn, eye, ear, front and rear legs, and ground. The second hubbing is to the northwest and is close in strength to the first. The hubbings are still very distinct in EDS and MDS coins.

DIE MARKERS

Obverse: Stage A - None. Stage B - Heavy die polish lines NE to SW. Die clash under chin. Stage C - Die crack SE from braid under ribbon to shoulder; heavy die polish lines NW to SE. Stage D - Die crack from the second S of STATES to the O in OF.

Reverse: Stage A - None. Stage B - Heavy die polish lines NE to SE. Die clash under EPU. Stage C - Heavy die polish lines NE to SW.

COMMENTS

The third of the "Big 3" major doubled dies in the series. It has become an integral part of a collection of Buffalo varieties. Readily available in Good through Fine, scarce in VF, very scarce in XF, and truely rare in AU and Mint State. It appears that an attempt to efface the doubling was made by heavily polishing the die. Some coins are VLDS, having the appearance of a Class VI, which would indicate that the die ran its full production in spite of repeated polishings and die breaks.

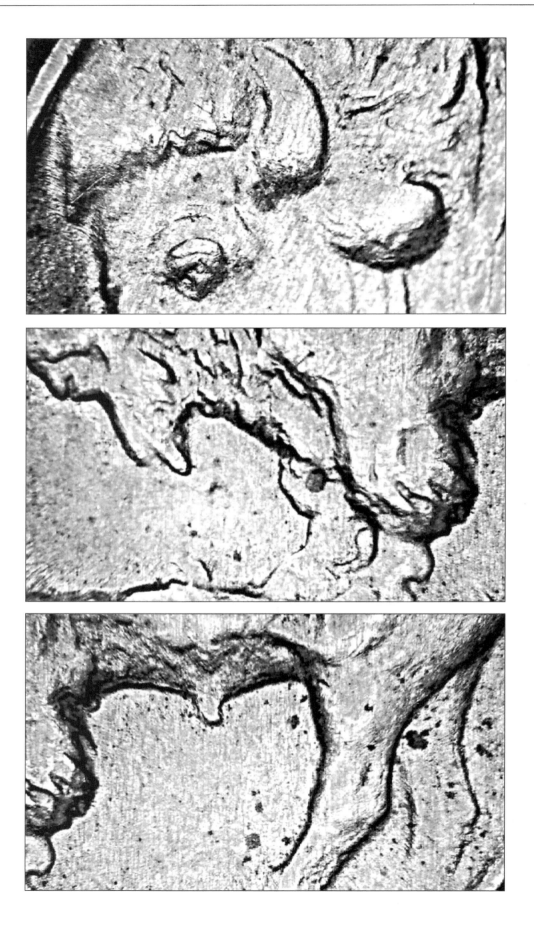

1935

DDR-002

Cross Reference	WDDR-002
Overall Rarity	Unknown
Interest Level	Moderate

CLASS VI
Distended Hub Doubling

GRADE	VF	XF	AU	MS60	MS63	MS65
VALUE	25	35	45	60	75	150

DESCRIPTION

Moderate extra thickness seen on UNITED STATES OF AMERICA, the dots and E PLURIBUS UNUM.

DIE MARKERS

Obverse: Die scratches through IBE of LIBERTY.

Reverse: Die scratches through UNITED.

COMMENTS

A decent Class VI doubled die with noticeable thickness in the lettering, especially at the bottom of FIVE CENTS.

1935

DDR-003

Cross Reference	WDDR-003
Overall Rarity	URS-05
Interest Level	Moderate

CLASS V
Pivoted Hub Doubling

GRADE	VF	XF	AU	MS60	MS63	MS65
VALUE	50	100	200	250	300	400

DESCRIPTION

Moderate doubling on FIVE CENTS, UNITED, and the back of the front legs. Slight doubling can be seen on STATES. Clockwise rotation from a pivot point at or near 2 o'clock.

DIE MARKERS

Obverse: None noted.

Reverse: Circular die scratches seen on the entire reverse.

COMMENTS

This variety is currently very scarce, but that may change as it becomes more well known. Do not confuse this coin with the very strong and valuable DDR-001. This DDR-003 is the second best of the DDRs for 1935, with a sale recorded in AU58 for $210.

1935

DDR-004

Cross Reference	WDDR-004
Overall Rarity	URS-05
Interest Level	Moderate

CLASS V
Pivoted Hub Doubling

GRADE	VF	XF	AU	MS60	MS63	MS65
VALUE	20	50	90	125	150	225

DESCRIPTION

Strong doubling below L in PLURIBUS. Minor doubling seen slightly behind the left rear leg.

DIE MARKERS

Obverse: None noted.

Reverse: None noted.

COMMENTS

It is very similar to some of the 1930 and 1935-S doubled dies, where the primary doubling is seen on the motto. A better grade specimen is needed to check for any die markers.

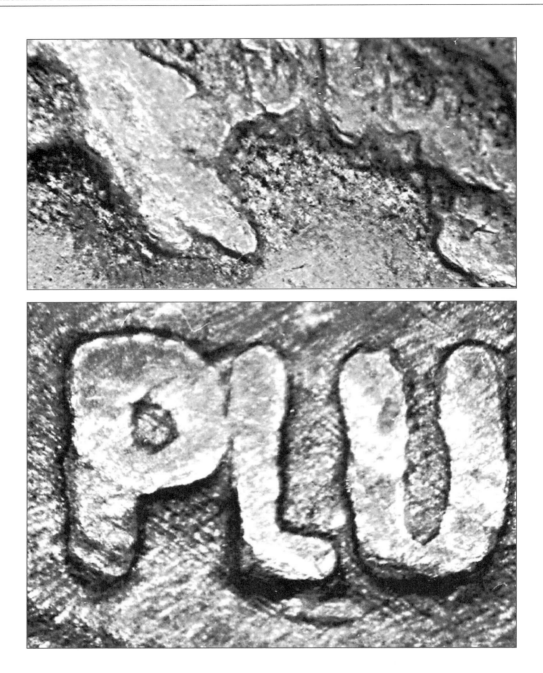

1935-S

DDO-001

Cross Reference	1-O-VI, WDDO-001
Overall Rarity	URS-06
Interest Level	Low

CLASS VI
Distended Hub Doubling

GRADE	VF	XF	AU	MS60	MS63	MS65
VALUE	10	20	30	65	115	225

DESCRIPTION

Moderate extra thickness seen on LIBERTY.

DIE MARKERS

Obverse: None noted.

Reverse: RPM-001.

COMMENTS

The spread is minor and is probably impossible to verify on anything less than a VF. Only later die states of the RPM also show the DDO.

1935-S

DDR-001

Cross Reference	1-R-III, WDDR-001
Overall Rarity	URS-09
Interest Level	Moderate to High

CLASS IV
Offset Hub Doubling

GRADE	VF	XF	AU	MS60	MS63	MS65
VALUE	35	45	75	110	175	300

DESCRIPTION

Strong doubling appears on PLU of PLURIBUS and U of UNUM. Obvious doubling also shows on E of FIVE and CENTS, on some of the letters of UNITED, and on the buffalo's belly. The second hubbing is offset to the northwest.

DIE MARKERS

Obverse: None noted.

Reverse: None noted.

COMMENTS

This is the best known of the three reverse doubled dies for this year and mint. It is scarce in high grades, but can be found without too much trouble in Good through VF.

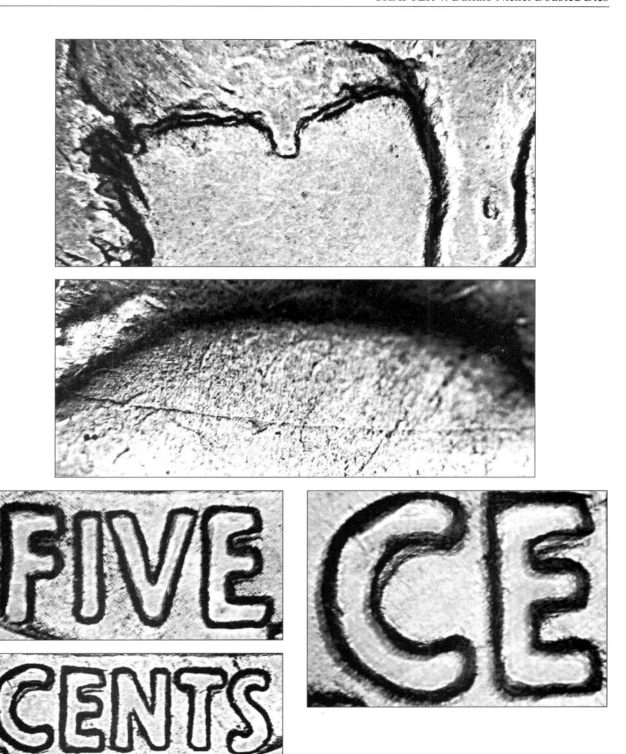

1935-S

DDR-002

CLASS IV
Offset Hub Doubling

Cross Reference	WDDR-002
Overall Rarity	URS-06
Interest Level	Moderate

GRADE	VF	XF	AU	MS60	MS63	MS65
VALUE	15	30	50	65	90	225

DESCRIPTION

Moderate doubling seen on the right side of IVE of FIVE, and inside the U of UNITED.

DIE MARKERS

Obverse: None noted.

Reverse: None noted.

COMMENTS

The first hubbing is weak and incomplete. A higher grade coin is needed to confirm die markers and any additional doubling that may be present.

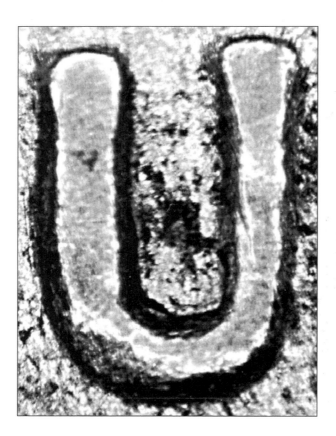

1935-S   DDR-003

CLASS IV
Offset Hub Doubling

Cross Reference	WDDR-003
Overall Rarity	URS-05
Interest Level	Moderate

GRADE	VF	XF	AU	MS60	MS63	MS65
VALUE	20	30	40	75	100	225

DESCRIPTION

Strong doubling seen on the P of PLURIBUS. Traces of doubling show on the rest of the motto. Doubling is also evident on some of the hair detail along the top of the buffalo's back. The second hubbing is offset to the southwest.

DIE MARKERS

Obverse: Die clashing of EPU seen in front of and below chin.

Reverse: Small raised lump seen in the middle of the rear leg.

COMMENTS

As with the last variety, this first hubbing is incomplete. Had it been stronger and more complete, this may have been a major variety. It is a recent discovery and rarity has not been established with much precision.

1936

DDO-001

Cross Reference	WDDO-001
Overall Rarity	URS-12
Interest Level	High

CLASS VI
Distended Hub Doubling

GRADE	VF	XF	AU	MS60	MS63	MS65
VALUE	50	100	125	200	350	750

DESCRIPTION

Dramatic extra thickness seen on LIBERTY and the date. The feather tips and nostril also show distortion.

DIE MARKERS

Obverse: Stage A - None. Stage B - Die scratches seen from the third feather. Stage C - Additional die polishing is seen on the lower lip.

Reverse: None noted.

COMMENTS

By far the strongest Class VI in the series. It certainly ranks within the top ten doubled die Buffalo nickels. It is, however, a relatively common coin, easy to find in most circulated grades and moderately available even in MS65, as a number that have been certified in this grade. These probably came from original rolls. Some sold at auction at extraordinary levels—$1500 and more. It is currently listed at very high levels in the CPG. It is possible that the prices for the two 1936 doubled dies listed there (DDO-001 and DDR-001) may have been inadvertently transposed, as the latter variety is also a major doubled die and is many times rarer than the obverse doubled die.

1936

DDO-002

Cross Reference	WDDO-002
Overall Rarity	URS-09
Interest Level	Moderate

CLASS VI
Distended Hub Doubling

GRADE	VF	XF	AU	MS60	MS63	MS65
VALUE	20	30	40	75	100	150

DESCRIPTION

Strong extra thickness seen on LIBERTY and the date.

DIE MARKERS

Obverse: None noted.

Reverse: Die scratch through the bottom of IC of AMERICA.

COMMENTS

This is similar to DDO-001, but much less dramatic and, therefore, demand is much lower. It may be difficult to attribute in low grade.

1936　　DDR-001

Cross Reference	WDDR-001
Overall Rarity	URS-06
Interest Level	High

CLASS II
Distorted Hub Doubling

GRADE	VF	XF	AU	MS60	MS63	MS65
VALUE	75	100	250	350	500	1250

DESCRIPTION

Strong doubling toward the center seen on UNITED STATES OF AMERICA and FIVE CENTS. Nice doubling also seen on E PLURIBUS UNUM, the rear legs, and the horn.

DIE MARKERS

Obverse: None noted.

Reverse: Die crack through the top of NITED to the top of S of STATES.

COMMENTS

By far the strongest Class II Buffalo nickel. This is a quadrupled die and shows multiple hubbings clearly on most of the reverse peripheral lettering. It definitely belongs in the top ten Buffalo nickel die varieties. Even though this is not near the importance of the 1916 DDO or the 1918-D 8/7 varieties, it should still be considered as one of the best doubled dies in the series—about the same strength and significance as the 1917 DDR-001 (though not quite as rare)—and makes a nice combination of doubled die varieties when paired with the 1936 DDO-001. It is, by far, the strongest Class II doubled die Buffalo nickel and is listed in the top ten. It is *many* times rarer than the major 1936 DDO-001 and appears to be a severely underrated variety.

1936-D DDR-001

CLASS VI
Distended Hub Doubling

Cross Reference	WDDR-001
Overall Rarity	Unknown
Interest Level	Low

GRADE	VF	XF	AU	MS60	MS63	MS65
VALUE	10	15	20	35	50	125

DESCRIPTION

Moderate extra thickness seen on UNITED STATES OF AMERICA.

DIE MARKERS

Obverse: Strike doubling seen on obverse on the neck, date, profile, ribbon, hair braids, and feathers.

Reverse: None noted.

COMMENTS

This is the only known doubled die for any branch mint 1936 Buffalo. A quick pick-up point is the very thick dot between UNITED and STATES.

1937

DDO-001

Cross Reference	WDDO-001
Overall Rarity	URS-07
Interest Level	Low

CLASS VI
Distended Hub Doubling

GRADE	VF	XF	AU	MS60	MS63	MS65
VALUE	10	20	30	40	45	65

DESCRIPTION

Moderate extra thickness seen on the date and LIBERTY.

DIE MARKERS

Obverse: None noted.

Reverse: Die polishing seen through STATES.

COMMENTS

The date shows moderate extra thickness, while it is of minor strength on LIBERTY, much like the 1936 DDO-002 previously listed.

1937

DDR-001

Cross Reference	None
Overall Rarity	URS-07
Interest Level	Medium

CLASS V

Pivoted Hub Doubling

GRADE	VF	XF	AU	MS60	MS63	MS65
VALUE	10	15	20	35	50	125

DESCRIPTION

Nice doubling seen on FIVE CENTS and E PLURIBUS UNUM. Doubling also seen on all four legs, the eye, tail, and parts of AMERICA.

DIE MARKERS

Obverse: Several die scratches between the neck and feathers. Several die scratches on the large feather.

Reverse: None noted.

COMMENTS

Very similar to 1935 DDR-003.

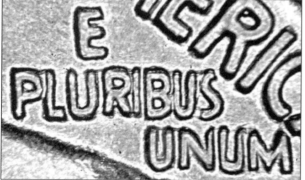

1938-D/S

DDR-001
(OMM-003)

Cross Reference	1-R-III, WDDR-001
Overall Rarity	Unknown
Interest Level	Moderate

CLASS II
Distorted Hub Doubling

GRADE	VF	XF	AU	MS60	MS63	MS65
VALUE	7	10	15	25	30	45

DESCRIPTION

Minor doubling seen on E PLURIBUS UNUM.

DIE MARKERS

Obverse: None noted.

Reverse: OMM-003.

COMMENTS

Both the doubling and the over mintmark are of a minor nature. This variety is of primary interest due to the D/S feature.

Chapter 5

Buffalo Nickel Over Mintmarks (OMM)

Over Mintmark Overview

An over mintmark occurs when two different lettered mintmarks have been punched into the die showing both mintmarks as overlapping or totally separate images.

Until recently, mintmarks were added to the working dies as part of the final step of production. They identified the mint that would use the working dies in the production of coins. All working dies used were prepared at the Philadelphia Mint. The mintmarks were added with a hand punch and a mallet. There was no mechanical aid used in aligning or hammering the punch.

There have been eight different mints that produced U.S. coins at various times, each of which had a different mintmark to represent it. There are a few reasons why working dies prepared for a particular branch mint might not be needed by that mint:

1. The branch mint is closed down.

2. The branch mint already has too many working dies.

In either case, good working dies that are already struck with mintmarks are left over and can be used by another branch mint if that mint is set up to strike the same denomination. The engraver can try to remove the old mintmark with abrasives or simply punch in the mintmark of the branch mint to where the working die will now be sent. This was probably the case for the 1900-O O/CC dollars and 1955 D/S nickels. The other possibility causing two different mintmarks to be punched into a working die is an error by the engraver.

Both examples (above) are of a 1944-D Lincoln cent. The working dies were first struck with an S for San Francisco, and with a D over top for Denver. Die #1 on the left shows the S much more strongly and commands a greater premium.

Date-by-Date Analysis

1936-D — Delisted Over Mintmark

Cross Reference	FS-19.8

GRADE	XF	AU	MS60	MS63	MS64	MS65
VALUE	------	------	------	------	------	------

DESCRIPTION

This variety has been described as an over mintmark. It was believed that the diagonal bar of an S is seen through the middle of the D. A small portion of the upper left side of the S is seen to the left of the D below the top serif.

Several high grade specimens were examined. There is not enough conclusive evidence of an S mintmark.

COMMENTS

The metal is diagonal across the center of the D. Looking at the 1938-D OMM-001 and OMM-002, and studying the S mintmark on 1936-S Buffalos, it was concluded that the center bar should curve and not go straight across as seen here.

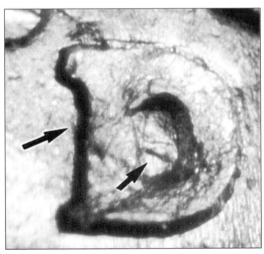

1938-D/S

OMM-001

Cross Reference	OMM #1

GRADE	XF	AU	MS60	MS63	MS64	MS65
VALUE	10	18	25	50	70	90

DESCRIPTION: *OVER MINTMARK D/D/S*

Repunched D over S mintmark. The top of the S is seen above the D. The left curve is seen below the top serif of the D. The diagonal bar of the S is seen through the middle of the D. The top of the bottom bar of the S is seen above the bottom of the D. Two repunched Ds south seen below the bottom and bottom right.

COMMENTS

The usual D/S variety offered in price lists, though OMM-002 is sometimes sold as the D over S. When it was discovered in 1962, it was considered to be a great rarity. This variety is easily distinguishable from the other five 1938-D OMMs because it is the only one that shows the top of an S above the top of the D. Late die states do not show the repunched D below the bottom of the D.

1938-D/S

OMM-002

Cross Reference	OMM #2

GRADE	XF	AU	MS60	MS63	MS64	MS65
VALUE	8	12	18	30	40	50

DESCRIPTION: *OVER MINTMARK D/S*

The diagonal bar of the S is seen through the middle of the D. The top left curve of the S is seen below the top serif of the D.

COMMENTS

Nearly as desirable as OMM-001, it shows the underlying curve very clearly. The diagonal bar of the S in the middle of the D is stronger than that on OMM-001. It is also in the same relative location as OMM-001, which is why these two varieties are sometimes confused. Why are there such strong remnants of the S in the middle of the D and none seen on the outside of the D?

1938-D

OMM-003

Cross Reference	OMM #3

GRADE	XF	AU	MS60	MS63	MS64	MS65
VALUE	10	15	25	35	40	50

DESCRIPTION

Repunched D over S mintmark. The diagonal bar of the S is seen through the middle of the D.

COMMENTS

This variety is also a doubled die reverse listed as DDR-001. Please refer to the doubled die chapter to see photos of the doubling. The remnants of the S are very light, but the shape and contour of the metal inside the D leads to the conclusion that this is an S.

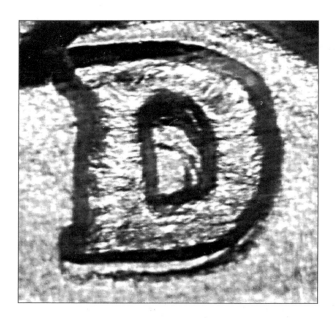 

1938-D

Delisted Over Mintmark

Cross Reference	OMM #4

GRADE	XF	AU	MS60	MS63	MS64	MS65
VALUE	------	------	------	------	------	------

DESCRIPTION: *REPUNCHED D/D/D*

This variety was previously listed as an over mintmark. The evidence is not sufficient enough to warrant this variety to be listed as an OMM.

COMMENTS

This variety was listed as an OMM in Wexler and Miller's RPM book and the first edition of this book. Most likely it was listed as an OMM because of the 1938-D/S OMM-001 and OMM-002. A line is seen across the center of the D. The line is straight, and does not follow the shape or contour of the center of an S mintmark. What appears to be two extra serifs are seen above the bottom serif of the D, however, these are most likely the remnants of a repunched D mintmark. If the crossbar was the center of an S mintmark, the extra serifs would be too high to be part of an S mintmark.

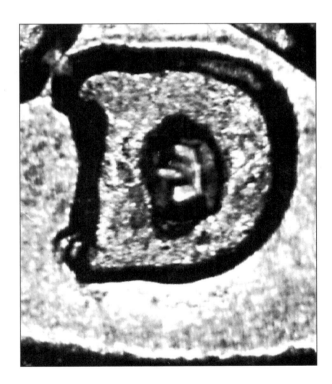

1938-D/S   Delisted Over Mintmark

Cross Reference	OMM #5

GRADE	XF	AU	MS60	MS63	MS64	MS65
VALUE	------	------	------	------	------	------

DESCRIPTION

This variety was previously listed as an over mintmark. The evidence is not sufficient to warrant this variety to be listed as an OMM.

COMMENTS

This variety was listed as an OMM in Wexler and Miller's RPM book and in the first edition of this book. Most likely it was listed as an OMM because of the 1938-D/S OMM-001 and OMM-002. One reason these varieties were reexamined was because of ANACS. Speaking to some of the graders at ANACS, they believed there was insufficient evidence of an OMM. We agree and are therefore delisting these as OMMs.

It was believed that the line protruding from the bottom right of the D was part of the center of an S mintmark. There are no parts of an extra digit seen in the middle of the D or anywhere else. The shape and contour of this line does not follow the shape and contour of the center of an S mintmark. The location of the alleged S mintmark is too low. This is simply a die scratch or another type of die defect.

1938-D/S

OMM-006

Cross Reference	None

GRADE	XF	AU	MS60	MS63	MS64	MS65
VALUE	10	18	25	50	70	90

DESCRIPTION: *OVER MINTMARK D/S*

Repunched D over S mintmark. The diagonal bar of the S is seen through the middle of the D. The bottom of an S is seen below the bottom of the D.

COMMENTS

Only one of these OMMs have been found to date. This is also the first time this variety has been published. With so many collectors looking for the first five OMMs, how was this one missed for so long? The bottom serif is very bold, the lower right curve of the S is obvious. There is no mistaking that this is an S.

Chapter 6
Buffalo Nickel Repunched Mintmarks (RPM)

Repunched Mintmark Overview

A repunched mintmark occurs when a mintmark has been punched into the die in more than one location, showing the mintmark or parts of the mintmark as overlapping or totally separate images.

Until recently, the mintmarks were added to the working dies as part of the final step of production. They identify the mint that would use the working dies in the production of coins. All working dies used were prepared at the Philadelphia Mint. The mintmarks were added with a hand punch and a mallet. There was no mechanical aid used in aligning or hammering the punch. If, between blows of the mallet, the punch was moved slightly out of alignment of the first impression, a double mintmark occurred. The number of mintmarks visible will depend on how many times the punch was moved and restruck.

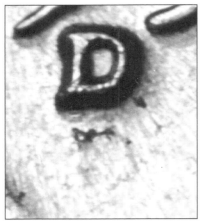

The top photo and bottom left photo are of the 1956-D Lincoln cent where the D was first punched far to the south of the final D. The photo on the bottom center is of a 1942-D Jefferson nickel where the first D was punched horizontal to the final D. The photo on the bottom right is of a 1946-D Jefferson nickel where the first D was punched inverted to the final D.

1913-D
RPM-001

Cross Reference	WRPM-001

GRADE	XF	AU	MS60	MS63	MS65
VALUE	40	70	100	180	400

DESCRIPTION: *RPM D/D*

Repunched D north west.

1913-S
RPM-001

Cross Reference	WRPM-001

GRADE	XF	AU	MS60	MS63	MS65
VALUE	40	70	100	180	400

DESCRIPTION: *RPM D/D*

Repunched D north west.

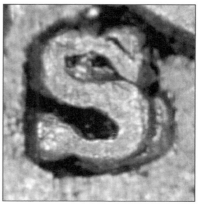

1914-S
RPM-001

Cross Reference	WRPM-001

GRADE	XF	AU	MS60	MS63	MS65
VALUE	40	70	100	180	400

DESCRIPTION: *RPM S/S*

Repunched D north west.

1915-D
RPM-001

Cross Reference	RPM-1, FS-15, WRPM-001

GRADE	XF	AU	MS60	MS63	MS65
VALUE	75	130	195	400	2000

DESCRIPTION: *RPM D/D*

Repunched D north west.

1915-S

RPM-001

Cross Reference	FS-015.6, WRPM-001

GRADE	XF	AU	MS60	MS63	MS65
VALUE	165	250	400	1500	2400

DESCRIPTION: *RPM S/S/S*

Repunched north and south.

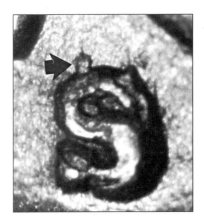

1915-S

RPM-002

Cross Reference	FS-15.5, WRPM-002

GRADE	XF	AU	MS60	MS63	MS65
VALUE	165	250	400	1500	2400

DESCRIPTION: *RPM S/S/S*

Repunched S north and south.

1918-D

RPM-001

Cross Reference	RPM-1, FS-15, WRPM-001

GRADE	XF	AU	MS60	MS63	MS65
VALUE	75	130	195	400	2000

DESCRIPTION: *RPM D/D*

Repunched D south.

1920-D

RPM-001

Cross Reference	RPM #1, WRPM-001

GRADE	XF	AU	MS60	MS63	MS65
VALUE	5	10	15	20	35

DESCRIPTION: *RPM D/D*

Repunched D west.

1924-D

RPM-001

Cross Reference	WRPM-001

GRADE	XF	AU	MS60	MS63	MS65
VALUE	150	250	500	1000	3400

DESCRIPTION: *RPM D/D*

Repunched D south.

1924-D

RPM-002

Cross Reference	WRPM-003

GRADE	XF	AU	MS60	MS63	MS65
VALUE	150	250	500	1000	3400

DESCRIPTION: *RPM D/D*

Repunched D south west.

1924-D

RPM-003

Cross Reference	WRPM-004

GRADE	XF	AU	MS60	MS63	MS65
VALUE	150	250	500	1000	3400

DESCRIPTION: *RPM D/D*

Repunched D south.

1924-S

RPM-001

Cross Reference	WRPM-001

GRADE	XF	AU	MS60	MS63	MS65
VALUE	1100	1400	1800	3300	9000

DESCRIPTION: *RPM S/S/S*

Repunched S south and east.

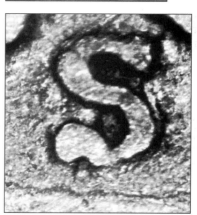

1924-S

RPM-002

Cross Reference	WRPM-001

GRADE	XF	AU	MS60	MS63	MS65
VALUE	1100	1400	1800	3300	9000

DESCRIPTION: *RPM S/S/S*

Repunched S south and east.

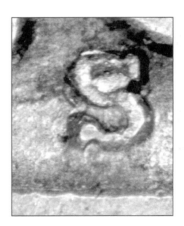

1925-S

RPM-001

Cross Reference	WRPM-001

GRADE	XF	AU	MS60	MS63	MS65
VALUE	1100	1400	1800	3300	9000

DESCRIPTION: *RPM S/S*

Repunched S east.

1925-S

RPM-002

Cross Reference	WRPM-002

GRADE	XF	AU	MS60	MS63	MS65
VALUE	1100	1400	1800	3300	9000

DESCRIPTION: *RPM S/S*

Strong repunched S east.

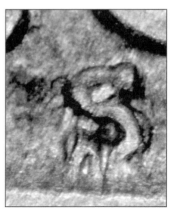

1925-S

RPM-003

Cross Reference	WRPM-003

GRADE	XF	AU	MS60	MS63	MS65
VALUE	1100	1400	1800	3300	9000

DESCRIPTION: *RPM S/S*

Strong repunched S northeast.

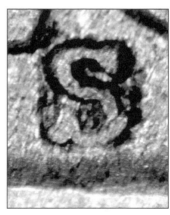

1925-S

RPM-004

Cross Reference	WRPM-001

GRADE	XF	AU	MS60	MS63	MS65
VALUE	1100	1400	1800	3300	9000

DESCRIPTION: *RPM S/S*

Strong repunched S northeast.

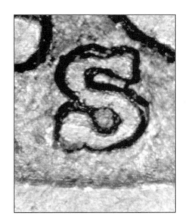

1925-S

RPM-005

Cross Reference	WRPM-001

GRADE	XF	AU	MS60	MS63	MS65
VALUE	1100	1400	1800	3300	9000

DESCRIPTION: *RPM S/S*

Strong repunched S northeast.

1927-D

RPM-001

Cross Reference	FS-16.7, WRPM-001

GRADE	XF	AU	MS60	MS63	MS65
VALUE	125	250	650	2500	3200

DESCRIPTION: *RPM D/D/D*

Repunched D north, and wide south.

1927-D

RPM-002

Cross Reference	WRPM-002

GRADE	XF	AU	MS60	MS63	MS65
VALUE	125	250	620	2400	3000

DESCRIPTION: *RPM D/D*

Repunched D north.

1929-D

RPM-001

Cross Reference	WRPM-001

GRADE	XF	AU	MS60	MS63	MS65
VALUE	25	60	90	180	1300

DESCRIPTION: *RPM D/D*

Repunched D east.

1929-S

RPM-001

Cross Reference	RPM #1, WRPM-001

GRADE	XF	AU	MS60	MS63	MS65
VALUE	15	30	75	125	400

DESCRIPTION: *RPM S/S*

Repunched S north east.

1929-S

RPM-002

Cross Reference	WRPM-002

GRADE	XF	AU	MS60	MS63	MS65
VALUE	10	25	65	95	350

DESCRIPTION: *RPM S/S/S*

Repunched S east and north east.

1929-S

RPM-003

Cross Reference	WRPM-003

GRADE	XF	AU	MS60	MS63	MS65
VALUE	10	25	65	95	350

DESCRIPTION: *RPM S/S*

Repunched S east.

1929-S

RPM-004

Cross Reference	WRPM-004

GRADE	XF	AU	MS60	MS63	MS65
VALUE	30	70	150	200	500

DESCRIPTION: *RPM S/S/S*

Repunched S wide south. The bottom of the S is in the rim. Second S north.

1929-S

RPM-005

Cross Reference	WRPM-005

GRADE	XF	AU	MS60	MS63	MS65
VALUE	30	70	150	200	500

DESCRIPTION: *RPM S/S*

Repunched S east.

1930-S

RPM-001

Cross Reference	RPM #1, WRPM-001

GRADE	XF	AU	MS60	MS63	MS65
VALUE	15	50	60	80	450

DESCRIPTION: *RPM S/S*

Repunched S west.

1930-S

RPM-002

Cross Reference	RPM #2, WRPM-002

GRADE	XF	AU	MS60	MS63	MS65
VALUE	10	25	35	70	375

DESCRIPTION: *RPM S/S*

Repunched S east.

1930-S

RPM-003

Cross Reference	WRPM-003

GRADE	XF	AU	MS60	MS63	MS65
VALUE	10	25	35	70	350

DESCRIPTION: *RPM S/S*

Repunched S west.

1930-S

RPM-004

Cross Reference	WRPM-004

GRADE	XF	AU	MS60	MS63	MS65
VALUE	20	30	70	85	400

DESCRIPTION: *RPM S/S/S*

Repunched S north east and south east.

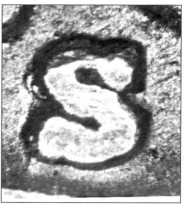

1930-S

RPM-005

Cross Reference	WRPM-005

GRADE	XF	AU	MS60	MS63	MS65
VALUE	15	50	70	90	450

DESCRIPTION: *RPM S/S*

Repunched S north.

1930-S

RPM-006

Cross Reference	WRPM-006

GRADE	XF	AU	MS60	MS63	MS65
VALUE	15	50	70	90	450

DESCRIPTION: *RPM S/S*

Repunched S west.

1930-S
RPM-007

Cross Reference	WRPM-007			

GRADE	XF	AU	MS60	MS63	MS65
VALUE	15	50	70	90	450

DESCRIPTION: *RPM S/S/S*

Repunched S north west and east.

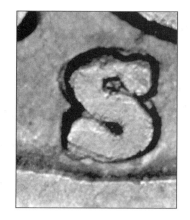

1930-S
RPM-008

Cross Reference	WRPM-008			

GRADE	XF	AU	MS60	MS63	MS65
VALUE	15	50	70	90	450

DESCRIPTION: *RPM S/S*

Repunched S north east.

1931-S
RPM-001

Cross Reference	RPM #1, WRPM-001			

GRADE	XF	AU	MS60	MS63	MS65
VALUE	20	40	75	95	225

DESCRIPTION: *RPM S/S*

Repunched S west.

1934-D
RPM-001

Cross Reference	RPM #1, WRPM-001			

GRADE	XF	AU	MS60	MS63	MS65
VALUE	20	40	75	95	225

DESCRIPTION: *RPM D/D*

Repunched D west.

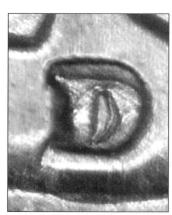

1935-D

RPM-001

Cross Reference	WRPM-001

GRADE	XF	AU	MS60	MS63	MS65
VALUE	15	50	60	80	425

DESCRIPTION: *RPM D/D*

Repunched wide D west.

1935-D

RPM-002

Cross Reference	FS 18.5, WRPM-002

GRADE	XF	AU	MS60	MS63	MS65
VALUE	30	75	95	150	475

DESCRIPTION: *RPM D/D*

Repunched D south west and east.

1935-D

RPM-003

Cross Reference	RPM #2, WRPM-003

GRADE	XF	AU	MS60	MS63	MS65
VALUE	12	30	40	70	325

DESCRIPTION: *RPM D/D/D*

Repunched D south west and east.

1935-D

RPM-004

Cross Reference	WRPM-004

GRADE	XF	AU	MS60	MS63	MS65
VALUE	15	40	55	75	375

DESCRIPTION: *RPM D/D*

Repunched D west.

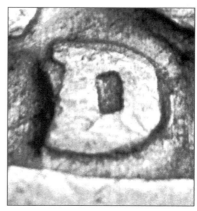

1935-D

RPM-005

Cross Reference	WRPM-005

GRADE	XF	AU	MS60	MS63	MS65
VALUE	15	30	40	70	325

DESCRIPTION: *RPM D/D*

Repunched D south west.

1935-D

RPM-006

Cross Reference	WRPM-006

GRADE	XF	AU	MS60	MS63	MS65
VALUE	18	40	50	70	350

DESCRIPTION: *RPM D/D*

Repunched D south.

1935-D

RPM-007

Cross Reference	WRPM-007

GRADE	XF	AU	MS60	MS63	MS65
VALUE	15	40	50	75	350

DESCRIPTION: *RPM D/D*

Repunched D south.

1935-D

RPM-008

Cross Reference	WRPM-008

GRADE	XF	AU	MS60	MS63	MS65
VALUE	20	45	55	75	375

DESCRIPTION: *RPM D/D*

Repunched D north.

1935-D

RPM-009

Cross Reference	None

GRADE	XF	AU	MS60	MS63	MS65
VALUE	15	40	50	75	350

DESCRIPTION: *RPM D/D*

What looks like the upper serif of a D is seen above the lower serif.

1935-D

RPM-010

Cross Reference	None

GRADE	XF	AU	MS60	MS63	MS65
VALUE	20	45	55	75	375

DESCRIPTION: *RPM D/D*

Repunched D west and east.

1935-D

RPM-011

Cross Reference	None

GRADE	XF	AU	MS60	MS63	MS65
VALUE	15	40	50	75	350

DESCRIPTION: *RPM D/D*

Repunched D east.

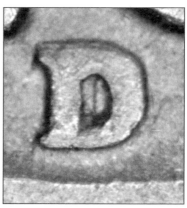

1935-S

RPM-001

Cross Reference	WRPM-001

GRADE	XF	AU	MS60	MS63	MS65
VALUE	8	20	40	75	125

DESCRIPTION: *RPM S/S/S*

Repunched S east and west.

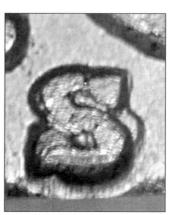

1935-S

RPM-002

Cross Reference	RPM #1, WRPM-002

GRADE	XF	AU	MS60	MS63	MS65
VALUE	5	35	70	95	150

DESCRIPTION: *RPM S/S*

Repunched S east.

1935-S

RPM-002

Cross Reference	RPM #2, WRPM-002

GRADE	XF	AU	MS60	MS63	MS65
VALUE	5	15	35	65	120

DESCRIPTION: *RPM S/S*

Repunched S east.

1935-S

RPM-004

Cross Reference	RPM #3, WRPM-004

GRADE	XF	AU	MS60	MS63	MS65
VALUE	5	20	35	70	130

DESCRIPTION: *RPM S/S*

Repunched S north.

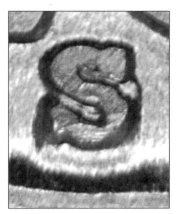

1935-S

RPM-005

Cross Reference	WRPM-005

GRADE	XF	AU	MS60	MS63	MS65
VALUE	8	15	35	70	135

DESCRIPTION: *RPM S/S*

Repunched S east.

1935-S

RPM-006

Cross Reference	RPM #4, WRPM-006

GRADE	XF	AU	MS60	MS63	MS65
VALUE	5	20	35	65	125

DESCRIPTION: *RPM S/S*

Repunched S north.

1935-S

RPM-007

Cross Reference	WRPM-007

GRADE	XF	AU	MS60	MS63	MS65
VALUE	15	30	70	105	200

DESCRIPTION: *RPM S/S*

Repunched S south.

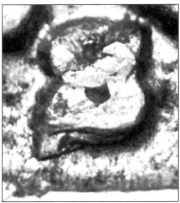

1935-S

RPM-008

Cross Reference	WRPM-008

GRADE	XF	AU	MS60	MS63	MS65
VALUE	5	15	30	60	130

DESCRIPTION: *RPM S/S*

Repunched S north east.

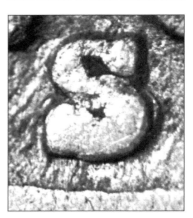

1935-S

RPM-009

Cross Reference	WRPM-009

GRADE	XF	AU	MS60	MS63	MS65
VALUE	5	15	30	60	130

DESCRIPTION: *RPM S/S*

Repunched S north east.

1935-S

RPM-010

Cross Reference	WRPM-010

GRADE	XF	AU	MS60	MS63	MS65
VALUE	15	35	75	125	175

DESCRIPTION: *RPM S/S*

Repunched S wide south.

1935-S

RPM-011

Cross Reference	WRPM-011

GRADE	XF	AU	MS60	MS63	MS65
VALUE	5	10	15	20	35

DESCRIPTION: *RPM S/S*

Repunched S south.

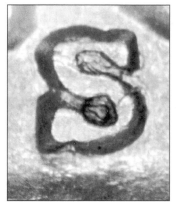

1936-D

RPM-011

Cross Reference	RPM #1, WRPM-001

GRADE	XF	AU	MS60	MS63	MS65
VALUE	8	15	20	35	80

DESCRIPTION: *RPM D/D*

Repunched D west.

1936-D

RPM-002

Cross Reference	RPM #2, WRPM-002

GRADE	XF	AU	MS60	MS63	MS65
VALUE	8	15	25	35	80

DESCRIPTION: *RPM D/D*

Repunched D north west.

1936-D

RPM-003

Cross Reference	RPM #3, WRPM-003

GRADE	XF	AU	MS60	MS63	MS65
VALUE	5	15	25	30	75

DESCRIPTION: *RPM D/D*

Repunched D north.

1936-D

RPM-004

Cross Reference	RPM #4, WRPM-004

GRADE	XF	AU	MS60	MS63	MS65
VALUE	5	17	30	45	60

DESCRIPTION: *RPM D/D*

Repunched D north east.

1936-D

RPM-005

Cross Reference	RPM #5, WRPM-005

GRADE	XF	AU	MS60	MS63	MS65
VALUE	5	15	25	30	80

DESCRIPTION: *RPM D/D*

Repunched D north east.

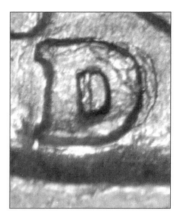

1936-D

RPM-006

Cross Reference	RPM #6, WRPM-006

GRADE	XF	AU	MS60	MS63	MS65
VALUE	5	15	25	30	60

DESCRIPTION: *RPM D/D/D*

Repunched D east and south.

1936-D

RPM-007

Cross Reference	WRPM-007

GRADE	XF	AU	MS60	MS63	MS65
VALUE	8	15	20	35	70

DESCRIPTION: *RPM D/D*

Repunched D east.

1936-D

RPM-008

Cross Reference	WRPM-008

GRADE	XF	AU	MS60	MS63	MS65
VALUE	5	12	20	30	60

DESCRIPTION: *RPM D/D*

Repunched D west.

1936-D

RPM-009

Cross Reference	WRPM-009

GRADE	XF	AU	MS60	MS63	MS65
VALUE	8	15	20	30	75

DESCRIPTION: *RPM D/D*

Repunched D north.

1936-D

RPM-010

Cross Reference	WRPM-010

GRADE	XF	AU	MS60	MS63	MS65
VALUE	5	12	20	30	60

DESCRIPTION: *RPM D/D*

Repunched D west.

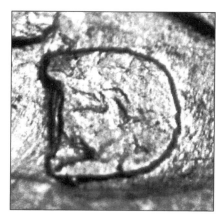

1936-D

RPM-011

Cross Reference	WRPM-011

GRADE	XF	AU	MS60	MS63	MS65
VALUE	5	12	20	30	60

DESCRIPTION: *RPM D/D*

Repunched D west.

1936-D

RPM-012

Cross Reference	WRPM-012

GRADE	XF	AU	MS60	MS63	MS65
VALUE	5	12	20	30	60

DESCRIPTION: *RPM D/D*

Repunched D east.

1936-D

RPM-013

Cross Reference	WRPM-014, FS-19.8

GRADE	XF	AU	MS60	MS63	MS65
VALUE	5	12	20	30	60

DESCRIPTION: *RPM D/D*

Repunched D tilted east.

1936-D

RPM-014

Cross Reference	WOMM-001

GRADE	XF	AU	MS60	MS63	MS65
VALUE	5	12	20	30	60

DESCRIPTION: *RPM D/D*

Repunched D east.

1936-D

RPM-015

Cross Reference	WRPM-015

GRADE	XF	AU	MS60	MS63	MS65
VALUE	5	12	20	30	60

DESCRIPTION: *RPM D/D*

Repunched D north west.

1936-S

RPM-001

Cross Reference	RPM #1, WRPM-001

GRADE	XF	AU	MS60	MS63	MS65
VALUE	35	65	90	150	220

DESCRIPTION: *RPM S/S*

Repunched S wide south.

1936-S

RPM-002

Cross Reference	RPM #2, WRPM-002

GRADE	XF	AU	MS60	MS63	MS65
VALUE	9	20	25	45	100

DESCRIPTION: *RPM S/S*

Repunched S east.

1936-S

RPM-003

Cross Reference	WRPM-003

GRADE	XF	AU	MS60	MS63	MS65
VALUE	10	25	35	45	125

DESCRIPTION: *RPM S/S/S/S*

Repunched S east and east and south.

1936-S

RPM-004

Cross Reference	WRPM-004

GRADE	XF	AU	MS60	MS63	MS65
VALUE	5	15	20	30	85

DESCRIPTION: *RPM S/S*

Repunched S east.

1936-S

RPM-005

Cross Reference	WOMM-005

GRADE	XF	AU	MS60	MS63	MS65
VALUE	15	25	35	50	125

DESCRIPTION: *RPM S/S*

Repunched S south west.

1936-S

RPM-006

Cross Reference	WRPM-006

GRADE	XF	AU	MS60	MS63	MS65
VALUE	5	15	20	25	75

DESCRIPTION: *RPM S/S/S*

Repunched S north and north.

1936-S

RPM-007

Cross Reference	WRPM-007

GRADE	XF	AU	MS60	MS63	MS65
VALUE	5	15	20	30	75

DESCRIPTION: *RPM S/S*

Repunched S north.

1936-S

RPM-008

Cross Reference	WRPM-008

GRADE	XF	AU	MS60	MS63	MS65
VALUE	5	15	20	30	75

DESCRIPTION: *RPM S/S/S*

Repunched S north and north east.

1936-S

RPM-009

Cross Reference	WRPM-009

GRADE	XF	AU	MS60	MS63	MS65
VALUE	5	15	20	30	75

DESCRIPTION: *RPM S/S*

Repunched S north east.

1936-S

RPM-010

Cross Reference	WRPM-010

GRADE	XF	AU	MS60	MS63	MS65
VALUE	8	18	25	35	85

DESCRIPTION: *RPM S/S*

Repunched S north.

1936-S

RPM-011

Cross Reference	WRPM-013

GRADE	XF	AU	MS60	MS63	MS65
VALUE	8	18	25	35	85

DESCRIPTION: *RPM S/S*

Repunched S east.

1937-D

RPM-001

Cross Reference	RPM #1, WRPM-001

GRADE	XF	AU	MS60	MS63	MS65
VALUE	5	10	27	33	55

DESCRIPTION: *RPM D/D*

Repunched D east.

1937-D

RPM-002

Cross Reference	RPM #2, WRPM-002

GRADE	XF	AU	MS60	MS63	MS65
VALUE	5	10	15	20	42

DESCRIPTION: *RPM D/D*

Repunched D east.

1937-D

RPM-003

Cross Reference	RPM #3, WRPM-003

GRADE	XF	AU	MS60	MS63	MS65
VALUE	5	10	15	20	35

DESCRIPTION: *RPM D/D*

Repunched D south east.

1937-D

RPM-004

Cross Reference	RPM #4, WRPM-004

GRADE	XF	AU	MS60	MS63	MS65
VALUE	5	15	20	30	35

DESCRIPTION: *RPM D/D*

Repunched D north west.

1937-D

RPM-005

Cross Reference	RPM #5, WRPM-005

GRADE	XF	AU	MS60	MS63	MS65
VALUE	5	17	30	40	80

DESCRIPTION: *RPM D/D/D*

Repunched D south and south east.

1937-D

RPM-006

Cross Reference	WRPM-006

GRADE	XF	AU	MS60	MS63	MS65
VALUE	5	10	15	20	35

DESCRIPTION: *RPM D/D*

Repunched D east.

1937-D

RPM-007

Cross Reference	WRPM-007

GRADE	XF	AU	MS60	MS63	MS65
VALUE	5	10	15	20	35

DESCRIPTION: *RPM D/D/D/D*

Repunched D east, east, and east.

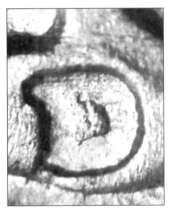

1937-D

RPM-008

Cross Reference	WRPM-008

GRADE	XF	AU	MS60	MS63	MS65
VALUE	5	12	20	35	40

DESCRIPTION: *RPM D/D*

Repunched D south.

1937-D

RPM-009

Cross Reference	WRPM-009

GRADE	XF	AU	MS60	MS63	MS65
VALUE	5	10	15	20	35

DESCRIPTION: *RPM D/D*

Repunched D east.

1937-D

RPM-010

Cross Reference	WRPM-010

GRADE	XF	AU	MS60	MS63	MS65
VALUE	5	12	20	30	43

DESCRIPTION: *RPM D/D*

Repunched D south.

1937-D

RPM-011

Cross Reference	WRPM-011

GRADE	XF	AU	MS60	MS63	MS65
VALUE	5	10	15	20	35

DESCRIPTION: *RPM D/D*

Repunched D east.

1937-D

RPM-012

Cross Reference	WRPM-012

GRADE	XF	AU	MS60	MS63	MS65
VALUE	5	10	15	30	35

DESCRIPTION: *RPM D/D*

Repunched D north west.

1937-D

RPM-013

Cross Reference	WRPM-013

GRADE	XF	AU	MS60	MS63	MS65
VALUE	5	10	15	20	35

DESCRIPTION: *RPM D/D*

Repunched D wide north.

1937-D

RPM-014

Cross Reference	WRPM-017

GRADE	XF	AU	MS60	MS63	MS65
VALUE	5	10	15	20	35

DESCRIPTION: *RPM D/D*

Repunched D east.

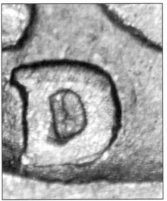

1937-D

RPM-015

Cross Reference	WRPM-019

GRADE	XF	AU	MS60	MS63	MS65
VALUE	5	10	15	20	35

DESCRIPTION: *RPM D/D*

Repunched D south.

1937-S

RPM-001

Cross Reference	RPM #1, WRPM-001

GRADE	XF	AU	MS60	MS63	MS65
VALUE	5	15	27	30	90

DESCRIPTION: *RPM S/S/S*

Repunched S west and north east.

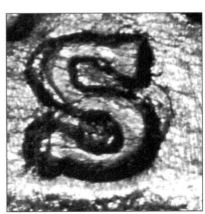

1937-S
RPM-002

Cross Reference	RPM #2, WRPM-002

GRADE	XF	AU	MS60	MS63	MS65
VALUE	7	15	30	35	60

DESCRIPTION: *RPM S/S*

Repunched S north east.

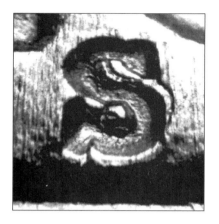

1937-S
RPM-003

Cross Reference	RPM #4, WRPM-003

GRADE	XF	AU	MS60	MS63	MS65
VALUE	5	10	20	25	35

DESCRIPTION: *RPM S/S*

Repunched S north.

1937-S
RPM-004

Cross Reference	WRPM-004

GRADE	XF	AU	MS60	MS63	MS65
VALUE	7	15	30	35	60

DESCRIPTION: *RPM S/S*

Repunched S west.

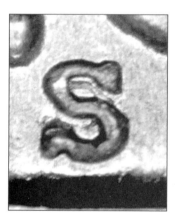

1937-S
RPM-005

Cross Reference	WRPM-005

GRADE	XF	AU	MS60	MS63	MS65
VALUE	5	15	27	30	90

DESCRIPTION: *RPM S/S*

Repunched S wide south.

1937-S

RPM-006

Cross Reference	WRPM-007

GRADE	XF	AU	MS60	MS63	MS65
VALUE	7	15	30	35	60

DESCRIPTION: *RPM S/S*

Repunched S east.

1937-S

RPM-007

Cross Reference	WRPM-009

GRADE	XF	AU	MS60	MS63	MS65
VALUE	5	15	27	30	90

DESCRIPTION: *RPM S/S*

Repunched S north.

1938-D

RPM-001

Cross Reference	RPM #1, WRPM-001

GRADE	XF	AU	MS60	MS63	MS65
VALUE	6	13	20	25	50

DESCRIPTION: *RPM D/D*

Repunched D south.

1938-D

RPM-002

Cross Reference	RPM #2, WRPM-002

GRADE	XF	AU	MS60	MS63	MS65
VALUE	7	15	20	30	50

DESCRIPTION: *RPM D/D*

Repunched D west.

1938-D
RPM-003

Cross Reference	RPM #3, WRPM-003

GRADE	XF	AU	MS60	MS63	MS65
VALUE	5	12	25	35	50

DESCRIPTION: *RPM D/D*

Repunched D west.

1938-D
RPM-004

Cross Reference	RPM #4, WRPM-004

GRADE	XF	AU	MS60	MS63	MS65
VALUE	5	10	15	20	35

DESCRIPTION: *RPM D/D/D*

Repunched D west and south.

1938-D
RPM-005

Cross Reference	WRPM-005

GRADE	XF	AU	MS60	MS63	MS65
VALUE	5	10	15	20	35

DESCRIPTION: *RPM D/D*

Repunched D south.

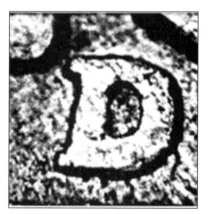

1938-D
RPM-006

Cross Reference	WRPM-006

GRADE	XF	AU	MS60	MS63	MS65
VALUE	5	10	15	20	35

DESCRIPTION: *RPM D/D*

Repunched D east.

1938-D

RPM-007

Cross Reference	WRPM-007

GRADE	XF	AU	MS60	MS63	MS65
VALUE	5	10	15	20	35

DESCRIPTION: *RPM D/D*

Repunched D west.

1938-D

RPM-008

Cross Reference	WRPM-008

GRADE	XF	AU	MS60	MS63	MS65
VALUE	5	10	15	20	35

DESCRIPTION: *RPM D/D*

Repunched D west.

1938-D

RPM-009

Cross Reference	WRPM-009

GRADE	XF	AU	MS60	MS63	MS65
VALUE	5	10	15	20	35

DESCRIPTION: *RPM D/D*

Repunched D east.

1938-D

RPM-010

Cross Reference	WRPM-010

GRADE	XF	AU	MS60	MS63	MS65
VALUE	5	10	15	20	35

DESCRIPTION: *RPM D/D*

Repunched D west.

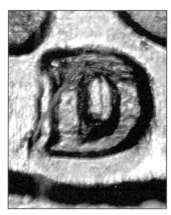

1938-D

RPM-011

Cross Reference	WRPM-011

GRADE	XF	AU	MS60	MS63	MS65
VALUE	5	10	15	20	35

DESCRIPTION: *RPM D/D*

Repunched D east.

1938-D

RPM-012

Cross Reference	WRPM-013

GRADE	XF	AU	MS60	MS63	MS65
VALUE	5	10	15	20	35

DESCRIPTION: *RPM D/D*

Repunched D north.

Chapter 7
Buffalo Nickel
3 ½ Legged Varieties

3 ½ Legged Variety Overview

When the obverse and reverse of properly functioning dies strike a blank planchet in the coining press, the metal from the planchet is pushed into the incused area of the die. The result is the raised design and image we see on most coins today.

During the minting process, it is often necessary to polish the dies. The die might be dirty, filled with grease or other elements. If the incused design elements become partially filled, it raises the depth of the design element closer to the surface of the die, thereby reducing the raised portion of the design element struck on the coin.

The die might also have become clashed, cracked, or damaged in the coining press. To fix these problems, the surface of the working die is polished with an abrasive element. Polishing the die lowers the surface of the die, thereby decreasing the depth of the design elements. In addition, the surface of the die begins to wear away through constant use in the coining press, blurring the distinction between the flat surface of the working die and the incused design elements. At the point when the surface of the working die is lowered to the depth of the design, the full design element no longer appears distinct on the struck coin.

In the case of the 3 ½ Legged varieties, overzealous polishing in the area around the right front leg of the Buffalo blurred the line between the design elements and the flat surface of the die. This blurring caused traces of the right front leg to be removed from the working die and, by extension, from subsequent coins struck from the die.

One of the most common reasons why a working die is polished is to mitigate the effects of die clashing.

Die clashing occurs when the obverse and reverse working dies strike each other in the coining press without a planchet between them. The clashing causes the outline of the design elements to be incused into the opposite die. The fields and the bottom edge, or outline of the design element, are the highest point on the working dies and will be the first to touch and penetrate into the opposite die. Under the right conditions, the lower design images of the die will be incused into the opposite die. How deep the design penetrates depends on the force applied, temperature of the dies, and number of times the dies clash.

Unless the clashing is effaced from the dies by polishing, or the surfaces of the dies become worn from use, all coins stuck by these dies will show evidence of die clashing. It is interesting to note that despite efforts to remove the effects of clashing some of the 3 ½ Legged Buffalo nickels show remnants of die clashing. It would be extremely interesting to assemble a collection of coins from these dies at each stage in the process, including the original die before any clashing occurred, from the clashed die before it was polished, and, of course, from the polished 3 ½ Legged variety with evidence of clashing.

Date-by-Date Analysis

1913 Type I

3 ½ Legged Buffalo

Cross Reference	FS-14.85

GRADE	G4	VG	F12	VF	XF	AU	MS60	MS63	MS65
VALUE	650	1000	2250	3500	5000	7500	10000	17500	47500

DESCRIPTION

Part of the right front leg of the Buffalo was removed from over-polishing.

DIE MARKERS

Obverse: None noted.

Reverse: None noted.

COMMENTS

Presently, there are probably less than a dozen known in all grades, with three or possibly four in Mint State. Of all other doubled dies, RPMs, and abraded die varieties, this is arguably the rarest significant Buffalo nickel die variety. No sale records are recorded for a circulated example, so values listed for these are only rough estimates. However, two sale records exist for Mint State coins: an MS64 sold for $20,500 in 2004 and an NGC MS65 (crossed from a PCGS MS64), the finest known of the variety, sold for $47,500 at the 2004 ANA show in Pittsburgh. Another specimen with a grade of Fine sold for more than $3,000.

This coin is also a 2 ½ feather variety but is rarely recognized for this feature; the die damage (clash) on the obverse is actually more impressive on that side of the coin than on the reverse.

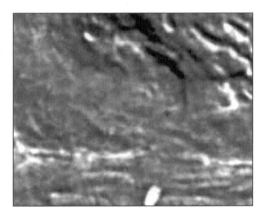

1917-D   3 ½ Legged Buffalo

Cross Reference	None

GRADE	G4	VG	F12	VF	XF	AU	MS60	MS63	MS65
VALUE	100	175	300	500	700	1350	1750	3250	------

DESCRIPTION

Part of the right front leg of the Buffalo was removed from over-polishing.

DIE MARKERS

Obverse: Several small die scratches between the ribbons.

Reverse: Several broken letters on AMERICA. Small die chips above the rim below FIVE CENTS. A vertical die scratch or gouge in the very center of the V of FIVE. A short 'spike' extending up from the bison's back below the 'E' of STATES. A die crack connecting the bison's tail to the rim.

COMMENTS

The most common of this variety and the most common in Mint State. A number are known in Uncirculated grade. Some show virtually no leg while others show an almost complete leg. These should be worth little or no premium and the values listed are for those with a weak leg.

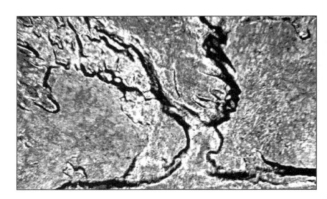

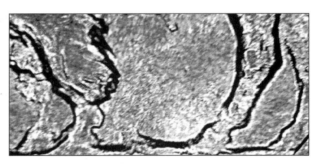

1926-D

3 ½ Legged Buffalo

Cross Reference	None

GRADE	G4	VG	F12	VF	XF	AU	MS60	MS63	MS65
VALUE	85	150	275	400	750	1750	3250	------	------

DESCRIPTION

Part of the right front leg of the Buffalo was removed from over-polishing.

DIE MARKERS

Obverse: None noted.

Reverse: None noted.

COMMENTS

Like the 1913, most also show a partial small feather and should be considered a 2 ½ feather + 3 ½ legged variety. Some have a very weak leg and the leg is a little stronger on others, but this date does not show the extreme variance that the 1917-D shows. Very rare in any grade above Fine.

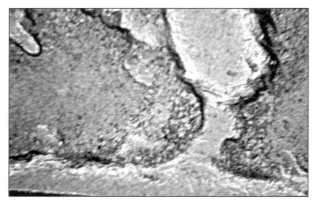

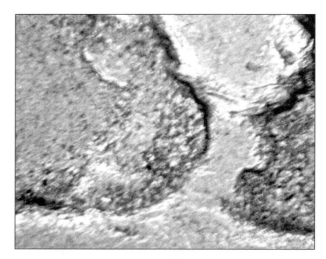

1927-D

3 ½ Legged Buffalo

Cross Reference	None

GRADE	G4	VG	F12	VF	XF	AU	MS60	MS63	MS65
VALUE	100	185	275	450	750	1500	2750	------	------

DESCRIPTION

Part of the right front leg of the Buffalo was removed from over-polishing.

DIE MARKERS

Obverse: None noted.

Reverse: None noted.

COMMENTS

The attenuated leg on this variety resembles the 1913, where the entire leg is weak rather than partially weak like the 1917-D, 1926-D, and 1936-D. It seems to be the second scarcest after the 1913. The weakness of the leg varies to a moderate degree. Almost never seen any better than Fine.

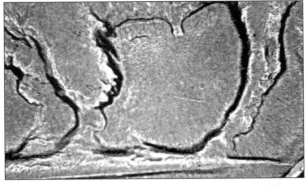

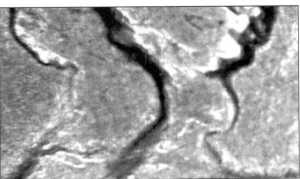
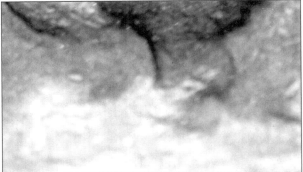

1936-D — 3 ½ Legged Buffalo

Cross Reference	FS-19

GRADE	G4	VG	F12	VF	XF	AU	MS60	MS63	MS65
VALUE	500	650	850	1150	3000	5000	11500	17500	------

DESCRIPTION

Part of the right front leg of the Buffalo was removed from over-polishing.

DIE MARKERS

Obverse: None noted.

Reverse: None noted.

COMMENTS

The best known of the variety. It has been recognized for nearly 30 years and is the only 3 ½ legged currently listed in the *Red Book*. Many sales records exist, so stated values should be very accurate. Only one, or possibly two, are known in Mint State. A few have a very weak leg rivaling the 1937-D for eye appeal. These should be worth an additional premium. Care should be exercised when purchasing these as altered coins have recently been seen.

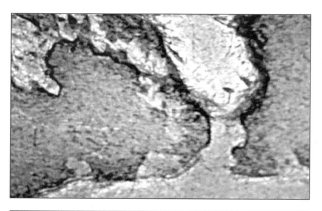

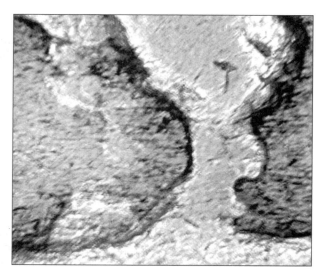

1937-D

3 Legged Buffalo

Cross Reference	None

GRADE	G4	VG	F12	VF	XF	AU	MS60	MS63	MS65
VALUE	575	650	925	1150	1350	1650	2650	5750	27,500

DESCRIPTION

The entire right front leg of the Buffalo was removed from over-polishing.

DIE MARKERS

Obverse: Die chips in hair on front of head. Die chip on braid.

Reverse: None noted.

COMMENTS

The rarity of this coin is almost always vastly overstated. It is not rare or, for that matter, even scarce. Thousands exist. The high values are the result of very high demand. Recognized as a novelty from the time of minting, a majority were saved shortly thereafter and XF/AU examples are the most commonly encountered grade. Low end Mint State coins are also not uncommon. The knowledgeable collector should never be fooled by the many altered coins offered as this variety has many distinctive die markers that distinguish a genuine piece.

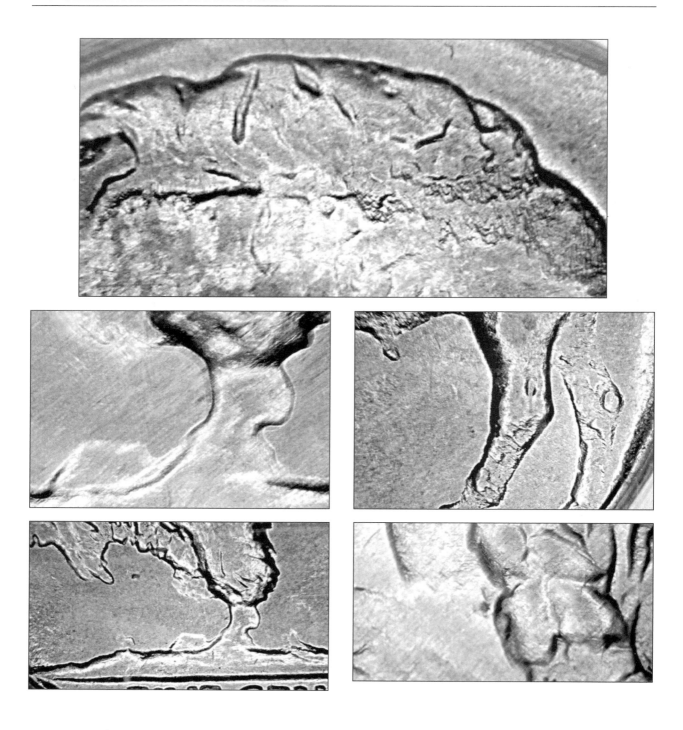

Submitters' Cross Reference

DOUBLED DIES

1913 T2	DDO-001	Ron Pope
1913 T2	DDR-001	Larry Briggs
1913 T2	DDR-002	Kevin Flynn
1914/3	DDO-001	Tom McCarrow
1914/3	DDO-002	JT Stanton
1914/3	DDO-003	Brian Raines
1914/3	Delisted #4	Larry Briggs
1914/3	Delisted #5	Kevin Flynn
1914/3	DDO-006	Daniel Carr
1915	DDO-001	Jim/Mark Lafferty
1916	DDO-001	JT Stanton
1917	DDR-001	Tom Arch
1917	DDR-002	Kevin Flynn
1918	DDR-001	JT Stanton
1918-D/7	DDO-001	JT Stanton
1919	DDO-001	Larry Briggs
1919	DDR-001	Leroy VanAllen
1921	DDO-001	Bill VanNote
1923-S	DDO-001	Tom Arch
1925 PDS	DDO-001	Bill VanNote
1926	DDO-001	Ron Pope
1927	DDO-001	Leroy VanAllen
1927-S	DDO-001	Ron Pope
1927-S	DDR-001	Tom Arch
1929	DDO-001	Ron Pope
1929	DDR-001	Ron Pope
1930	DDO-001	Ron Pope
1930	DDO-002	Brian Raines
1930	DDO-003	Leroy VanAllen
1930	DDO-004	Ron Pope
1930	DDO-005	Bill VanNote
1930	DDO-006	Brian Raines
1930	DDO-007	Brian Ranies
1930	DDR-001	Sam Lukes
1930	DDR-002	Ron Pope
1930	DDR-003	Brian Raines
1930	DDR-004	Mark Lafferty
1930	DDR-005	Leroy VanAllen
1930	DDR-006	Larry Briggs
1930	DDR-006	Dennis Paulsen
1931-S	DDR-001	Larry Briggs
1931-S	DDR-002	Ron Pope
1934	DDR-001	Leroy VanAllen
1934	DDR-002	Larry Briggs
1934-D	DDR-001	Leroy VanAlen
1934-D	DDR-002	Leroy VanAllen
1935	DDO-001	Jennifer Casazza
1935	DDR-001	Jim Lafferty Sr.
1935	DDR-002	Larry Briggs
1935	DDR-003	Ron Pope
1935	DDR-004	Leroy VanAllen
1935-S	DDO-001	Larry Briggs
1935-S	DDR-001	Leroy VanAllen
1935-S	DDR-002	Leroy VanAllen
1935-S	DDR-003	Leroy VanAllen
1936	DDO-001	Ron Pope
1936	DDO-002	Ron Pope

1936	DDR-001	Bill VanNote
1936-D	DDO-001	Larry Briggs
1937	DDO-001	Kevin Flynn
1938-D	DDR-001	Brian Raines

OVER MINTMARKS

1936-D/S	Delisted #1	JT Stanton
1938-D/S	OMM-001	Kevin Flynn
1938-D/S	OMM-002	Kevin Flynn
1938-D/S	OMM-003	Kevin Flynn
1938-D/S	Delisted #4	Kevin Flynn
1938-D/S	Delisted #5	Lloyd Hanson
1938-D/S	OMM-006	Lloyd Hanson

REPUNCHED MINTMARKS

1913-D	RPM-001	Jim/Mark Lafferty
1913-S	RPM-001	Lloyd Hanson
1914-S	RPM-001	Lloyd Hanson
1915-D	RPM-001	Lloyd Hanson
1915-S	RPM-001	JT Stanton
1915-S	RPM-002	JT Stanton
1918-D	RPM-001	Lloyd Hanson
1920-D	RPM-001	
1924-D	RPM-001	Lloyd Hanson
1924-D	RPM-002	Lloyd Hanson
1924-D	RPM-003	Lloyd Hanson
1925-S	RPM-001	Lloyd Hanson
1925-S	RPM-002	Lloyd Hanson
1925-S	RPM-003	Lloyd Hanson
1925-S	RPM-004	Lloyd Hanson
1925-S	RPM-005	Lloyd Hanson
1927-D	RPM-001	Ron Pope
1927-D	RPM-002	Lloyd Hanson

1929-S	RPM-001	Lloyd Hanson
1929-S	RPM-002	Lloyd Hanson
1929-S	RPM-003	Jim/Mark Lafferty
1929-S	RPM-004	Jim/Mark Lafferty
1929-S	RPM-005	Lloyd Hanson
1930-S	RPM-001	Lloyd Hanson
1930-S	RPM-002	Lloyd Hanson
1930-S	RPM-003	Lloyd Hanson
1930-S	RPM-004	Lloyd Hanson
1930-S	RPM-005	Lloyd Hanson
1930-S	RPM-006	Lloyd Hanson
1930-S	RPM-007	Lloyd Hanson
1930-S	RPM-008	Lloyd Hanson
1931-S	RPM-001	Lloyd Hanson
1934-D	RPM-001	Lloyd Hanson
1935-D	RPM-001	Lloyd Hanson
1935-D	RPM-002	Lloyd Hanson
1935-D	RPM-003	Lloyd Hanson
1935-D	RPM-004	Lloyd Hanson
1935-D	RPM-005	Lloyd Hanson
1935-D	RPM-006	Lloyd Hanson
1935-D	RPM-007	Lloyd Hanson
1935-D	RPM-008	Jim/Mark Lafferty
1935-S	RPM-001	Lloyd Hanson
1935-S	RPM-002	Lloyd Hanson
1935-S	RPM-003	Jim/Mark Lafferty
1935-S	RPM-004	Lloyd Hanson
1935-S	RPM-005	Lloyd Hanson
1935-S	RPM-006	Lloyd Hanson
1935-S	RPM-007	Lloyd Hanson
1935-S	RPM-008	Lloyd Hanson

1935-S	RPM-009	Lloyd Hanson	1937-D	RPM-004	Lloyd Hanson
1935-S	RPM-010	Jim/Mark Lafferty	1937-D	RPM-005	Kevin Flynn
1935-S	RPM-011	Ron Pope	1937-D	RPM-006	Lloyd Hanson
1936-D	RPM-001	Lloyd Hanson	1937-D	RPM-007	Lloyd Hanson
1936-D	RPM-002	Lloyd Hanson	1937-D	RPM-008	Lloyd Hanson
1936-D	RPM-003	Lloyd Hanson	1937-D	RPM-009	Lloyd Hanson
1936-D	RPM-004	Lloyd Hanson	1937-D	RPM-010	Lloyd Hanson
1936-D	RPM-005	Lloyd Hanson	1937-D	RPM-011	Lloyd Hanson
1936-D	RPM-006	Lloyd Hanson	1937-D	RPM-012	Lloyd Hanson
1936-D	RPM-007	Lloyd Hanson	1937-D	RPM-013	Jim/Mark Lafferty
1936-D	RPM-008	Lloyd Hanson	1937-D	RPM-014	Lloyd Hanson
1936-D	RPM-009	Lloyd Hanson	1937-D	RPM-015	Lloyd Hanson
1936-D	RPM-010	Lloyd Hanson	1937-S	RPM-001	Kevin Flynn
1936-D	RPM-011	Lloyd Hanson	1937-S	RPM-002	Lloyd Hanson
1936-D	RPM-012	Lloyd Hanson	1937-S	RPM-003	Lloyd Hanson
1936-D	RPM-013	Lloyd Hanson	1937-S	RPM-004	Lloyd Hanson
1936-D	RPM-014	Lloyd Hanson	1937-S	RPM-005	Lloyd Hanson
1936-S	RPM-001	Sam Lukes	1937-S	RPM-006	Lloyd Hanson
1936-S	RPM-002	Kevin Flynn	1937-S	RPM-007	Lloyd Hanson
1936-S	RPM-003	Lloyd Hanson	1938-D	RPM-001	Kevin Flynn
1936-S	RPM-004	Lloyd Hanson	1938-D	RPM-002	Kevin Flynn
1936-S	RPM-005	Lloyd Hanson	1938-D	RPM-003	Kevin Flynn
1936-S	RPM-006	Lloyd Hanson	1938-D	RPM-004	Lloyd Hanson
1936-S	RPM-007	Lloyd Hanson	1938-D	RPM-005	Lloyd Hanson
1936-S	RPM-008	Lloyd Hanson	1938-D	RPM-006	Lloyd Hanson
1936-S	RPM-009	Lloyd Hanson	1938-D	RPM-007	Lloyd Hanson
1936-S	RPM-010	Lloyd Hanson	1938-D	RPM-008	Lloyd Hanson
1936-S	RPM-011	Lloyd Hanson	1938-D	RPM-009	Lloyd Hanson
1937-D	RPM-001	Kevin Flynn	1938-D	RPM-010	Lloyd Hanson
1937-D	RPM-002	Lloyd Hanson	1938-D	RPM-011	Lloyd Hanson
1937-D	RPM-003	Kevin Flynn	1938-D	RPM-012	Lloyd Hanson

Bibliography

ANACS Population Report, February, 1998

Breen, Walter. *Walter Breen's Complete Encyclopedia of U.S. and Colonial Coins*. New York, New York: Doubleday, 1988.

Flynn, Kevin. *Getting Your Two Cents Worth*. Kevin Flynn, 1994.

Flynn, Kevin and John Wexler. *The Authoritative Reference on Lincoln Cents*, 1996.

Flynn, Kevin. *A Collector's Guide to Misplaced Dates*, 1997.

Flynn, Kevin John Wexler, and Bill Crawford. *The Authoritative Reference on Eisenhower Dollars*, 1998.

Flynn, Kevin. *Morgan Dollar Overdates, Over Mintmarks, Misplaced Dates and Clashed E Reverses*, 1998.

Flynn, Kevin. *Treasure Hunting in the Flying Eagle and Indian Cent Series*, 1998.

Flynn, Kevin. *A Quick Reference to the Top Misplaced Dates*, 1998.

Flynn, Kevin, Gary Wagnon, Karen Peterson. *A Quick Reference to the Top Lincoln Cent Die Varieties*, 1998.

Flynn, Kevin, Edward Fletcher. *The Authoritative Reference on Three Cent Nickels*, 1999.

Flynn, Kevin. *Flying Eagle, Indian Cent, Two Cent, and Three Cent Doubled Dies*, 1999.

Flynn, Kevin, John Wexler, and Ron Pope. *Treasure Hunting Buffalo Nickels*, 1999.

Flynn, Kevin, John Wexler. *Treasure Hunting Mercury Dimes*, 1999.

Flynn, Kevin, Bill Van Note. *Treasure Hunting on Liberty Head Nickels*, 1999.

Flynn, Kevin, Ron Volpe, and Kelsey Flynn. *Those Amazing Coins, A Kid's Guide to Collecting*, 2000.

Flynn, Kevin, Ron Volpe, and Kelsey Flynn. *Kid's Statehood Quarters Collector's Folder with information on collecting other cool coins*, 2000.

Flynn, Kevin, Kelsey Flynn. *Statehood Quarters and other cool coins*, 2000.

Flynn, Kevin. *The Authoritative Reference on Roosevelt Dimes*, 2002.

Flynn, Kevin and John Wexler. *Over Mintmarks and Hot Repunched Mintmarks*, 2003.

Flynn, Kevin and John Wexler. *Treasure Hunting Franklin and Kennedy Half Dollar Doubled Dies*, 2003.

Flynn, Kevin. *The Authoritative Reference on Barber Dimes*, 2004.

Flynn, Kevin. *The Authoritative Reference on Barber Quarters*, 2005.

Flynn, Kevin. *The Authoritative Reference on Barber Half Dollars*, 2005.

Flynn, Kevin. *Treasure Hunting on Walking Liberty Half Dollars*, second edition, 2005.

Flynn, Kevin. *The 1894-S Dime, A Mystery Unraveled*, 2005.

Fivaz, Bill and J.T. Stanton. *The Cherrypickers' Guide to Rare Die Varieties*. Third Edition. Wolfeboro, NH: Bowers & Merena Galleries, Inc., 1994.

Wexler, John. *The Encyclopedia of Doubled Dies*, Volume 1, 1981.

Wexler, John. *The Encyclopedia of Doubled Dies*, Volume 2, 1981.

Wexler, John. *The Lincoln Cent Doubled Die,* 1984.

Wexler, John and Tom Miller. *The RPM Book,* 1983.

Wexler, John. *The Complete Guide To The 1995 Doubled Die Cent Varieties,* John Wexler, 1996.

Wexler, John. *The Best of The Jefferson Nickel Doubled Die Varieties,* John Wexler, 1998.

Wexler, John, Brian Ribar. *The Best of The Jefferson Nickel Doubled Die Varieties,* 2002.

Wexler, John, Kevin Flynn. *The Best of The Washington Quarter Doubled Die Varieties,* 1999.

Yeoman, R.S. and Kenneth Bressett, ed. *A Guide Book of United States Coins,* 51st Edition, Racine, WI: Wextren Publishing Company, Inc., 1998

Kevin Flynn

The Boy Scouts deserve credit for introducing generations of young Americans to coin collecting. Kevin Flynn is no exception. The merit badge he earned in coin collecting as a Boy Scout provided his first glimpse into what is a fulfilling hobby and great passion today.

While an interest in coins never ventured far from his heart, school and studies consumed most of his time in the late 1970s and '80s. He received an undergraduate degree at Temple University in Computer Science, and a Masters of Engineering in Computers at Penn State. After a six years stint as an Aviation Electronic Technician in the Naval Reserves, Kevin became deeply involved with volunteer service and the American Red Cross. There he taught swimming, lifesaving, CPR, first aid, sailing, canoeing, and adapted aquatics. For the last 20 years, Kevin has worked as a Computer Programmer.

In 1989, Kevin caught the coin collecting bug again. He began studying the Two Cent series and found more questions than answers. His passion for coins and the history that surrounds them led Kevin to the National Archives in Philadelphia, where he spent his Saturdays poring through original Mint documents. The abundance of 19th century official Mint records at the National Archives lends much to Kevin's primary interests: the study of Mint history and learning what actually took place from the letters of the individuals involved in the creation of U.S. coinage, and the study of the die making process.

After five years of research, Kevin wrote his first book on coins, *Getting Your Two Cents Worth*. Now, twelve years since this first title was published, Kevin is widely known as one of the most prolific authors in the numismatic field.

Kevin is currently working on several new coin collecting books. Some pertain to die varieties, others to general numismatics. Some focus on unanswered questions in numismatics that sparks Kevin's insatiable curiosity. Kevin enjoys fishing, swimming, and spending time with his family.

John Wexler

At the age of eight, John came up with a novel way to assemble his first collection. Taking the side from a large corrugated box, he carefully cut coin-size slits into the face. His collection, of course, consisted of Lincoln cents, which he inserted into his new coin board.

Eventually, John replaced his coin board with a traditional Whitman folder, (1941 to date), and grew his collection until just one hole remained. John recalls the incredible excitement when his uncle provided him the missing coin: a 1955-S. John immediately noticed something peculiar about the coin. It had extra metal, resembling the letter I, between the B and E of LIBERTY. According to Spadone's *Variety & Oddity Guide*, the coin was an error known as a BIE. The discovery plunged John into the world of errors and varieties. From then on, he scrutinized every coin.

In 1971, John found a 1971 cent on which all the letters of LIBERTY and many of the letters of IN GOD WE TRUST appeared to be doubled. Having read an article about error coins by Alan Herbert in *COINs Magazine,* John sent the coin to Mr. Herbert. Mr. Herbert responded with amazing news: the coin was a new doubled die discovery—Obverse Die #1. On the invitation of Mr. Herbert, John joined CONE (Collector's of Numismatic Errors). This, along with the discovery of a 1972 Obverse Die #1 Lincoln cent and several other lesser varieties in the following year, led to his passion to research doubled die varieties.

In 1978, John and Robert Wilharm began publishing a monthly magazine, *ERROR-VARIETY NEWS.* John went on to become the Chairman of the Board of CONE. With the help of then NECA President, L.G. Davenport, he was instrumental in the merger of CONE and NECA (Numismatic Error Collectors of America) into CONECA. John's doubled die research led to the publication of *The Encyclopedia of Doubled Dies*, Volume 1 in 1978 and Volume 2 in 1981. In 1983 he co-authored a book about RPM's (RePunched Mintmarks) with Tom Miller, and in 1984 he authored *The Lincoln Cent Doubled Die* book. Eventually he sold *ERROR-VARIETY NEWS* to another publisher. Suffering from burnout, he left the hobby in 1987.

In the summer of 1993, his interest in coins resurfaced. In 1996, John's research into 1995 Lincoln cents doubled dies led to the publication of his book *The Complete Guide to the 1995 Doubled Die Cent Varieties*. In 1997, John was asked to do a bi-monthly column in *Coin World* Magazine with Ken Potter called "Varieties Notebook." By 1998 John's research into Jefferson Nickel doubled dies led to the publication of *The Best of the Jefferson Nickel Doubled Die Varieties*.

John is currently a member of the ANA, CONECA, SDDCA (The Society of Doubled Die Collectors of America), and LCS (Lincoln Cent Society).

Ron Pope

Ron's introduction to coin collecting began in the 1960s. Like the vast majority of new collectors at the time, he started collecting with a blue Whitman Lincoln cent folder #2. Ron quickly moved on to Buffalo nickels. Buffalo nickels featured an attractive design and, in the '60s, could still be found in circulation, even in XF and AU grades. While Ron was basically a traditional "date and mintmark" collector, he always kept an eye open for full strikes.

Ron first took up an interest in "cherrypicking" the Buffalo series after finding six 1918-D 8/7s. At the time, the only available source on varieties was Spadone's *Variety & Oddity Guide*. Most varieties know today were yet to be discovered, and one can only speculated at the number of the 1916 DDOs, 1917 and 1935 DDRs, and 1936-D 3 legged Buffalos that went unnoticed.

In 1989, after a hiatus of nearly twenty years, (part of this time was two and a half years stationed in Okinawa with the U.S. Army), Ron re-entered the coin variety hobby in a big way when he found his first 1935 DDR-001 Buffalo nickel. He has continued in the doubled die/variety segment of the hobby at a frantic pace ever since. For a time, Ron's two boys, Robbie and Timmy, accompanied him to shows and shops and made many good finds of their own. (In spite of his best efforts, both have since lost interest in varieties—Robbie still collects coins and paper money.) Since then, Ron has cherrypicked every major variety in the series, except for the 1916 and the 1937-D 3 legged.

Ron has a keen interest in doubled dies and specializes in doubled die Washington quarters, Walking Liberty half dollars, Roosevelt dimes, Kennedy halves and Ike dollars, as well as the Buffalos. In addition to the Buffalo doubled dies, he collects most of the die polishing errors in the series such as the 3 legged and 2 feather varieties. Ron is also in the process of assembling a Mint State, full struck date set of Buffalos—a tougher project than many might think. (The 1929 is very tough, and doubts persist if a 1931-S exists.)

The pursuit of varieties re-energized Ron's interest in numismatics. He strongly believes that the mainstream date/mintmark collectors, most of whom overlook the importance of varieties, continue to miss out on a truly fascinating part of the hobby. Nearly all doubled dies are from one die only. In most cases their mintage is but a fraction of that date and mintmark—the die could have lasted 5 coins, 500 coins, 5000 coins or 500,000 coins—making them extremely rare and exciting to find.